IF YOU DON'T BUY THIS BOOK
EVERYBODY DIES

By Tracy Smothers
and John Cosper

Copyright 2020 by Tracy Smothers and Eat Sleep Wrestle, LLC
All rights reserved.

www.eatsleepwrestle.com

FOREWORD #2
Tim Denison

I have been fortunate enough to have been involved in the wrestling business in some capacity or another since the age of ten and have seen and/or met virtually every wrestler who wrestled in the late sixties through the present day, although admittedly it's becoming more and more difficult to keep up with all the indies these days. Wrestlers come in all shapes, sizes and personas, but every now and then comes a talent with the "it" factor: the combination of speed, skill, size, ability, psychology, knowledge, athleticism, charisma and someone who just gets the business and how "it" all fits together. Tracy Smothers is one such talent. With a career that now spans into five decades, Tracy has heard it all, seen it all and done it all in a very grueling and demanding business…and lived to tell about it. My old friend Jason Boland always said, "At the edge of hell, there's a choice to make, to go around or through…" For Tracy, it's never been a choice, it's always been only one way. Through. Straight. On. Through.

In a world filled with gypsies, tramps and thieves, Tracy is one honest, hardworking, humble, unpretentious and unassuming guy. As you will see in reading this book, he is also a great wrestling historian and storyteller, not only about his adventures but the adventures and misadventures of his colleagues and brothers in the ring. While there are many great wrestling historians and archivists of the business, I would daresay that the only man who knows and recalls more history than Tracy is the one and only Jimmy Cornette. You'll hear from him as well.

What many people do not realize about Tracy is that he has done more for (yet is appreciated far less) and helped more of the young wrestlers in the business than virtually any other wrestler of his time. Tracy is never too busy to lend a hand or an ear when asked his opinion or advice on any aspect of the wrestling business. In addition to the School of Smothers, which he founded with professional wrestler Joey Grunge in 2014 to train young aspiring wrestlers, Tracy has watched countless matches, critiqued countless moves, and explained the psychology of the business to anyone desiring his knowledge, all for free. Yet he remains gravely undervalued.

Tracy Smothers is a gritty and tireless grappler and truly one of the nicest guys ever to work in the wrestling business. Whether wrestling as a babyface or as a heel, Tracy weaves it all together with his magic for all the fans to see. But make no mistake about this nice guy though, because if wronged or betrayed, the old legendary "Smothers temper" is unleashed, and he is just as mean, nasty and ornery of a sonofabitch as his father and uncles whom he describes in this book. Seen it firsthand. True story.

Finally, I encourage you to read this saga of the "Bear Expert", who after becoming a "Wild-eyed Southern Boy", a "T.H.U.G.", a "Young Pistol", "Freddie Joe Floyd", and a member of the "F.B.I", went on to forge his own unique mark and legacy in the wrestling business. The stories are true, authentic and unadulterated. And remember, "If You Don't Buy This Book, Everybody Dies."

Tim Denison
Louisville, Kentucky
February 8, 2020

FOREWORD #3

Hy Zaya

If you had told me the first time I ever laid eyes on Tracy Smothers that I would come to see him as a father figure, I'd have thought you were crazy.

I grew up in Louisville, Kentucky, so my first exposure to Tracy was on the USWA wrestling show on WAVE-3 TV and also at the Louisville Gardens. Tracy was a heel at that time, and when I saw him waving that Confederate flag, I despised him. I always saw the flag different than most Southern folks having grown up in the black community, so when I saw Tracy waving the flag, I thought, "Fuck that dude!"

In my teenage years I fell in love with independent wrestling. I attended a lot of IWA Mid-South shows in Louisville, and Tracy was pretty much the top hero in the promotion in 1996. Even though I hated him as a kid, I got a different energy off of him as a teen. I saw the charisma Tracy had, how he could hold the crowd in the palm of his hand.

A few years later, I was finally old enough to get a license to train (i.e. when I was old enough to lie about my age and get away with it). American Kickboxer gave me my initial training, but Tracy Smothers was the focal point for wisdom for all the young guys in the IWA-Mid South locker room. He was to the kids in IWA Mid-South what Rip Rogers was to the guys training at Ohio Valley Wrestling across the river.

The first time I wrestled him, I was so nervous. I was rushing everything, which is what you do when you're first starting out. I was a complete wreck, and I didn't understand the business. I was a little bit better the second time. I slowed down and was a bit more consistent.

The match that finally clicked with me and Tracy happened at the Veteran's Memorial Coliseum in Evansville in 2010. I had worked that building for several guys over the years, and at that time, I was working for Sam Cosby's CCW promotion. Sam was running a joint show with Juggalo Championship Wrestling, and even though I was a JCW Original, I was on the CCW side working against Tracy.

I was in the corner catching back-fists from Tracy, which were no joke when Tracy threw them. He was talking to me, asking me, "Man, how old are you now, Hy Zaya?"

I told him how old I was, and he snatched me up in a headlock takeover. "Damn, I've known you since you were what, sixteen years old?"

I'm in the middle of the ring, trying to maneuver as I answer back, "Yes, sir."

Tracy let me go and called a spot for Derek Neal, who was his manager, and the referee. He worked the crowd for a minute and then came back to me and picked up our conversation. "Okay, get up. Go ahead and do your come back. I'll cut you off when I need to."

That was really the moment when Tracy became my Mr. Miyagi. I felt the chemistry we had in that moment, and a light bulb went on as if I finally got it. Once he saw I was pliable to work with, we didn't need to call a thing. He trusted me to do my come back and roll with it.

A lot of younger guys have a different attitude where they don't want to listen to the older guys. I never had that problem. American Kickboxer taught me when to talk and more importantly, when not to talk. I surrounded myself with the "O.G.'s" in the locker room, and I was always willing to listen and learn.

Being willing to listen gave me an "in" with Tracy. I remember one time sitting listening to him and Gypsy Joe in the dungeon of the Coliseum. Tracy looked at me at one point and said, "Man, Hy, say something!" I wasn't talking because I wanted to be respectful and learn from these two men.

Tracy's always admired my ninja attitude and my drive to fight the powers that be. I think he sees himself in me. Or maybe it's because we're both Virgos. One night at Heroes and Legends, I bought Tracy a beer. One beer led to two or three, and the next thing I knew, he was banging on the door of Ric Flair's dressing room, challenging him to a fight. Tracy loves to fight, and I know he sees we have that in common.

Tracy and I were both in Evansville one night working the J.C. Bailey Memorial Tournament. The plan was for me to go over and win the tournament, but when I got to the building, I felt a disturbance in the Force. Something wasn't right, and during my first match, I took a brain buster that was so hard, I knew someone had it in for me. I stopped wrestling and started fighting back hard.

I won the first match, but I had a few more to go. Tracy saw what had happened, and he came and found me after the opening match. He gave me a few ibuprofens. "Take this. When your adrenaline goes down, it'll help with the pain." Tracy helped me to stretch out before my second match and my third. As I was headed to the ring, he came and checked on me once again.

"Be careful, man, you're doing a good job," he said. He was looking into my eyes to make sure I was okay. It was literally like the Karate Kid being coached through the show by Mr. Miyagi. That's who Tracy Smothers really is.

When Tracy is in the building, he watches the entire show Every single match. It doesn't matter if Tracy's wrestling or not. If he's there, he's going to watch every match. He's going to give everyone willing to listen feedback that will help them get better. He gives more of himself in that way than he's ever received back.

Tracy watches every match for another reason: he doesn't want to duplicate anything that's already been done on the show in his match. That's one thing that most of his kids take away from him. I always keep an eye out on what's been done in the matches before mine so I don't repeat anyone else's spots.

Tracy really gets fired up when guys call him an old man. I've seen guys get brave on Facebook, calling veterans like him old, and I know that's a bad move. Tracy comes from a different time, and even at his age, he can switch from wrestling to fighting and beat someone's ass.

Tracy's been beat up, but he's not old, and he's still sharp. He remembers the things that make guys special. One time he and I were locking up, and he asked me, "Do you still do that roundhouse kick you used to do?" I said yes, and he told me to go for it. Tracy did an evasive move while I did my ninja thing, and we got a huge pop from the crowd. It was another light bulb moment for me, seeing Tracy's situational awareness and his ability to recall just the right move from years before to fire up the energy in the room.

One thing I am very proud of is that I have held the same OVW Southern Tag Titles as Tracy. Tracy and Steve Armstrong won the belts back in 2000 during a TV taping for OVW in Knoxville. They lost them to the Disciples of Synn a few weeks later. I won the belts as part of the

Legacy of Brutality with Big Zo, Cash Flo, and Jay Bradley, and we defended them under Freebird rules. Guys like Tracy are the reason we are called the Legacy of Brutality. They are our legacy, and it was at times a brutal one.

      It's no secret how the Confederate flag makes people feel, especially today. It's always funny though when I show up at a building and Tracy's already there wearing his Confederate shirt. He'll look over at me and yell, "There's my son!" while I yell back, "Pops!" People looking on always have this look like, "Something's about to go down," and then their mouths drop open when they see us hugging like family. We are family, and I am proud to be one of his kids.

Hy Zaya
Louisville, Kentucky
January 30, 2020

THE BEAR EXPERT

I'll never forget the second bear I ever wrestled.

I'll never forget the first bear I wrestled, either. Nor will I forget the third bear. The night I worked that third bear, I also had to wrestle a tag match and a singles match that same evening. Then I had to come back and do it all over again the next night - tag, bear, and singles - and again the next night. Three nights in a row! I spent the next several days home in bed, barely able to move.

But I'm getting ahead of myself.

It was 1986, and I was working for Mid-South Wrestling at that time. I was spending a lot of time on the road with Chavo Guerrero, Sr., and D.J. Peterson, both of whom have since passed on. One night after working a show in Alexandria, Louisiana, a bunch of the boys congregated at a huge bar called the Lighthouse (or as we called it, the Fighthouse) for a party. The Fighthouse was a very popular joint, and just about any night, you'd see these huge Louisiana boys who worked two weeks on/ two weeks off on the off-shore oil rigs drinking at the bar who were as big as the bar bouncers that we knew from the gym.

The place was crowded every night of the week, but it was especially busy that evening. Nick Adams had a grizzly bear he had raised from a cub that was seven-feet tall and weighed 1500 pounds, and the bear was taking on all comers at the Fighthouse.

A lot of wrestlers and fans turned out at the bar that evening to watch the action. Many of them came hoping to see someone they knew try their luck with the bear, and a few brave (or foolish?) souls went in with the intention of doing just that. I was not one of those men. I was freshly showered, having wrestled earlier that evening, and dressed in a nice shirt and pants. I was also single and hoping to meet some ladies!

I was no stranger to hanging out in bars, but before that evening in Alexandria, I had never had a sip of alcohol. I don't know why I gave in that evening, but sitting at the bar with Chavo and D.J., I had a beer and a shot while we watched these big football players and bouncers and Cajun boys try to tangle with that bear. Not one of those guys knew anything about working a bear, and I was sure that sooner or later, one of them was going to get seriously hurt. The alcohol started to loosen my tongue, and I started to voice my opinions on the matter.

"Naw, naw, naw, don't piss the bear off," I said out loud. "Stay on the defense. Stay away from him. Don't piss him off. Don't make him mad."

Chavo and D.J. asked me how I knew so much about wrestling bears. That's when I let it slip. I had wrestled a bear before, and not just any bear. I had wrestled the world famous wrestling bear Ginger back in my days as a college football player. I knew how bad a bear could fuck you up, and I knew the first rule of wrestling bears.

Don't piss the bear off!

"So I guess you're the bear expert, huh?" one of them said, nudging the other.

"I know enough to know that you don't want to make the bear mad," I said. They finally got it out of me that I had wrestled a bear before. I was in college at the time playing football, and my first opponent had been none other than Ginger the Wrestling Bear. Sure, I had done it once, but I had no desire to do it again.

Chavo and D.J. were amused at my lecture on bear wrestling, but I didn't think anything of it. I wandered away from the boys and found a tall, beautiful blonde who I had seen at the bar before. This was why I had come to the bar, not some stupid bear. I forgot all about Nick's bear and focused on the girl instead.

Nick Adams had capped the number of bear wrestling matches at eight. It was the same deal on the night I wrestled Ginger. Wrestling was really play for the bears, but after about eight guys, they started to get tired. Seven men had tried their luck with Nick's bear, and it was time to announce the final contestant of the night. The host got on the microphone and called out:

"Tracy Smothers!!"

I heard my name and looked up in horror. I turned to where Chavo and D.J. were sitting and realized I had been ribbed. After I ran my mouth and acted like the expert, telling everybody how to do it, they went and signed me up.

"No!" I said. "I'm not dressed for this, and I don't want to do it!" I really had no interest in ever wrestling a bear again. I was doing

2

well with the blonde, and I did not want to mess up my clothes. I did my best to beg off, but there were too many boys in the bar to allow me an opportunity to run. I had to leave the girl at the bar and step into the ring with the grizzly.

A lot of people think it's cruel to make animals wrestle, and it's probably a good thing for the bears (and humans) they don't allow it anymore. But bears love to wrestle. Bears do it all the time in the wild. It's how they play with each other.

I knew better than to take the bear head on, and I knew to go easy. If you're easy on the bear, he's more likely to be easy on you, but when you get aggressive, it's lights out.

I was doing what I could to avoid provoking the bear, but that 1500 pound grizzly kept leaning on me with all his weight. I couldn't get him off me, no matter what I did. The bear had me against the ropes, and my head was right against its chest. I was desperate to get him to back off, so I head butted him right in the chest.

Big mistake.

The bear went from playing to meaning business. I could feel the full strength of that bear coming at me. It had a muzzle on, but the bear was doing everything it could to gnaw on my head with its back teeth.

I hadn't meant to hurt the bear or come at the bear so hard, but once I did, I was in a fight for my life. I was swinging hard, throwing haymakers and screaming at Nick, "Get this mother fucker off me!"

Nick dove on top of the bear and wrapped his arms around the bear, using a chain to get the animal under control. Nick had had the bear since it was a cub, and he was able to distract the bear enough for me to get away. I was sweating and completely blown up, and my nice clothes were ripped to shreds.

The bear roared and lunged at me one more time as I leapt out of the ring. I took a bump on the floor and shit my pants as soon as I landed. I thought I was having a heart attack, my heart was racing so hard. Thankfully I had a pair of sweats out in the car, so I was able to go into the bathroom and put on some fresh clothes after I cleaned myself off.

By the time I got back to the bar, the blonde was already talking to one of the bouncers. She was laughing pretty hard at what happened to me, and I knew my window of opportunity was closed. To be honest, I wasn't even thinking about her.

I was just thankful I had survived my second time in the ring with a bear.

Little did I know, it wasn't to be my last!

SMOTHERS TOUGH

It takes a special kind of tough to step into the ring with three bears. You only need to look back a generation or two to see where the Smothers temper comes from. The Smothers family has German and Native American blood, and that combination packs a real punch.

My grandfather on my Dad's side lived to be 98 years old. I knew him as Pa. His kids knew him as Pop. Everyone else called him Mr. Albert. He was 5'10", 195 pounds, and wiry without an ounce of fat on him. He was a hard working man from Camden, Tennessee, where he raised beef cattle, dairy cattle, chickens, and roosters. He had a catfish pond and an orchard, and he made his own jelly from the apples he grew.

In his younger days, Pa was a bare knuckle boxer. He used to walk eight miles just to get to the fights. He owned a horse and buggy he could have ridden to the fight, but he preferred to walk so he could think about it. He never lost a fight. He'd walk five miles to the store by himself to get things for his kids. He never let anyone go with him. He always went and carried things back by himself - ten miles total. I can't even walk fifty feet these days!

Pa had three heart attacks and was pronounced dead twice but came back. He lived to see grandkids, great-grandkids, and great-great-grandkids. They don't make 'em like Pa anymore.

My grandma wasn't a boxer or a fighter, but she was as hard working and tough as my grandfather. She had nine children all together: six boys and three girls. She actually went into labor with one of them while she was out working in the garden.

My dad was Bob Smothers, and he grew up on the farm with his eight siblings. He was a Golden Gloves boxer, and his parents put him to work on the farm at a young age.

My dad's brother Troy was a big, bad dude. Until I was in the seventh grade, I thought Uncle Troy was actually Hoss Cartwright from *Bonanza*. He was college educated at the University of Tennessee at Martin. He was a banker, and he was a very smart man.

Uncle Lloyd was a fighter pilot during World War II and was awarded a Purple Heart. He was shot down over the ocean and floated on some debris for three days, watching some of his friends be eaten by sharks, before he was rescued.

Uncle Dennis was an Army Ranger who was deployed twice. He liked war, and he liked killing people. He was a bit crazy. After he left the service, he became a lumberjack in a logging camp. Uncle Dennis was 6'7" and 275 pounds. He couldn't spell weights or steroids. When we went to visit him, he'd stick his arms out and we'd run, jump, and hang off his arms. "Chin ups, boys," he'd say, and we'd do chin ups on his arms. He was a beast!

Uncle Dallas served in the war as well. He was an undertaker, and he loved to shoot guns. Aunt Louise was about 6'2" and a school teacher. Uncle Leon was a preacher, but he was tougher and meaner than all of them!

Uncle Troy owned a lodge back in the 50s or 60s, and a bunch of people owed him money. One of the guys who owed Uncle Troy money got cute with my Uncle Lloyd. Uncle Lloyd was a negotiator, not a fighter, but all the other brothers, including my Dad, loved a good fight.

The brothers went down to take care of business and met up with the guys who owed money. They were outnumbered, but they didn't care. They had that "Smothers temper" fired up, and they took those guys out. My dad was the sniper, picking off the strays that tried to break away and run. My uncles still talk about that fight to this day.

I don't remember much about my grandfather on my mother's side. He died when I was only twelve. My grandmother worked for the Brown Shoe Company her whole adult life and retired from there.

My mother Wanda grew up on a farm like my dad, picking cotton. She went to college at the University of Tennessee at Martin, which is where she met my Dad. A bunch of freshmen boys went out one night to the girls' dorm and threw rocks at the windows. My mom was in the dorm that night, and that's how the two of them met. They stayed together from the age of eighteen until my father passed away at the age of 69.

I was born in Bruceton, Tennessee on September 2, 1962. When I was born, I already had two older brothers, Jeff and Sammy. My younger sister named Allison came along a few years later.

When I was about four or five years old, we moved to Springfield, Tennessee, a little town about twenty five miles north of

Nashville near the border with Kentucky. Springfield was a rural town in Robertson County with a population of just over 9000 people.

My mom worked for the Department of Human Services and was supervisor over three counties. My dad had a farm where he raised beef cattle, and he was also part owner of a car lot.

Growing up with them in a small town, I learned the importance of working hard. All of us kids worked on the farm, taking care of the cattle and chopping wood, both for firewood and to sell. If you didn't get up on time to go out and help, my Dad would throw a bucket of water on you and send you out to work. He was really old school, and while we didn't understand why he did it at the time, both he and my mom taught us the value of a hard day's work.

When I was eight years old I started working at the car lot. I started out washing cars but soon progressed to moving cars around. At eight years old, that was pretty cool.

I went to Cheatham Park Elementary School, Bransford Elementary School, and Springfield High School. I wasn't always the best student, but I did okay. Everybody played sports in Springfield, and I was no exception. I played football, baseball, and golf, and of course, I was on the wrestling team. I wasn't the greatest at any sport, but I got to play a lot because it was a small school. There just weren't that many people to play.

My brother Sammy played a little football himself in school, but that was his only sport. Sammy drives a truck for Roadway, which is owned by Yellow Freight. He has two daughters named Cammie and Brooke.

Jeff wasn't into sports as much as he was racing. Any kind of race, Jeff was up for it. He was really smart, and he now works for a Japanese company. His wife works for the same company, and they've done really well.

Allison is in real estate in Memphis. They all hate wrestling and never wanted anything to do with it, but they've all done well, and I'm proud of them.

Springfield was very backwoods even in those days. The folks who lived around Springfield lumped us together and referred to us as Robertson County Rednecks. If they only knew how many different factions there were.

The Southtown Rinky Dinks were a bunch of white guys, while the group known just as Southtown was all African American. There was also a group called Rose Hill, a bunch of guys who lived up on a hill, and the Goat Boys. The Goat Boys were the real backwoods rednecks of the bunch with four-wheel drives and everything.

The group I ran around with was known as the Thugs, with a capital T. As a matter of fact the Thugs is where I got one of my best known catchphrases:

T is for terrible.

H is for Hell.

U is for ugly.

G is for jail, because a Thug can't spell.

The Thugs were all older than me, but they let me hang around from an early age. There was Papai, who we named Papai because he looked like his dog. That poor dog got run over by cars a hundred times and never got killed. Beano got his nickname because when he was born, they said there would "be no more!" My buddy Gin was called Gin because that was her father's favorite drink. She was the only girl in the Thugs. Then there was also Big Stud, Cockbite, Jambo, Walldog, Snoopy, Terp, Dab, Blockhead, Superman, and Schmitty, all good buddies of mine.

All of the Thugs were characters, but they were also good athletes. They were also older than me. I ran with them from age 13 to 21. They didn't wear gang colors or anything, and we didn't get into too much trouble, but you can trace one of my famous catchphrases and T-shirts back to those boys.

In addition to the Thugs, I spent a lot of time with the Goat Boys, which made the Thugs mad, but I related more to the Goat Boys than the Thugs. They were closer to my age, and I went to trade school with a lot of them.

All of the guys in our cliques worked on farms during the day, but at night, we'd get together to have fun. We'd meet some place up near the Kentucky state line, build bonfires, play horseshoes, play cards, or go cruising around. We all hung out together, black guys and white guys, just having a good time.

We usually got along pretty well, but whenever two guys had a problem, they'd settle it with a fight. No guns, no knives, just their fists.

They would beat each other up, and then that would be it. They wouldn't kill each other like some guys do today.

When the fights broke out, everybody would take bets. I was still just a young teen and sometimes I'd be fighting guys as old as thirty years old. We'd even create our own angles for the fights. Not that we were smart to the business of pro wrestling and called them angles, but that's what we did without realizing it.

There was a hill we used to hang out that had an institution on top of it. Everybody used to gather up there to hang out. Sometimes we'd catch a glimpse at some of the people who lived in the institution, and some of those folks looked pretty strange. I remember there was a security guard about 6'7" who roamed around the outside. He was kind of strange looking, but he was tough, and we knew not to mess with him.

You had to pass through the town of Greenbriar to get to the hill. Greenbriar was home to a motorcycle gang called the Chosen Few. Those guys would come out to the hill and hang out with us as well. I remember one time the Chosen Few had some issues with the Hell's Angels, and a few people were killed during the feud. No one was ever convicted.

Greenbriar was an all-white town, and the Klan was there too. Those guys were real assholes. One time when I was home from college, something happened on the square. The Klan was marching and came up on Papai, Cockbite, Bucky, and Benny. They were going to jump my boys, but the boys talked their way out of it. That really pissed the rest of us off.

The next night a bunch of us went to Greenbriar and saw some of the Klansmen in a bar. Benny went inside to stir something up with them, and when the Klansmen chased him outside, the Thugs jumped them. They wouldn't let me join in because they didn't want to jeopardize my athletic scholarship at Carson-Newman.

The Thugs had a softball team and a flag football team. Sometimes we'd go down to Nashville and find some college boys to challenge in football. We'd start out playing flag football, but after egging the other guys on, we'd get them to play tackle.

One day Cockbite, Bucky, and Bow Wow got together and robbed a dollar store and a couple of convenience stores. They parked their cars at the high school before their little crime spree, and the next day, when they came back to get their cars, the cops grabbed them. The Thugs disbanded after that, and that was the end of an era for us.

When I turned fifteen I got a little more independence thanks to a motorcycle, a Suzuki 185. About that same time, we started to hear rumors about some troll-like guy who lived way, way out in the woods. He lived in a cabin that supposedly had running water, an outhouse, and a farm. They said he loved to drink and made his own moonshine. He also used to wander back and forth across the nearby road with a big old hat on. Nobody messed with this guy. Everyone left him alone. But me and a few of my buddies wanted to catch a peek at him.

Me and two friends of mine went out on our bikes. We went out at night and rode up and down the road where he was known to walk and sometimes fish around midnight. We went back and forth a few times and didn't spot anything, but just as we were making our last pass down by a ravine, we heard a noise.

All of a sudden we saw him walking across the street, the meanest looking dude I ever saw. We hit the gas on our bikes and we booked it out of there. We never dared go back for a second look.

There were all whispers of a mysterious creature near Springfield known as the Carr's Creek Critter. They said it was a half wolf-half dog, or half wolf-half fox that killed farm animals like hogs, goats, and chickens. There was even a story about a man who lured one of his co-workers out to one of the bridges and shot and killed him. They never found the body because the Carr's Creek Critter ate him.

There were two or three bridges that crossed Carr's Creek in the county, and we used to ride over the bridges looking for it. We never spotted the Critter, but we could hear it howling.

Years later when I went to WWF, I wanted to use the Carr's Creek Critter as my gimmick. I pitched it to creative, but obviously, they didn't go for it.

I had a good upbringing in Springfield, but the town had a real dark side to it. As small a town as Springfield was, it was ranked in the top 20 for murders during that time. There was a lot of drug trafficking going on as well. The sad thing is some folks were actually proud of that. It was a different era and a different time, but I had a lot of friends there.

I had a friend named Jughead, who went to a party one night. His car got blocked in by another guy at the party, and Jughead asked cut by an NFL team, either the Cowboys or Chiefs, but he played a few years in the Canadian Football League.

him if he could move his car. The other guy was drunk and gave Jughead the keys, but when Jughead moved the car, he accidentally flattened the guy's tire.

Jughead went back into the party and told the guy what happened. He offered to change the guy's tire. The guy pulled out a gun and shot Jughead dead right there. These were two guys who had grown up with one another! That's how crazy it was!

I'm happy to say I wasn't the only one who managed to move beyond Springfield. There were a lot of guys from the Thugs, the Rinky Dinks, Southtown, the Southtown Rinky Dinks, and the Goat Boys who were pretty good athletes. A lot of those guys went to college on athletic scholarships, and many of them turned out to do pretty well as adults.

Big Stud wrestled at Middle Tennessee State for one year and beat Notre Dame's star wrestler. He was six foot tall, 350 pounds, with forearms that were eighteen inches in diameter. He could bench 500 pounds and deadlift 700 pounds. He was built like a power lifter and so tough.

Papai went to the Senior prom wearing his Thugs T-shirt with the sleeves cut off. His dad had played football at Notre Dame. Papai was a good football and baseball player himself who walked on and played football at Tennessee. He got kicked off the team after a game in which he took down an All-American wide receiver who decided to take a swing at him. Papai beat the crap out of him, and that was it for his football career. Papai boxed, but he couldn't wrestle because he wanted to fight with his fists. Papai was an Irish redhead, 5'10", 205 pounds. He would have been great for our business, but he ended up working in a factory with Dab.

Jesse Gray, who we called Blockhead, was a great athlete who ran a 4.5 40 yard dash. He was a terrific pitcher and shortstop, and he could have played baseball at any SEC school he wanted. Senior year, he started messing around with a girl and failed English. That ended his hopes at a college scholarship. He ended up walking on at Austin Peay University and led the conference in ERA. Jesse was killed in a car accident in 2004, but his son, Sonny Gray, played for the Oakland A's and the New York Yankees.

Jeff Chapman was a friend of mine who belonged to Southtown. He played football at Tennessee State University. He was

WHEN TRACY MET GINGER

Like a lot of professional wrestlers, I got into wrestling when I was young. All of my friends and I were big wrestling fans. Nick Gulas was the big promoter in Tennessee when I first started watching, but in 1977, Jerry Jarrett split away from Nick and took Memphis, Louisville, and the northern part of Nick's territory from him. Angelo Poffo ran an outlaw promotion out of Lexington for a while, and they came to our area a few times, with Angelo's sons Lanny Poffo and Randy Savage as the main attractions.

I remember Nick Gulas would go on TV every week and declare, "This is the biggest show I ever signed!" He would pump and promote that show to the point that you believed him. He always kept heat on the heels like Johnny Long, Tojo Yamamoto, Len Rossi, Dutch Mantell, and Bearcat Brown. The heels would always beat down babyfaces like Jerry Jarrett, who sold those beatings to the point that it made the girls in the crowd cry!

There were so many great characters working in Tennessee during that time, men like the Mighty Yankees, the Fabulous Ones, Eddie Marlin, Jackie Fargo, Dennis Condrey, Phil Hickerson, and the French Angel. They didn't do moonsaults and flips, but they didn't have to. You knew they were tough guys who could beat your ass. They always kept something going, week to week, and the crowds were red hot. There were fights in the stands some nights, and they also had to have security around the heels' cars to keep the fans from slashing their tires or doing something worse.

There was a gentleman I worked for as a boy named Mr. Perry who used to take me to see the matches live. I did work for him on his farm, picking tobacco and strawberries. I'd be out in the field on a Wednesday evening, and he'd pull up in his truck and blow the horn. If my mom and dad gave me the okay, I'd hop in, and we'd go to the Nashville Fairgrounds. I was about twelve the first time he took me, and I used to love riding in the back of his truck down to the Fairgrounds for the show.

When I got my motorcycle at the age of fifteen, I was only allowed to ride it five miles from the house. When the wrestlers were in town, they'd workout at a gym fifteen minutes from my house, so I'd ride out there to get a look at them.

Wrestling back then was still kayfabe, and guys protected the business. They wanted the fans to believe it was real. There were a few guys I believed were the real deal, but even though I knew something wasn't on the level, I still respected it. It was a bit like watching Houdini or a master magician. You didn't know how he was doing it, but he did it, and you respected him for it.

I remember how real it felt watching Tojo Yamamoto turn on Jerry Jarrett. That was a real shock when it happened. Jerry Jarrett was the good ol' country boy with the blonde hair, and he knew how to sell when Tojo went after him.

I remember watching the matches when Jackie Fargo passed the torch to Jerry Lawler and seeing Lawler become the guy in Memphis. I didn't realize that was what was happening at the time, but it sure stuck with me.

Dutch Mantell was one of my favorite guys. So was Randy Savage when he came along. Len Rossi and Bearcat Brown were real tough guys I loved too. Bill Dundee worked out in the gym where I started working out as a kid. I've known him since I was in the eighth grade, and I used to talk to him a lot.

I really enjoyed watching wrestling. I enjoyed the action and the drama. Jerry Lawler was a heel in those days, and he was so good at everything. Jerry Jarrett had a great mind for the business when he was really into it. A lot of the gimmicks you saw Vince McMahon do in the 1980s that put WWF on top were borrowed from Jerry Jarrett and Jerry Lawler. My buddies and I used to watch wrestling and then we'd have some matches of our own.

I joined the high school wrestling team in my sophomore year and wrestled three years. We'd only had a team for two years when I joined up, and our coach really only knew the basic maneuvers. I won district in my junior year as a natural 185 pounder and took fourth in the region, which meant I was the first kid from my school to ever wrestle at state.

In my senior year I wasn't as serious about it but I still came second in the district. I had a lot of trouble with my weight that year, and I was always trying to cut weight at the last minute. I was also distracted chasing a cheerleader from White's Creek named Donna Clark. She's a grandmother now and a friend on Facebook. I tease her every now and then that she cost me the state championship. The guy who won state in my senior year was a guy I had beaten in my sophomore and junior. He beat me a few times, including district in my senior year, but I had beaten him easily four or five times before that.

In a sign of things to come, I lost a match at a dual meet in high school when I picked up a guy and body slammed him. That's perfectly legal in pro wrestling, but you can't do it in high school. The coach of the opposing team was George Weingeroff, who was a former high school and professional wrestler. My coach was mad because he really wanted to beat George.

Wrestling was hardly my only sport. I was on the golf team and came in third in the district in my senior year. I played catcher on the baseball team, but I quit baseball before my senior year. During football season I played defensive tackle, center, and several other positions in football. I was All-District in football.

The highlight of my senior year on the gridiron was beating Gallatin, a team that had a long undefeated streak and had beaten us many times before. We weren't good enough to make state, but we had some good players. One of them made it to the pros and played in the Canadian league for a few years after being cut by the Cowboys and Chiefs.

In my senior year I was offered an athletic scholarship to Carson-Newman College. Everyone was really excited for me, and they all had my life planned out. I'd play four years of college football, graduate, and come home to Springfield to be the high school football and wrestling coach.

My future plans started to change as soon as I got to Carson-Newman. Although scholarship was for football and wrestling, I only played football because I couldn't keep my grades up. I made varsity in my freshman year as a backup defensive tackle, and I was in on all passing downs. I was also on all special teams and played as a wedge buster, which resulted in quite a few concussions. Back then people weren't as concerned about head injuries, of course, so I hardly missed any playing time for those.

The football team won the SAC 8 championship while I was there, but during the spring of my freshman year, I tore my knee up. I was able to get back on the field by the fall, but after cracking a vertebrae in my neck on a kickoff, I was forced to redshirt my sophomore year. I trained hard at the gym that spring trying to put on weight, going from 215 to 245. Every time I went to the local gym, I saw the wrestlers working out.

I saw the Fabulous Ones, Stan Lane and Steve Keirn. I saw Bill Dundee and a lot of the other guys. The more I got a look at some of them, I began thinking maybe I might want to give professional wrestling a shot.

I had watched Memphis wrestling on TV growing up, but it was during my college days that wrestling took off on cable TV. I discovered Georgia Championship Wrestling and started watching guys I'd never seen before like Dusty Rhodes, the Road Warriors, and Superstar Billy Graham.

During winter workouts, we'd get on the mats and do our own championship wrestling just like the guys we saw on TV. My friend Roy Stone was a big fan of Dirty Dick Slater. Roy would play Dick Slater and be the babyface, and I'd play myself as a heel. We didn't know what we were doing, of course, but we had some fun.

A group of us took a trip down to the Omni in Atlanta to see Georgia Championship Wrestling live. I remember seeing Butch Reed, King Kong Bundy, Tony Atlas, the Armstrongs, and the Road Warriors, who were the hottest thing going in the business at that time. You believed the Road Warriors because they beat the shit out of everyone.

Another time we went to Marietta, Georgia to see King Kong Bundy, who was doing a body slam challenge at the time. I tried to slam Bundy, but he wouldn't budge for me. One of my teammates, a guy named Jeff Carman, took a crack at Bundy. Bundy went up for Jeff, just a little, to tease the crowd and make them think it was possible he could be taken down. He didn't go down for Jeff, but looking back, it was cool seeing Bundy give him that little rub. He didn't give me anything that night, but that was really the hook for me wanting to become a wrestler.

I was struggling to stay on the football team with my grades as it was, and when a new coaching regime came into the school, there were some politics going on that rubbed me the wrong way. I was frustrated, but I wasn't ready to give up on football just yet. My real dream was to play at the University of Tennessee. I spoke with the coaches at Tennessee, and I ended up transferring to a junior college, hoping that I could pull my grades up enough to get into UT and become a walk-on for the Volunteers.

It was at Volunteer State Community College, even before I started training to become a professional wrestler, that I had my match with Ginger the wrestling bear. Now there have been a number of Gingers in the wrestling business going back to the 1940s, so this wasn't the original Ginger, but the Ginger I faced was a formidable opponent, a black bear weighing 750 pounds. Her claws had been cut and she wore a muzzle, but Ginger was a seasoned and dangerous veteran. In the early 1980s she was the oldest and meanest of the wrestling bears.

This match took place inside a big bar in Murfreesboro, Tennessee. I had seen the advertisements about Ginger, and I wanted to go check it out mostly because I love animals, especially bears. I started talking about taking on Ginger myself, and one of the guys dared me. That's all it took.

We got a big passenger van and packed about twelve guys inside to go to the bar that night. I was the only one who didn't drink, so I was the driver that night. I don't know what those guys would have done to get home if Ginger had messed me up that night.

They only allowed eight people a night to wrestle Ginger, and in order to step in the ring with Ginger, you had to sign a waiver stating that the venue and Ginger's trainers were not liable for any injuries. If you fought Ginger, you were doing so at your own risk. That makes you stop and think a little bit. I thought for a few minutes, but I knew I was going to sign the waiver anyway. That was the whole reason we had come out that night, and I wasn't backing down.

Ginger's owner was right behind her with a cattle prod in his hands. Before the action started, he warned all of us not to try anything stupid with his bear.

"If you get cute with Ginger, I'll give her a jab with the cattle prod, and she'll really mess you up. Don't punch my bear, don't tackle my bear, or I will turn her loose on you."

The first guy to face Ginger that night was a football player from Middle Tennessee State. This was a big guy, probably 6'4" and 270 pounds. He was an All-American type and a serious pro football prospect. He heard the warnings from Ginger's owner the same as the rest of us, but he was feeling really cocky. He went down into a three-point stance as they were counting down to the start of the match.

Big mistake. Ginger took a zap from that cattle prod, and she leg-sweeped that boy so fast, he didn't know what hit him. He went flat on his back and busted his head open on the bar room floor. There was blood on his face and blood on the floor beneath his head. We thought he was dead.

We were warned that if Ginger got us down, we should cover up because she'd try to bite us. That poor boy didn't have time or the wits to react. Ginger was right on top of him, head-butting his face until she broke his nose and pushed the cartilage of his nose up into his brain. The owner called Ginger off of him, and the bar called an ambulance. Ginger's first opponent not only lost in a squash match, he never played a down of football again.

I had the same thought as some of the other guys waiting to face Ginger. "Fuck this!" I took the keys to the van and raced out to the parking lot A few guys who had also signed up made it out of the bar and didn't come back, but my friends were not about to let me quit. "No, no, no, you said you'd do this, and you're going to do it! You already signed the waiver! We're placing bets!"

I went back into the bar and watched the remaining guys ahead of me take their turn with Ginger. I drank a few cups of coffee and watched the few remaining guys try to take on the bear. I noted that a lot of the guys tried to take her head on, and that only made her mad. I came up with a different strategy: the best offense is a good defense.

I went three three-minute rounds with Ginger, mostly ducking and dodging and just trying to survive The wrestling was mostly play for Ginger, who didn't need to be fast or even that strong to knock you down. Hell, she weighed three times what I did! She really only got dangerous when her owner stuck her with that cattle prod. I was lucky he didn't sick her on me, and I lasted the time limit draw in my first ever wrestling match.

I've wrestled three bears in my life, and out of the three, Ginger was the toughest. She was older, she was smarter, and she didn't mess around.

I was lucky to survive that match with Ginger, but as dangerous as that encounter was, I was hooked on wrestling. I was tired of school and the politics of football, and the more I thought about it, the more wrestling appealed to me.

Everyone back home was less than thrilled when it came out I had left school to become a wrestler. They were still counting on me to be the high school coach of the future. Needless to say, they were pretty angry when I dropped out of college. Some of them still aren't over it!

I didn't become the hometown football coach, but I still lived in Springfield all the way up until about 1995, when I moved to Nashville. I don't get back to Springfield very often. It was a rough place when I lived there, and from what I hear, it's only gotten worse.

A "FABULOUS" EDUCATION

I was very fortunate to break into the business with Memphis and Jerry Jarrett, and it was all thanks to my dad. My father and Jerry Jarrett almost went into business together and opened a car lot. The business didn't happen, but my dad and Jerry remained close friends. It was my dad who told Jerry I was interested in becoming a wrestler, and Jerry suggested I talk to Stan Lane and Steve Keirn.

Stan and Steve were the biggest babyface tag team in Memphis, the Fabulous Ones. It was a brilliant gimmick created by, who else? Jerry Jarrett. They made a number of MTV-style videos with Stan and Steve to hype their debut, all set to ZZ Top's "Sharp Dressed Man," and the boys were red hot from the moment they made their debut.

Stan and Steve were really the only guys with a school in the area at that time. They were traveling six days a week and working two shows on Saturdays, and they kept putting me off at first because of their schedule. It took about a year of talking before they were able to work me in, but the Fabs gave me my initial training.

I only got to workout and train with them five or six times, but they spent several hours with me and taught me a lot. One of the things I learned from Stan and Steve was just how real wrestling was. Many people look at certain moves like the sleeper hold and think it's all fake. I once asked Steve to put a sleeper on me for real, and I learned quick - it's a real hold, and if you apply it right, it will choke someone right out!

Stan and Steve let me ride with them a few times. A lot of stories have been told about how wild the Fabulous Ones were, and I can tell you the stories are true. Everywhere they went, they got mobbed, especially at the little spot shows. Week after week the ladies mobbed their gimmick table to buy new photos of the boys. They had to have security to help us in and out of the building just like the heels, though the fans wanted to get their hands on the Fabs for very different reasons.

I had a good job at Wedgewood Industries loading trucks. That was a great workout for me. My boss was a man named Don Barnhart. He knew I was trying to get into wrestling, and he was really lenient with my schedule. I could give him an hour's notice, and he'd let me go. He was really good to me.

I was working out at the gym a lot, preparing myself for the day when I would get to wrestle my first match. One day a great big guy walked in wearing a toboggan and sweats in the middle of summer. He was hard to miss, he was so big. It turned out to be King Tonga. Tonga was a former Sumo wrestler and a native from the island of Tonga who had come to America with his friend Haku. Tonga later became famous as the Barbarian in WWF.

Tonga was huge, bigger than the Road Warriors, and he put on a show that afternoon in the gym. After hanging from the bar for a bit, Tonga went to the bench press and did 135 pounds ten times, then 225 ten times, 315 ten times, 405 ten times. By the time he reached 315, the entire gym was watching him. Tonga didn't even acknowledge them. He was just doing his workout. He then went to 495 on the bar and did that ten times. He went over to the incline bench and did 405 fifteen times. He went to the flat bench and did close grip presses with 315 pounds fifteen times. He went and hung on the bar a bit longer and then left.

Two or three days later, Steve Keirn called me at home (because there were no cell phones back then!). He told me someone had dropped off a card Jerry Lawler was booking and they had a match for me. I was going to be wrestling for the first time in Columbia, Kentucky.

"Who am I wrestling?" I asked.

Steve said, "You'll be in the ring with King Tonga."

I'd only trained like a handful of times, and they were throwing me straight into the fire. I brought a pair of boots from home, and Steve let me borrow an old singlet because I didn't have any ring gear. The strap of the singlet kept falling off because it was too big for me, and the guys ribbed me. "You better keep that strap on your shoulder! You can't drop the strap! That's Lawler's gimmick!"

The dressing rooms weren't connected, which was fine because back then, you didn't go over your match with your opponent. You called it all in the ring.

I went out to the ring and stood next to referee Paul Morton, Ricky's father. "You know who you're in the ring with, right?" said Paul.

"Yeah," I said.

"Okay," said Paul, "Just listen to him."

A fan yelled out, "Hey, you're gonna get your ass kicked!"

"Not by you!" I said.

About that time, Tonga came out of the dressing room. He looked huge, walking down the aisle toward me. I turned to Paul and said, "I might need to go back to college or drive a bus."

It was a squash match with Tonga going over, and it was a horrible match. Tonga tried to lead me, but there wasn't much I could do. Word got back to Lawler how bad it was, and that put a bad taste in his mouth.

I continued to train with the Fabs, hoping it might lead to another opportunity. One day one of the boys was unable to make a show in Louisville, and that led to a falling out with Lawler. Steve and Stan were huge in Louisville, but things got so bad they left the territory, heading to Minnesota to work for Verne Gagne and the AWA.

I had heat on me because I was Steve and Stan's student, and that kept me from getting a job in Memphis. I was able to get on a smaller show at a roller rink, and I got paid five dollars, half of it in change. During the match, another wrestler hit the ring, and I beat his ass, just like I was told to do. One guy at the show liked it and came up to me afterwards, inviting me to a TV taping in Gallatin, Tennessee the following week. I worked the TV taping and didn't get paid, but I was told to come back the next day so I could meet Tojo Yamamoto and Gypsy Joe.

Tojo Yamamoto was one of the long time Memphis stars and the guy who trained Jerry Jarrett. He was a native of Hawaii who adopted the evil Japanese gimmick to get over as a heel. Gypsy Joe was one of the craziest guys ever to work in the wrestling business. He started way back in 1951 and didn't retire until 2011, sixty years later!

Tojo and Joe looked me over. Tojo did all the talking while Joe just stared at me. "You've got a good look. You work out, that's good." They excused themselves to go to another room and talk for a moment. They came out a few moments later.

"Your name is Steve Lane," they said, a ring name inspired by my trainers. I didn't argue with them because I had already learned not to question anything.

I tagged up with Tojo that night against Joe and another guy. Tojo turned heel on me during the match, and Joe gave me my first blade job that night.

I worked a few matches with Gorgeous George, Jr., against Tojo and Joe. George, Jr., was semiretired at that time. He had a good job as a construction foreman, but I learned a lot working with him.

Two other guys who helped me a lot were Roger Howell and Tommy Higge. Tommy was a very good worker who tagged with me a lot against the New York Dolls, and both he and Roger taught me a lot about how to work babyface.

Tojo and Joe got me my first regular job in wrestling, not in Memphis but in Nashville and with Nick and his son George Gulas. George Gulas was one of the main reasons Jerry Jarrett split away from Nick Gulas in 1977. Nick was booking his son as a top star, but Jerry, who knew George wasn't main event material, refused to go along with it. The fans were refusing to buy him as a top star as well, and everyone could see it - except Nick and George.

When Jerry Jarrett split away from Gulas, Tojo stayed with Gulas. Even though he had mentored Jerry in his early days on the road, he stayed with Nick and George out of loyalty until the early 1980s.

Tojo was a guy who made people believe wrestling was real. There was more than one time when the police tried to arrest him for attempted murder after seeing him in the ring.

One night down we were in Tupelo, Mississippi, in the same building where they once did the concession stand brawl between the Blonde Bombers and Jerry Lawler and Bill Dundee. We were in the ring afterwards, waiting to get paid, and there were two guys getting into it with the manager of the building. The manager had enough and came over to where Tojo and I were waiting.

"Tojo," he said, "I'll give you a hundred bucks to beat that guy's ass."

"Come on, Tojo," I said, "Let's get out of here," I had to work the next morning at 7 am and then wrestle the next night, so I just wanted to get home.

Tojo turned to the manager and said, "Give me three hundred, and give the kid one hundred."

Next thing I knew, I was in the ring with Tojo, fighting these two guys. I was holding one of the guys down at one point, and Tojo hit the guy with his wooden shoe, right between the eyes.

Working as Tojo's partner meant some nights I had to fight my way to the ring and then back to the dressing room. We had a gimmick table where we sold pictures, but we could never work the table ourselves. We had another guy sell pictures for us so the fans could rip them up in front of us. It was crazy, but those were the times that hooked me on the business. You couldn't get away with any of that shit now. One hit from Tojo with his stick on a fan, and he'd get sued, but it was a different time then. I could get in a fight or cause a riot and get away with it.

When Tojo made amends with Jerry and rejoined him in Memphis, I wanted to follow him. Tojo told me I needed to talk to Eddie Marlin, so I came to the shows every week and bugged Eddie, asking him to give me a chance. Eddie liked me, and he finally booked me in West Tennessee against guys like Kurt Von Hess. Kurt wouldn't work with me for some reason, and the match didn't go too well. I didn't hear from Eddie again, so I went back to Nashville to work for Nick Gulas a while longer.

Finally, one day, I got a chance to meet Jerry Jarrett. I went backstage with Tojo, expecting Tojo to put me over. Jerry asked his old mentor how I was in the ring.

"Oh Jerry," said Tojo, "This kid, his work is horrible. His headlock is bad. His hook up is bad. Steve and Stan tried to teach him. He's crazy. He wants to fight all the time. He chases girls all the time. He gets mad when I discipline him."

I said, "Yeah, I get mad! I work forty hours a week loading and unloading trucks! I'm working out all the time! I'm on call for you all the time! I'm napping on my rest breaks, getting in at two or three in the morning!"

Of course I got in trouble for that. Jerry would shake his head and say, "Well, we're not going to use you unless you work in Tojo's school. He's got a class every Sunday." I agreed to train with Tojo, and Jerry started booking me on the weekends for TV and in Buddy Wayne's towns down south.

I was smart to the business by the time I started training with Tojo and his students, but he had not smartened any of his students up at that time. A lot of my training with Tojo was me shooting one on one with the other students. Tojo was as tough a trainer as he was a wrestler. If you didn't do something right, he had a stick and would hit you in the ear or the leg or whatever to make you remember!

Once everyone was worn out from working in the ring, Tojo would make us climb to the top of the Fairgrounds arena. We'd get on our knees with our hands behind out back, and Tojo would kick us in the front ten times in a row. Then he'd take that stick and baseball hit us with it right in the stomach ten times while we stayed still and took our licks.

Even though I was already smart to the business, Tojo made me go through the same torture. Matter of fact when he got to me, he kicked me twenty times and hit me with the stick twenty times. I'd scream and cuss at him, "Muther fucker, I'm gonna kill you!" You couldn't train like that these days, or you'd be arrested for attempted murder. Looking back, I'm glad Tojo was as hard on me as he was, but I was mad at him.

I only worked out with Tojo for six months, but I spent three years working full-time loading trucks, 7 am to 3:30 pm Monday through Friday, while wresting part-time for Jerry. We trained from 10 am to 4 pm on Sundays. I lived about an hour away, and half way in between was the gym. I'd leave at 4 pm, get in the jacuzzi and sauna, then get up and go to work in the morning.

Jerry ran shows in Memphis on Monday night, Louisville on Tuesday, Evansville on Wednesday, spot shows on Thursday and Friday, TV taping in Memphis Saturday morning, Nashville Saturday night, and another spot show on Sunday. I wasn't on the road full-time, but I was always on call if someone were to cancel. I'd drive to the show, wrestle, get home at 1 or 2 am, and wake up a few hours later to go to work.

I got a hell of an education working for Jerry Jarrett. Jerry is a genius. He is one of the greatest minds in the history of the business. He's been successful at everything he's ever done, and not just in wrestling. He's a pretty smart businessman as well.

One thing I never forgot was how he taught me the importance of getting heat on the heel. "If there's no dragons to slay," he said, "there's no knight in shining armor, and no damsel in distress." It was the simplest, smartest thing I ever heard said about the wrestling business. You could have the greatest babyface in the business, but if there's no heel, there is no business at the box office.

I remember sometimes watching him come up with an angle for a storyline on the fly, and all of us standing there would shake our heads wondering, where did he come up with that? That's how the Tupelo Concession Stand Brawl came to be. Jerry had lost all his heels in one mass exodus, and he needed to create some new heels quickly. He sent a TV crew down to Tupelo for a spot show and planned this whole angle with Lawler and Dundee fighting with the Blonde Bombers, Wayne Farris and Larry Latham, out of the ring and into the concession stand.

When the footage aired on Memphis TV that Saturday, it was one of the wildest and bloodiest matches the fans had ever seen. There was blood and mustard everywhere. Even the popcorn machine bit the dust, in spite of the pleas from the building owner. The plan worked perfectly, and on Monday night, the Coliseum in Memphis was sold out.

Jerry Lawler was Jerry Jarrett's partner and his top star. Jerry grew up watching Memphis wrestling, and he first got on television as a teenager showing some art work he had done of the matches at the Coliseum. Jerry was and still is a hell of an artist.

It didn't take long for Lawler to become the big star once he started wrestling. Lawler not only starred on the top rated TV show in Memphis with the weekly wrestling program, he recorded some songs and had a long-running talk show. Even though the King of Rock 'n' Roll lived in the same town, Jerry Lawler was the true king of Memphis.

The two Jerrys invented a lot of the things the WWE does now. Whenever you see a video package set to music or some backstage skit involving wrestlers, that started with Jerry Jarrett and Jerry Lawler. They crafted the video packages that turned the Fabulous Ones into top babyfaces and Kamala into a feared monster. The WWF saw what they were doing and started to copy it on their TV programs.

When Jerry Jarrett started to step away and focus on his other interests, Lawler was the guy who stepped in and kept us going. They were creative, brilliant guys who brought out the best in the company.

Vince McMahon didn't show much respect for many of the old territory guys he put out of business, but he had a great deal of respect for Lawler and Jarrett. I think the biggest testimony to Jerry Jarrett's brilliance as a promoter is what happened during the WWF steroid trial. Vince brought Jerry into the WWF to help out with booking during the trial. No one was sure how the trial would end, and the plan was for Jerry to run the company if Vince had to go to jail.

If Vince McMahon had the confidence to hand Jerry Jarrett the keys to the kingdom like that, Jerry must have been doing something right.

There are two guys I'd like to mention that I rode with in those early days: Jerry O and Jay Youngblood. Jerry O was probably best known as Jerry Allen when he worked as enhancement talent for the WWF. Jay Youngblood had just come off a hot run in Charlotte working with Ricky Steamboat. Jay had some problems out of the ring, but he taught me a whole lot about the business, as did Jerry. I really miss those guys, and I appreciate that they took the time to teach me a lot about the business.

LEARNING THE ROPES

I hate sounding like the guys who say today's wrestlers don't have respect or don't know how to appreciate the past, but sometimes I can't help but wish more of the young guys did appreciate the opportunities they have to work with and learn from the guys who came before. When I was coming up, if I had the chance to work with someone I respected, I cleaned my ears with Q-Tips before the match. I was all ears and ready to learn everything, and some of my teachers were pretty amazing.

Around the time I finished training with Tojo, Stan and Steve came back to work for Jerry Jarrett. Tom Renesto had the book in Memphis at the time, and he liked me. He started booking me more on the weekends, and my old boss was really good about letting me off when I needed it.

When you're the booker, you tend to favor certain guys. Tom Renesto's guys just happened to be the Poffos: Angelo, his son Leaping Lanny, and his other son Randy Savage. I worked with all three of those guys, but I had more matches with Angelo than his sons. He was just unreal. His cardio was so good, he was like a machine. In fact he was once featured in the newspaper strip *Ripley's Believe It Or Not* for doing 6033 sit ups in four hours and ten minutes. If you weren't in shape when you stepped in the ring with Angelo Poffo, he would blow you up and beat your ass.

Randy was exactly like you saw on TV. He was crazy, but if he liked you, he liked you. I was still pretty green the one time I worked with Randy, which was right before he signed with WWF. Randy laid the whole match out and called it in the ring. It went eleven minutes, and Randy made me look terrific, which wasn't an easy thing to do. Randy was as crazy as people say, but he knew how to work. I remember him asking me, "Ever take a suplex on the floor?"

I said, "Nope!"

He said, "You are now!" He suplexed me hard onto the floor. I thought I was paralyzed for a second, and it hurt real bad after the match, but I got through it, and Randy finished me off with his flying elbow.

Randy was running all around the back after the match because he was helping Jerry Lawler book the territory at the time. I managed to grab him real quick and shake his hand. "Thanks for the match. That was the best match I ever had in my life!"

"Kid," Randy said, "Never thank a guy who suplexes you on the floor." A week later, Randy lost a 'loser leaves town' match in Memphis and was off to New York and the WWF.

Somewhere around 1984 Memphis worked a series of shows in partnership with Georgia Championship Wrestling. King Kong Bundy was part of their crew, along with Rick Rude, the Grapplers, Len Denton, Tony Anthony and Jimmy Hart.

Ronnie Garvin and I were working together during that stretch. He was a great guy and a great wrestler, but man, he chopped me harder than any man I ever wrestled. I was getting ready for my match when Jimmy Hart came racing upstairs and said, "We've got to do something! Randy and Rip are fighting downstairs!"

We found out that an old beef Rip Rogers and Randy Savage had going back to their ICW days had boiled over. When I got downstairs, Lanny Poffo had pinned Rip's then-wife to the floor to keep her out of the fray. Rip put a shoot headlock on Randy and wouldn't let go, so Randy bit a huge chunk out of Rip's side. It was pretty ugly, but we broke it up, and the guys cooled off.

I got to work with Iron Mike Sharpe a lot. He had just finished his WWF run and come back to Memphis. He was a big, rawboned guy and a good worker who liked to work with the younger guys.

Tommy Gilbert was working under a mask as a heel, and the two of us worked together a lot. We had a number of fifteen to twenty minute Broadways, and I learned so much from him. Later on, Jerry Lawler gave him a Freddy Krueger gimmick. Jerry was a big horror movie fan and used a lot of monster gimmicks, everything from Frankenstein to the Mummy. He even made "Dr. D" David Schultz dress up as the Riddler from Batman.

Speaking of Dr. D, one day in early 1985 I walked into the locker room and was surprised to see a familiar face. I did a double take and turned to someone and asked, "What the hell is David Schultz doing in here?"

It had been years since David had worked the Memphis territory. He was one of the baddest men in the business, and his promos were just awesome. He was a legitimate tough guy too. Eddie Marlin once told me a story about David having a confrontation with Billy Robinson. Billy was a great shooter from England, and if he ever sensed a guy wasn't an amateur wrestler, he'd put it on them.

Billy worked with David one night, and he shot on David. After the march, David went up to Billy and said, "Mr. Robinson, I don't know that rasslin' stuff, but if you try that on me again, we're gonna fight."

Billy laughed off the threat. The next night, they worked each other, and Billy took David down, shooting on him again. They got back up to their feet, and David nailed Billy, knocked him right out. Billy was one of the great shooters of his time, but he was no match for an angry Tennessee boy who loved to fight!

I was very surprised to see David back in Memphis. The last time I had seen David, he was on WWF television, showing off his gun collection on Tuesday Night Titans and wrestling guys like Sgt. Slaughter and Hulk Hogan.

Turns out David had just been fired by WWF. We had all seen the footage of David on TV slapping John Stossel backstage at Madison Square Garden for saying wrestling was fake. That wasn't the reason they fired him, but Schultz knew he was on the way out even before that incident.

If John Stossel had been in Nashville the night I had to wrestle David, he might have changed his mind about wrestling being "fake". I was literally fighting for my life! The two of us dressed in separate locker rooms because that's the way it was back then so there was no planning the match ahead of time. David had never wrestled like I did in high school, but he was just naturally tough. He didn't lift weights and didn't have to train. He was a naturally tough good old boy from Jackson, Tennessee.

Billy Travis was another guy who had just come off a run with WWF. We had a lot of matches, and my first real angle on TV was with him. I learned a lot working with Billy. The two of us worked a tag team program together against Dr. Tom Prichard and Pat Rosen with Buddy Wayne as their manager.

Steve and Scott Armstrong came into the territory during that time. They worked a program with Pat Rose and Tom Prichard with Buddy Wayne as their manager. Steve would soon play a huge part in my own career as my tag partner.

One guy who helped me a lot in those early days as far as in-ring training was Rick Rude. The two of us worked a lot of matches together, and Rick made me look good, which wasn't easy! Rick was an incredible wrestler and a good guy. He always liked to go on early so he could get out and hit the bar, but he'd often watch my matches and give me advice. I still appreciate all he did for me as a young guy still learning to work.

Jackie Fargo was still wrestling when I got in, and he taught me a lot in the ring. He was always telling me, "You gotta have more fire!" Jackie Fargo was the most over babyface ever in that territory. It makes me sad how few guys today even know his name, especially around Memphis.

The Bounty Hunters, Jerry and David Novak, had been a big tag team back in the 70s, and they taught me a lot. I used to run into David in the gym. He gave me a lot of great advice.

Eddie Gilbert and Tommy Rich were put together as a new version of the Fabulous Ones. The fans didn't accept it, partly because they preferred Stan and Steve but also because they didn't have the body of Stan and Steve. They were both over huge as singles wrestlers and didn't need to be in a tag team. They both took time to mentor me and give me advice.

Another guy who mentored me was Dutch Mantell. Dutch was one of my idols before I got into wrestling. He was a real prick to me when I first met him, but after I got to know him, I loved him even more than when I was just a fan. We traveled a lot together, and I learned so much.

Dutch could fire on you, and he loved to rib me. He's a very funny guy, and I always thought he could have made it as a comedian. He's funny without being funny. He's a smart guy who not only knows the wrestling business but really keeps up with current events. He's also a brilliant booker.

Wildcat Wendell Cooley was working a program with Dutch during that time. He was a hell of a worker who really should have gone further in the business. He was from the Florida panhandle, but he had a Texas cowboy gimmick.

Jerry Jarrett and Jerry Lawler get a lot of the credit for making Memphis into the territory that it was, but I have to say that Dutch

Mantell, Bill Dundee, and Randy Hales were really the glue that held that promotion together. Jerry Lawler worked the big cities like Memphis and Louisville, but Dutch, Randy, and Bill were on every show.

The Fabulous Moolah would send some of her ladies to work the territory every now and then. She ran a school and booking office in her hometown of Columbia, South Carolina, which was home base for pretty much all the lady wrestlers at that time. Leilani Kai was Moolah's right hand at that time, and she'd come in with Wendi Richter, Luna Vachon, Velvet McIntyre, and Princess Victoria. They'd all work with each other in singles, tags, or six-person matches.

Back then, none of the boys messed around with the girl wrestlers. Moolah was pretty strict about that, and it just wasn't done. The girls would mess with the boys some, just to piss us off. Wendi was really hot, and she'd come over and sit on my lap when I was tired just to tease me and piss the other boys off.

Sherri Martell came into Memphis as well. Many fans remember Sherri only as a valet from her WWF days, and they have no idea how good she was in the ring. Sherri was a hell of a worker. She was working a program with Candy Devine, and she stuck around for a while after to work as a valet. The two of us became pretty close, and I traveled a lot with her and Candy. Sherri and Candy were the ones who taught me how to do a standing drop kick.

I remember when the Fantastics, Tommy Rogers and Bobby Fulton, first came into Memphis. Back then I was driving a Mercury Lynx, which was similar to the old Ford Escort. I was driving near Somerset, Kentucky in that Lynx doing about 85 miles an hour in between shows. Tommy and Bobby came up behind us in Tommy's Ford Fiesta, and they passed us like we were tied to a tree. Tommy had a moon roof on the car, and as they drove past us, Bobby stood up and mooned us.

Tommy and Bobby came into Memphis off a hot run down in Dallas. The Fabulous Ones had just left, and the Fantastics were the new hot babyface tag team in town. I traveled with them and picked their brains as much as I could. I usually had to work the next day after shows, so I'd sit in the backseat and try to sleep. I had to sleep, because they drove so fast, it scared me to death!

A pair of big guys from California came into the territory under the name the Freedom Fighters: Steve Borden and Jim Hellwig, who became Sting and the Ultimate Warrior. They were competition body builders who idolized the Road Warriors. They had a great look, and I heard Sting got an audition to play Ivan Drago in *Rocky IV*, the role that went to Dolph Lundgren. In those early days though, the boys were pretty green, as we all saw from their first TV match.

I worked with those guys in their third match. I didn't have enough experience to call the match, but I had the edge on them and had to take the lead. I worked with them a few times during that run.

One time on a road trip, Tom Prichard hopped in the car with us and told us a story about the Freedom Fighters and Frank Morrell. Frank was an older guy who had wrestled for years and made the transition to working as a referee. Back in those days, the dressing rooms didn't always connect, and the refs had to go back and forth between the heel and babyface locker rooms to carry the finishes.

Frank didn't know Sting and Warrior's names yet, so when he went to talk to them, he referred to Sting as "the smaller one."

Sting glared at him and said, "Well, hey, I'm bigger than you!"

One day while I was working out in a gym in Memphis, I looked over and saw a giant of a man doing straight bar curls with 180 pounds on the bar like it was nothing. I went over to him and joking around said, "Damn you need to get into a gym."

He laughed and said he was trying. He recognized me from TV, as I was already making appearances doing jobs for the other guys. He introduced himself and told me that he was a football player and had recently tried out for the USFL. He was looking to get into wrestling, and he told me he was going to start training with Tojo Yamamoto.

"I'm excited, I can't wait to try it," he said. "Tojo thinks I have a good chance."

I looked up at this 6'9" monster and said, "Good chance? Hell, if all you have is a good chance, I need to go back to college right now." Back then, he was known as Sid Eudy, but fans of pro wrestling would later know him better as Psycho Sid and Sid Justice.

Sid was ahead of his time in so many ways. Not only was he big, he was cut like crazy, and he trained like a machine. I remember he used to take in 500 calories of protein a day. Glenn Jacobs, who later became Kane, took in 600 a day. That's a whole lot for any man, even a guy as big as them.

Sid was known for something else besides his workout ethic. He could roll and smoke the biggest, fattest blunt you ever saw. Even in his hands, that thing looked like a giant cigar. I never saw anyone come close.

As big as Sid was, there was one man who dwarfed even him: Andre the Giant. I had the opportunity to meet Andre in 1984 when Vince brought the WWF to Nashville for a show at the Municipal Auditorium. This was just before Hulkamania blew up and Hulk Hogan became the biggest star in the world.

Everybody knows that Andre and Dick Murdoch were drinking buddies and that after the show, they would be at the Stockyard Restaurant Bar where all the country stars used to drink. I headed over there with some friends after the show, and there was a line out the door. I got in, and I started stalking the two of them, hoping for a chance to meet them. I followed Murdoch into the bathroom, and after we both got done taking a piss, I introduced myself.

Dick knew Steve and Stan, so I told him I was a wrestler and that they had trained me. "Oh, okay," he said, looking me over. "You play football?"

"I did."

He asked, "Were you any good?"

"Not really," I laughed.

"Where did you play?" he asked.

"Carson-Newman," I told him.

"Newman," he said.

"Hey, I really wanted to meet you," I told him. "The Armstrongs really talk highly of you. Do you think there's any way I can meet Andre and shake his hand?"

He said, "We'll see. Depends how he feels."

We walked back out into the bar, and Andre had a crowd around him. There was security around him to keep the crowd away. I couldn't get over how massive he was. He looked about as wide as he was tall.

"Hey boss!" shouted Murdoch. Andre kind of looked his way and grunted, annoyed by the crowd. "Boss, Newman wants to shake your hand," said Dick.

"Newman?" said Andre.

Dick pointed to me. "This is Newman. He played football at Carson-Newman. We go way back. Like twenty minutes."

Andre shook my hand, and let me tell you, that hand was massive. Andre was all of seven feet four and a half inches wide as well as tall. I've been around Big Show, and he's a big guy, but even he was nothing next to Andre. Andre was drinking wine, and not from a wine glass. He had the whole pitcher, and even that looked small when he lifted it to drink. He ordered a pitcher of beer later, and he drank that the same way, holding it like I would hold a beer glass. I've never seen anyone do that.

I had one other encounter with Andre around 1990. I was with Brad Armstrong at the time, and we ran into him in an elevator. Andre didn't know who I was six years later, but Brad knew him well.

Andre got on the elevator, and I swear to God, he took up the whole elevator. He was so massive. Brad said, "Hey, Andre! Good to see you! How are you doing?" Andre didn't say a word to him. He was definitely not in the mood that day. Brad didn't mean to be a bother, of course, but Andre stayed silent until he got off the elevator.

"Tell your Dad I said hi," he said, and he walked away.

"Okay, Andre!" shouted Brad.

"Is he okay?" I asked Brad.

"He's in a lot of pain," said Brad. "He's not doing well. He still has people coming up to him everywhere he goes, and he just gets really frustrated." Andre could be moody, and he didn't like attention. Brad understood that from being around him so much. He was a real giant, he was hard to ignore, and that really bothered him at times.

MID-SOUTH

I spent three years wrestling part-time for Lawler and Jarrett while I loaded trucks full-time. I was lucky to have an understanding boss at Wedgewood Industries who would let me take time when I needed it, but I was frustrated not being able to get on full-time in wrestling.

I was exhausted, too, with the work and the travel. Usually when I got the call, it was too late to get ahold of one of the other guys to hitch a ride to whatever town they needed me. I'd end up driving myself to the show, driving home afterwards, going to bed about 2 am and having to be back at work by 7 am. I was taking naps on my ten minute break and thirty minute lunch, then when I wrestled the shows, the guys would tell me I had no fire in the ring.

"It's because I'm worn out!" I said. Part of it was me not wanting to be too aggressive in the ring, but it was also the fatigue.

Lawler and Jarrett didn't like to use the local guys full-time. They knew they could get us locals any time they needed us, but they also knew there was bigger box office in bringing in stars from out of town rather than featuring a guy who lives just down the street. I understood that, but I kept plugging, answering the call every time, eating right and working out and waiting for my chance.

One day in Blytheville, Arkansas, Bill Dundee walked into the dressing room. He had just returned from working for Bill Watts in Louisiana with Terry Taylor, the Midnight Express, and the Rock 'n' Roll Express. "I talked to Bill Watts today," said Bill. "He wants you, and you, and you." The "you's" in question were Koko Ware, Billy Travis, and me.

I said, "I'll go right now!" I didn't have to think twice about it. For a long time, I had resisted going on the road and leaving home, but I knew by now this was the only way to go full-time in the business.

Billy didn't want to leave, though. Having just finished a run with WWF, he liked being close to his hometown of Lexington, Kentucky. They had also put him in a father/son thing with Frank Morrell that was getting over big.

Koko was as ready to go as I was. He was always good to me,

as was Norvell Austin in my early days. Norvell ended up quitting wrestling and going into business for himself. Last I heard, he was doing really well.

When I went south to work for Bill Watts in 1986, Vince McMahon was already in the process of snatching away the top talent in the smaller territories so they would shrivel and die, but the boys in Mid-South were still working full-time and making a nice living. It wasn't as good as a few years before, when stars like Jim Duggan, Ted DiBiase, and the Midnight Express were killing it, but the $750 to $1000 a week I was making was still good money at that time.

The trade-off with the good money was the long trips the territory was famous for. We hit a lot of towns in Louisiana including Lafayette, Lake Charles, Baton Rouge, and New Orleans, but every two weeks we'd have to drive down to Houston and then drive 500 miles up to a spot show in Tulsa or Oklahoma City. Bill gave us $100 for transportation on Houston weeks, and a lot of guys would fly. I rode with Carl Fergie and saved the extra money. We also did overnights to Jackson, Mississippi and Little Rock, Arkansas once a month because the territory was so spread out. Those were some good times but a lot of miles. We didn't have quite as many Interstates in those days, either. There were a lot of back roads, and the speed limit wasn't anywhere near as high as it is today, not that everyone paid attention to that.

Bill was really strict about guys being on time. If you were late, he'd fine you. If you no-showed, you'd better have a pretty good excuse or he'd dock your pay. He was starting to get away from that a little bit when I got there, but that's the way the business was back then. Bill ran a tight ship, and he didn't take any nonsense from anybody.

Bill paid his wrestlers every two weeks, and he was always two weeks behind on what you were owed. Bill did that to keep people from walking out on him, and if they did, they wouldn't get the money they were owed.

Terry Taylor was taking over as the booker from Dick Slater when I arrived in Mid-South. My first show was in Shreveport, Louisiana. I'll never forget riding to the building and hearing an ad on the radio plugging that night's card: Terry Taylor vs. Eddie Gilbert, Dr. Death Steve Williams vs. Buzz Sawyer, and Jake "The Snake" Roberts vs. Dick Slater. I don't remember who they wrestled, but Ted DiBiase and Jim Duggan were on the card as well.

This was still the early days of wrestling being on cable TV, and only a few promotions were getting national attention. These were names that I knew from TV, and I was so nervous driving to the building that night knowing I'd be working with all these guys.

Jake Roberts was so hot as a babyface that when I pulled up to the building in Shreveport, the people in line were already chanting, "D-D-T!" They let the crowd into the building at 6:30 pm, and for a solid hour they kept on chanting, "D-D-T!" Jake put over Dick Slater that night because he was finishing up his run and going to WWF. The fans didn't know this because of course they kayfabed all that back then, but Jake did the honors for Dick on his way out the door.

I can't remember who I worked that first night in Shreveport, but they put me over as the new guy in town. Terry Taylor gave me Bill Dundee's old finish, a reverse cross body off the second rope. I was excited to have my first match out of the way and thrilled to be in Mid-South.

Tommy Gilbert helped me to get an apartment in Alexandria, Louisiana. My rent and my car payments were the only two bills I had as a single guy, and I started saving as much of my money as I could. I ate a ton of spicy food every day at an all-you-can-eat Cajun buffet, and I worked out every day.

I started traveling with Tommy, Terry Taylor, and D.J. Peterson, who had a look that reminded me of Magnum TA. Tommy Gilbert and Carl Fergie were both in Mid-South working as referees, and both of those guys taught me a lot in the ring.

I got to work with Dick Slater in a TV match one night. Slater really put me over and gave me the best match of my life to that point, but it got him a little heat with Bill Watts. Slater was working a program with Duggan, and Watts wanted him to look strong. Slater gave me a lot of offense that night, and Watts thought he went a bit too far. I appreciated Slater for doing that.

Buzz Sawyer took a liking to me after that match, and I got to work with him a little bit. He had just come off a run working with Duggan. One night in Jackson, Mississippi, I went out first to the ring for the opening match. I was the new guy, and my entrance went over like a fart in church. Then Buzz came out to the ring, and we got into a stare down.

"Hey, I think you're a good babyface," he said. "I think I can have a good match with you. Just listen to me, okay?"

"Okay, I'm all ears," I said.

Buzz made me look great. He knew how to make a babyface, and he really put me over big with the fans. We were wrestling to a ten minute time limit, but at 9:58, he caught me with a power slam for the pin. It was absolutely awesome.

Buzz had a lot of problems outside the ropes, but in between the ropes, he was absolutely amazing and way ahead of his time. His brother Brett Sawyer became a tag partner of mine later on, and he helped me a lot, too.

I mentioned that Buzz worked against Dr. Death Steve Williams on my first night in Mid-South. During that match Dr. Death pressed Buzz over his head five times! It was unbelievable.

Steve Williams got the name "Dr. Death" all the way back in the eighth grade. It had nothing to do with wrestling and everything to do with how tough he was. He was an absolute beast who could chew beer cans in half. He was the baddest man who ever lived. He played football in college and in the USFL, but he was "too short" for the NFL. Bill Watts trained him, and he quickly became one of the most feared men in the business.

Grizzly Smith was working as an agent, and he was always good to me. Grizzly was a real professional, and he knew everything that was going on. He would stooge on himself, he was so serious about things.

Jerry Jarrett sent the Freedom Fighters, Sting and the Ultimate Warrior to Bill Watts to get some more seasoning. They had changed their name to the Blade Runners, and Bill matched the boys up with Eddie Gilbert to act as their trainer, manager, and occasional tag partner. Eddie had a great mind, but Sting and Warrior had a body builder attitude that made them difficult to coach. Sting was really cocky in those days, and he was reckless, which led to him hurting Ricky Gibson and a few other guys.

One night in Baton Rouge I got to the locker room and saw Dick Slater playing cards with Terry Taylor. Those two never got along really well, so when I saw the two of them playing nice, I knew something was up. I shook hands and said my hellos to the two of them, and I noticed that Dick, who wasn't actively wrestling, had his hands taped up.

I went over to sit down and get my gear on with Tom Gilbert and D.J. Peterson. I turned to D.J. and made mention of the tape on Dick's hands. D.J. nodded and said, "Yeah, it's on."

We watched Dick get up from the card table and say, "Terry, I'll be right back," as he left the room.

I did not see what happened next, but this is the story I heard. Back then the heels and babyfaces came out of separate entrances, but the two locker rooms in the building that night connected so the guys could meet out of sight of the fans and talk to one another. Slater went around to see Sting.

Slater had been in a relationship with Dark Journey, a bi-racial female wrestler who had also worked ringside as Slater's valet. Word was that Sting had hooked up with her after she split from Slater, and Slater went over to Sting and said something about it.

Hooking up with another man's girl was something you just did not do in those days. Sting already had a ton of heat with the older guys from hurting people in the ring. According to Taylor, Slater asked Sting to go into the bathroom with him, and as soon as Sting set foot into the bathroom, Slater sucker punched him and then lit him up.

When Warrior heard the commotion in the bathroom, he tried to break things up. Dick Murdoch stepped in and hooked him while Slater had his way with Sting. He shoved Sting's face in the toilet, and Eddie Gilbert had to come running in to get Slater to stop before he killed Sting.

Now this is all hearsay because I wasn't anywhere near the bathroom, but when I saw Sting later on, he looked like a truck had hit him. To his credit Sting still went out and worked the show that night.

We all came away with a lot more respect for guys like Slater and Murdoch. They were older and didn't look as physically intimidating as those two body builders, but guys from their generation were different. They were trained different, and they still knew how to hook you. It didn't matter what age they were, you did not mess around with those boys.

Dick Murdoch didn't remember me from the bathroom Stockyards Bar in Nashville when we met in Mid-South. When we met again and I introduced myself, he said, "Smothers? You kin to the

Smothers Brothers?"

"No," I said.

"You oughta claim that you are!" he said. "They're over!"

Sting had one more learning moment coming involving Ricky Gibson. When my car arrived at the show that night, we saw Ricky outside talking with Dr. Death Steve Williams. The two of them were wrestling out in the yard, and Doc, who was a pretty good amateur wrestler, was showing Ricky all kinds of legitimate shoots and hooks.

We walked up to see what was going on. Back then guys would never drink before a match, but we could see Ricky had already had a few. He was also pretty worked up and angry.

"We're in a tag tonight," he said, indicating that Ricky and me would be against the Blade Runners. "Fuck those mother fuckers. You stay on the apron."

I said, "Ricky, whatever you gotta do is fine with me." Wrestlers back then had a certain way of settling their differences, and I knew better than to try and intervene.

When we got into the ring, Ricky repeated his demand for me to stay out of the way. Ricky got in the ring with Sting, and he beat his ass. Ricky wasn't really a shooter, but he was smarter than Sting and worked him over pretty good. After that match, they all sat down and talked out their differences, and that was the end of it.

One night in Greenville, Mississippi, Sting tried to take advantage of me. He could get a little roid rage at times, but when he came after me, I got behind him and took him down. They called me "Takedown Tracy" that night.

Sting started to come around after that. He started learning and working hard and he became a really great worker. If you followed WCW, you know the rest of the story about what a star he became.

I got a little heat in Mid-South riding around with Terry Taylor. Terry was the booker for part of the time I was there. Terry could be a smartass, and he rubbed some guys the wrong way. Some guys thought he was a stooge, but he was always pretty good to me.

Tommy Gilbert and D.J. Peterson rode with Terry and me on a lot of those long drives. Talk about oil and water, Tommy and Terry really didn't get along. They'd sit in that car and argue all day long.

One of the craziest things I ever saw happened on the road between Alexandra, Louisiana, and Houston, Texas. I was driving a car with D.J. Peterson, Terry Taylor, and Carl Fergie, and we were following Jim Duggan and Dr. Death Steve Williams. Steve and Jim had a Fuzz Buster - a police radar detector. The cops were all over the back roads of Louisiana in those days, and if they found anything on you, they would arrest you and make you pay the fines before you could go on. It was bad all over, but I remember Shreveport being the worst.

Terry Taylor was in the passenger seat next to me, coaching me on how to avoid speed traps. All of a sudden we saw a few station wagons and trucks full of young college guys fly past us. For some reason they started messing with Steve and Jim. These guys were coming back from a bonfire party or something, and they were looking for trouble.

After a few miles of this, Steve and Jim pulled over on the side of the road. The college kids pulled over as well, and they all started hopping out of their vehicles. This was at a time when if a fan fucked with you, you had to step up and go over. If you didn't go over, you could lose your job. I figured something was about to go down, so I pulled over and started to get out of the car.

Terry and D.J. reached over and grabbed me. "What the fuck are you doing?"

"Are you kidding? There's three car loads of those guys!" I said.

Terry said, "Mother fucker, do you really think they need you?"

I sat down and watched the scene unfold out the front window. Steve Williams got out of the car and started throwing Gatorade bottles left and right at their attackers. While the boys were busy dodging the bottles, Duggan got out of the car. It was then these college boys realized who they were dealing with, and they took off running. The lucky ones made it into the woods and got away, but Duggan and Dr. Death beat the hell out of these young, strong, athletic looking kids.

Bill Watts had a working relationship with Fritz Von Erich, who ran World Class Championship Wrestling from the "World Famous" Sportatorium in Dallas. Near the end of my run, Bill brought Ken Mantell in from WCCW to take the book from Terry Taylor. Ken brought the Freebirds, Missy Hyatt, John Tatum, One Man Gang, and

Jack Victory with him.

I saw the writing on the wall, and I started looking for other territories. I had become close with Brett Sawyer, and he called Don Owens in Portland, Oregon for me. Back then, we didn't have emails and social media. We didn't even really have video tapes at that time. We'd mail a few 8 x 10s to some promoters and hope for the best.

I sent a package to Don Owens and spoke to him by phone. "Well, you look good. Bret says you're kind of green, but you're learning and you're athletic. I'd like to have you, but I don't have a spot for you. I'd have to ask some of my guys to move, and these guys have wives and girlfriends, and babies on the way. I just can't do that to them."

I remember hanging up the phone and saying, "I can't believe he just said all that." I was genuinely surprised to talk to a promoter who actually cared about his wrestlers like that. Disappointed as I was, I thought he was a class act.

I tried to go to Kansas City, which was owned by Harley Race at the time. I spoke to Harley's booker "Bulldog" Bob Brown and Bob Geigel, the head of the NWA at that time. Kansas City was looking good. I spoke to Bob Brown on a Thursday, and he told me, "I'm going to talk to Harley about you on Monday."

"Great," I said.

The next day, I had a show in Lafayette, Louisiana. When I walked into the locker room I could sense something was up. Grizzly Smith came in and announced the rumor going around was true: Harley Race had signed with the WWF!

Everybody was stunned. At that time, Harley Race was the NWA. He had just passed the torch to Flair about a year earlier, but he was still the NWA in the eyes of most fans and the boys. It wasn't too long before that when WWF had tried to run in Kansas City. Harley went down there with a gun and shut them down. Now he was part of the WWF. No one could believe it.

"There goes Kansas City," I thought. I tried to call Bob Brown again, but I never got a hold of him after that.

I had one more crazy incident with Sting in Pine Bluff, Missouri near the end of my run. I was working out my notice with Bill Watts, and I was preparing to go back to Memphis. Sting's skin was broken out pretty bad, but he thought it was just from shaving his body hair. He got me in a rest-hold/bear hug, skin to skin, and the next thing I knew I was broken out.

Unfortunately for both of us, it had nothing to do with shaving. Sting had a staph infection, and now, I had staph as well. I broke out after that, and I called Bill Watts from home. Bill told me Sting was going to be out at least two weeks. I asked him what he wanted me to do. Bill said, "You've given me proper notice, and you've always done good business with me. We have plans for Sting but not for you going forward." I told Bill I already had a starting date back in Memphis, and he thanked me for my time.

I appreciated how straight forward Bill was. It was no-nonsense and all business with him. He ran Mid-South like a football coach. He had a great mind for the business, but he was an old school guy you didn't mess around with.

RETURN TO MEMPHIS

Bill Dundee had the book when I agreed to go back to Memphis, but by the time I got there, Jerry Lawler had taken the book. Lawler wasn't always the easiest guy to get along with in those days, but I had a few extra things going against me. I was local, and Jerry didn't like pushing the local guys. Plus Jerry was on the outs with Tojo and the Fabulous Ones. In wrestling, you're guilty by association, so I was in trouble just being connected to those guys.

I knew Jerry would start bringing in his own guys that he had plans with, and that's what happened. I really only had to deal with Jerry when we were in Memphis, as he wasn't making all the towns. Bill Dundee was still running Louisville, Evansville, and all the usual stops, but Dundee didn't have any pull as far as creative went.

Jerry Jarrett's mother Christine Jarrett was the lady who ran the building in Louisville and Evansville. She was in charge of all the promotion, ticket sales and the TV tapes. She was all business, and she did not mess around. She wanted you to dress nice and act professional at all times, and you could not be late. She stood by the back door with her watch, and if you walked in five minutes late, she wanted to know why.

Christine treated us all like her own kids. She was tough, but it was because she really cared. You towed the line when you worked for her because if you didn't - she WOULD find out. She was a hard-working lady, God rest her soul, and I have a lot of great memories of her.

I met a lot of new guys the second time around in Memphis. Randy Hales was starting to help out behind the scenes and took on more and more responsibility as time went on. Some other guys I remember from that time are Plowboy Frazier, Cousin Junior, J.R. Hall, Eddie Marlin, and Moondog Larry Latham.

There were some younger guys who made my second run in Memphis a lot of fun. I met Paul Diamond, who later worked as Max Moon in WWF. I also got to know Pat Tanaka, who was the son of the legendary Duke Keomuka. And then there was Jerry's son Jeff, who was just starting to break into the business.

The four of us spent a lot of time together. We'd go to Jerry Jarrett's house before shows to shoot promos, and afterwards we'd arrive at the wrestling show in a limousine. Of course, most of the time I was the guy driving the limousine. During the week, we would all carpool together, and each one of us would take turns driving with our car.

Pat Tanaka was crazy. He lived in an apartment out by the airport in Nashville, and he would throw parties like you would not believe. On the first and third Saturday night every month after the Nashville show, he'd rent out the clubhouse at his apartment complex and throw a huge party. Pat Xeroxed directions and handed them out to everyone: wrestlers, fans, and the girls. Unlike a lot of guys, Pat did not refer to the girls who slept with wrestlers as rats; he called them "talent."

I didn't drink or smoke or do anything back then, so I'd sip on orange juice while everyone else got wild, but I still had a good time. I'd stay at Pat's two or three nights a week, including those Saturday nights. We'd party most of the night, sleep until noon on Sunday, which was our off day, and play water volleyball in the afternoon.

Paul Diamond brought his then-wife to a party one Saturday. That lasted about ten minutes before she left. The Summer of 1986 was a good time for all of us, never to be forgotten!

Jeff Jarrett was a hell of a basketball player. He was a star in high school and played a few years in college, but like his father, he wanted to be a wrestler. Jeff was skinny back then and hadn't started lifting weights, but he was a really gifted athlete. Tojo Yamamoto and Tony Falk trained him and got him started, and once he was on the road, he started riding with me and my crew.

Jeff was a really smart kid, and he listened whenever his dad spoke. He understood his dad knew the business well, and he learned everything he could from him. It was no surprise to me when Jeff turned out to be a good promoter in his own right.

One of the best guys in the ring with Jeff Jarrett was another second generation star, Curt Hennig. Curt was from Minnesota and the song of another legend, Larry "The Axe" Hennig. Curt and Jeff had a great false finish that they used to do, and the two of them had some classic matches together in those early days.

As much fun as I was having with the guys, I knew I was never going to get a good push in Memphis. I was starting to feel worn out with the wrestling business and was considering getting out to go back to school and get into coaching. I gave my notice to say I was leaving, but then they ran an angle that changed my plans.

They had a tag team called Fire and Flame, Don Bass and Roger Smith. Don and Roger had worked a lot of gimmicks over the years, including Interns, the A-Team, and the Assassins. They drew a lot of money working as a heel tag team.

Roger and Don were tough guys, real shooters, but they liked me. So one day on a TV taping, they did a gimmick where they burned me. I took it face first, and they really got me. I sold the injury, which wasn't too hard because they really got me good, and it came across as looking pretty brutal on TV.

I was living at my mom and dad's house at the time, and the next day, Sunday, my mom hollered to tell me Jerry Lawler was on the phone.

"Hey," he said. "That thing you did on TV with the fire looked great. We're not going to have you wrestle Monday. Can you get there a little early and dress nice? I'll doctor you up to make you up like you really got burned."

I got to Memphis, and Jerry applied some makeup to make me look like a real burn victim. They were pushing Fire and Flame as strong heels, and the angle really got over. I went down to the ring to do a bit with Roger and Don, and Roger, who was helping Lawler with the booking, spoke to me.

"You took that flame really well," he said. "You're a really good babyface. We want to do something with you."

"You need to talk to Lawler about that," I said. "I don't think they have any plans for me, and I just gave my notice."

"No, no, no, you ain't giving no notice," he said. "We're helping King, so we'll talk to him."

I was serious when I gave my notice and said I wanted to quit. If it wasn't for Roger and Donny, I wouldn't be writing this book. I'd have gotten out of the business and gone into coaching.

Roger and Don got me some more matches, and I started to get some wins. Then I got booked in a tournament for the AWA Mid-American title. I had to work three times and get juice, but at the end of that night, I had the belt around my waist. It was the first belt I ever owned.

I dropped the belt a while later to Tony Falk, who had a Boy George type gimmick. Boy Tony in modern times would have to be a babyface, but Tennessee during the mid-1980s, he got serious heel heat playing a gay character. It's an angle you definitely can't do today for obvious reasons.

I worked with Tony for about six months. We had a stipulation one night where the loser had to be the other guy's maid for a day. I lost, and I had to be his maid for a day. We made a whole video of me working around his house, getting chased by his dog, and other stuff. It may be out on the Internet, if you want to go look for it.

One Saturday, on live Memphis TV, I got myself in big trouble. Tony had done something to cause me to lose a match on the show. We were headed to Jonesboro, Arkansas that night, and since Jonesboro got the show live, I came out of the ring to cut a promo on him.

This was long before Monday Night Raw, and it was completely unscripted. We all knew that there were certain words you could not say on television, and in the heat of the moment, I used a word to describe Boy Tony that made Dave Brown's eyes go as wide as saucers. I saw Lance react too out of the corner of my eye, and I knew I had messed up bad.

When I got to the back, Jerry Jarrett, Eddie Marlin, and Jerry Lawler all went off on me. I thought for sure that I was going to be fired and blackballed from the business.

Like I said, you couldn't do an angle like Boy Tony today, and if you used a word like I did on TV today, you would be done. Period! Somehow I survived the incident. They eventually had to pull back on the character for Tony's safety.

After the Tom Cruise movie *Top Gun* came out, they put Paul Diamond and me together in a tag team. They were going to dress us up like fighter pilots and call us the Top Guns. We worked a good program with another tag team called the Mod Squad.

One of the other angles that got over big at that time was Jeff Jarrett and Pat Tanaka versus Akio Sato and Tarzan Goto. Sato and Goto were great in the ring, and Jeff started getting better every night. They added Tojo Yamamoto to the angle as Sato and Goto's manager which led to Jerry Jarrett standing in Jeff and Pat's corner. That led to some three on three matches that went over big.

We all really learned how to work once our angles took off and we were all working more. Being in Memphis, Louisville, Evansville, and Nashville every week meant we had to constantly change things to stay fresh. We also had to match up our house shows with what was happening on TV. The Memphis show Monday always followed the live TV show on Saturday, but that TV episode wouldn't air in Louisville and Evansville until the following week. We'd do a new match on Monday in Memphis, then wrestle the match we'd done the previous week in Memphis when we got to Louisville and Evansville, who had just seen the previous week's TV show on tape.

Memphis was a really great place to learn because of the demanding schedule but also the talent. Everybody who was anybody came through Memphis: Hulk, Savage, the Rock, Austin. Not only that, before "Bret screwed Bret," Vince McMahon himself did an angle on Memphis TV, creating the evil "Mr. McMahon" persona that he would later use on WWF television. Go out and search for it on YouTube. It's all there.

FLORIDA

About a year after my return to Memphis, I was ready to move again. You didn't want to stay in a territory for too long because you didn't want your character to get stale with the fans. You always tried to leave on good terms, and you wanted to leave in such a way that when you came back, the fans would be excited to see you return one day.

Pat Tanaka got me connected with Florida Championship Wrestling. Pat told me to send my information to his father, Duke Keomuka, who was the booker for Florida Championship Wrestling. Steve Keirn was long-time friends with Mike Graham in the Florida office, and he put in a word for me as well. Duke reviewed my information with Mike, Kevin Sullivan, Luke Williams and Hiro Matsuda.

I had worked with Luke in Mid-South, and he really pushed for me with the guys. I got a call on my house phone from Hiro and Kevin Sullivan, who explained their plans. "We have Steve Armstrong down here, and we want to pair you with him to do a Confederate gimmick as babyfaces."

Now before my younger readers reach for a lighter to burn the rest of this book, let me explain. Back in the 1980s, waving the rebel flag didn't automatically make you a heel like it would today. A couple of good looking, younger guys named Bo and Luke Duke had already flown the stars and bars on top of their car on television and become a top hit, much to the surprise of TV executives. Hiro and Kevin knew that a pair of good looking babyfaces like Steve and me would get over huge. Having already met and worked with Steve, I was excited for the opportunity.

"We want to call you the Wild Eyed Southern Boys," they told us. "We will dress you up in Confederate uniforms and have you carry the rebel flag. We're going to put you right into a feud with our tag champions, the New Breed, Chris Champion and Sean Royal."

The New Breed, Chris Champion and Sean Royal, were red hot at the time, with their signature haircuts and their entrance theme: the Beastie Boys' "(You Gotta) Fight For Your Right to Party." If you paired a team like Steve and I against a team like the New Breed today, the New Breed would be the babyfaces and we would be the heels, not just because of the flag but because of the New Breed's gimmick. Instead, we were the babyfaces and they were the heels. Funny how times change.

They gave me a starting date, which allowed me to give two weeks' notice. That was how you did business back then, especially if you wanted to be welcomed back one day!

Kevin Sullivan was the booker when we got to Florida. He was a brilliant guy who knew the business well and knew how to draw money. I honestly don't know why he's still not in some sort of creative position somewhere. Not only did he have a great mind, he's a rare person who can handle the big egos and get everyone on board.

Mark Lewin was still involved at that time as well. He was an old time wrestler who went back to the 1950s. He was trained by his brother-in-law, "Dangerous" Danny McShain, a real tough character from back in the day, and when I met him, Mark was Kevin's mentor.

In Florida we did a house show in Tampa on Tuesdays and TV on Wednesdays at the Tampa Sportatorium. Then we would drive south through the Everglades to do Miami one week and Ft. Lauderdale the next. We'd do spot shows on Fridays, making stops once a month in places like Lakeland and Sarasota. Every Sunday was the Eddie Graham Sports Complex in Orlando.

My first day in Florida at the gym, I ran into Steve. We were thrilled to be teamed up together. I also met Scott Hall, who was several years away from getting his big break as Razor Ramon. The three of us traveled together every day, and if we were in Steve's van, we'd occasionally be joined by Ron Simmons, Big Ed Gantner, and the Mulkys. We made a lot of drives through the Everglades, looking at all those gators on the side of the road. I was never there to witness this, but I heard stories about Steve Keirn, Barry Windham, and Mike Graham shooting at animals on their way through the Everglades.

Occasionally we'd make a trip to the airport to pick up Wahoo McDaniel, Steve's dad Bob Armstrong, and Jimmy Valiant. Road Warrior Hawk would ride with us when he and Animal were in the territory, while Animal rode with someone else. Hawk was kind of wild, but he was a really cool guy.

One time in Steve's van, Hawk said to us, "Listen, guys, Joe is going to ask you to look out for his kid brother when he comes down to Florida."

Joe's kid brother was John Laurinitis, aka Johnny Ace. We had no idea what he looked like, and we were surprised to meet a good looking blonde kid who wasn't all muscled up like Animal.

Johnny was really cool, and we had some good times traveling with him, but occasionally we'd tell him, "There's no way you and Joe are brothers!"

Ron Simmons was a country boy from Warner-Robbins, Georgia. He was a great football player in high school and went on to become a hall of fame college player at Florida State. He played a little for the Cleveland Browns in the NFL and then for the Tampa Bay Bandits of the USFL, where he was teammates with Lex Luger.

Mitch Snow was in Florida. So was Samu, who was called the Tahitian Prince. He had already had a run in WWF by that time. Some of the other guys include Colt Steele, Tijo Carne, Pez Whatley, Brad Armstrong, Jimmy Del Ray, and Jimmy Backlund. Gordon Solie was our commentator. Every Wednesday Dusty Rhodes would come down for TV, and Jim Crockett would be there every now and then. He would later take over the territory.

Kevin Sullivan brought in a young manager and gave him his start while I was down there. Paul Heyman was managing a big guy named Tombstone, who worked with Scott Hall every night. Paul was a great talker even then, and he'd already done the angle in Memphis where he and Tommy Rich caused Jerry Lawler to get his head shaved. Tommy was actually the guy who vouched for Paul in Tennessee, and that's why years later Paul gave Tommy a job at ECW.

Mike Rotunda came in for a while and worked every night with Dory Funk, Jr. Dory was just a machine, and Mike was a consummate wrestler. They would go 30-40 minutes, and they were all classics.

Bob Cooke was a great worker I got to know down in Florida as well. He was from that area, and Steve and I worked with him a lot in Florida as well as WCW. He never would set foot in a gym, or else he might have gotten a big push in the business, but a great guy.

Steve Keirn was tag teaming with Mike Graham, working as heels. Steve got out of the business shortly after that. He had a family, and I think he had a farm where he raised alligators.

Stan Lane was there too. I remember when he got the call to go to WCW and work for Jim Crockett. He ended up replacing Dennis Condrey and teaming up with Bobby Eaton and Jim Cornette in the Midnight Express.

Right after they finished their run with me and Steve, the New Breed got the call to work for Crockett as well. Times were changing, and the New Breed, who had always been heels, started getting over a babyfaces. They have been sort of forgotten because there were so many good tag teams back then, but they had some great runs with the Mod Squad and the Midnight Express.

Florida was in a rough state when we arrived due to an incident involving Bruiser Brody and Lex Luger. Luger was new and green and in those days, pretty cocky, and prior to a steel cage match with the dangerous veteran Brody, he tried to tell the big man how the match was going to go down. That's a big no-no, especially when you're talking about a veteran like Brody.

The match started out okay, but then at one point Bruiser stopped selling for Luger. He no-sold every bit of offense that Luger threw at him. The fans knew something was wrong. Luger was terrified. He knew how tough Bruiser was, and he got spooked. Luger ended up climbing on the cage and escaping to the outside, ending the match. Lex was on his way out at that time anyway, bound for WCW, but rather than fulfill the dates he was booked during his last week, he no-showed them. It was a big blow for the Florida promotion, and it hurt business for a long time.

I got to meet Bruiser when he came into Florida for a one week loop. Kevin Sullivan brought him in to work against another hardcore guy, the original Sheik. Bruiser Brody was an absolute beast. He did a thousand squats a day. He was 6'8" and weighed 325 pounds in his prime and couldn't spell steroids. His leg strength was unreal, and when he got that adrenaline going, he was unstoppable.

Bruiser was a crazy looking guy with a faraway look in his eyes, but Steve Armstrong put me at ease. "I've known Frank all my life," he said, "He and my Dad have been friends a long time. He was Uncle Frank to us."

We had a packed house in Miami that night to see Bruiser wrestle the original Sheik. Steve turned to me before the match and said, "Let's go out and watch Big Frank tear up the building."

"What?" I said.

Steve said, "Just come with me." He took me up into the balcony to a spot he and his brothers had been going since they were kids, and we saw one of the damnedest matches I ever witnessed.

Bruiser Brody and the Sheik didn't even get in the ring. They fought all over the building and tore up everything that wasn't nailed down. After the match, Brody destroyed the place. He turned over a concession cart on wheels like it was nothing. After that, he came back into the dressing room calm as could be. I couldn't believe it.

One night we did a pull-apart where a bunch of us hit the ring to try to pull Bruiser and Kevin Sullivan apart. Kevin warned all of us, "Watch it when you go out there. Sometimes Big Frank gets excited."

Sure enough, when we got out there, Bruiser and Kevin were up in the bleachers. He grabbed me and whispered, "Sell your back, kid," and he brought that giant arm of his down on my back. BAM! I thought I was paralyzed. Then I heard him say, "Watch the boot to the stomach." He punted me, and I did a Cactus Jack bump down the steps. I didn't mean to do it, but his boot just lifted me in the air and sent me down the steps.

Bruiser Brody is one of two guys I think could take out today's shoot fighters. The other guy is Haku. I'm not talking about Haku in his prime. I mean Haku now, in his sixties, could still whip anybody in UFC. This is a man who knocked out six guys outside a bar in St. Louis without throwing a punch. It was all kicks. He got into a fight with Jimmy Jack Funk, a good friend of his, just a few years ago, and Haku pulled his eye out of the socket. That's how tough that guy is.

Haku is a great guy. Whenever I see him, he always pulls me in for a big hug. Let me tell you, I can feel the strength in that man when he wraps his arms around me. That's how I know he could whip any man in UFC even today. One blow, and you're done.

Sometimes when we were traveling, we would stop off at a bridge we knew was a good spot for gar fishing. Gar fish are no good to eat but fun to catch because they put up a fight. The Mulkey Brothers had these little fishing rods they always brought with them.

One time we had Scott Hall, Ron Simmons, Mulkey brothers, Bull Gantner, and Johnny Ace all loaded into Steve's van. We pulled over at our usual spot and were fishing when another car came by with Steve Keirn inside. We heard Steve shout, "Hey, watch this!"

Steve tossed two or three cherry bombs off the bridge into the water. Next thing we knew, BOOM! BOOM! BOOM! Those things went off and water and gar went flying everywhere. Scared us to death, but it was funny.

Some nights when we got home, Steve Armstrong and Samu would go fishing in a lake. One night they came in and said they had hooked an alligator. They didn't reel it in, but they hooked it in a lake where people went to swim and fish all the time. Ron Simmons was disappointed to learn they hadn't reeled it in. He was ready to skin it and cook it.

I wasn't there for this story but I heard about it. Barry Windham, Steve Keirn, and Mike Graham were driving through the Everglades in a van. They had the side door open, and they were shooting at alligators and wild hogs. They were aiming to miss, not to kill, just having a little fun on the road.

Another time when we were headed down south, a strange man pulled up next to us in a van and started waving a gun and yelling at us. We had trouble making out what he was yelling at first, but we soon realized he was accusing us of sleeping with his wife. The guy had us worried until we figured out it was Mike Graham in disguise ribbing us. Of course he didn't reveal himself until he'd already run us off the road.

Dusty Rhodes really liked Scott Hall, who was trained by Barry Windham. Scott and Curt Hennig had tagged in the AWA before he came to Florida. He really looked great, and you could tell he was going to be a star.

Like many wrestlers, Steve and I caught the eye of the ladies who came to the matches. Being two young, handsome babyfaces with a good ol' Southern boy gimmick, we had more than our share. Everybody did, really. I turned down a lot, but I had more than my share.

I was always single back then, and it fell to me to keep a "talent sheet" for myself and many of the boys. A lot of the guys had wives or girlfriends at home, so they weren't in a position to easily carry around the numbers of their favorite fans in certain towns. I kept the tablet for everyone, so when we hit this town or that, the guys could get the numbers they needed from me.

Every territory I worked in had a talent sheet. Smoky

Mountain, ECW, all of them. We had rules for how things were done, and if someone got out of line, we would hold wrestler's court. It was all in good fun.

There were plenty of wild times after the matches with the female fans, but it wasn't just about the sex. A lot of these girls had good jobs, and some had boyfriends. Some were willing to go get groceries for us. They brought us birthday presents and brought food to the matches. They would run errands for us. They'd clean our apartments when we were away.

The term "ring rats" is often used today in regards to the girls who liked to sleep with wrestlers, but we didn't call them that. You didn't disrespect them, and you didn't do anything to hurt the business. We got to know a lot of their families as well as the ladies. I'm still friends with some of them today.

We had a lot of folks willing to lend a hand and do us favors, not just the ladies who had a thing for the boys. Restaurants would give us discounted or free meals to eat at their establishments. Gyms would let us work out for free in exchange for us wearing their T-shirts on TV, which we were glad to do. The police were really cool to us, so long as we didn't put them in a bad spot.

Steve and I worked a lot of tag feuds and six man matches in Florida. They would bring in different guys to work as our third man against the New Breed and the Mod Squad. One time Bill Dundee came in, working as the manager of the Mod Squad against us. We did an angle where they made a big cake for Bill. Bob Armstrong came out and put Bill's face in the cake, just like they did with Jim Cornette and the Midnights. That led to a six man with Bob in our corner.

Boogie (Jimmy Valiant) was always a big hit when he came in. When he worked as our third, he would come in at the end, drop the elbow and do his dance in the ring. The fans just went crazy over it.

Boogie worked a lot with The Barbarian. They brought Barb in to TV on a Wednesday, and he jumped in the ring and went after Boogie. Boogie got some color, which you could do on TV back then, and afterwards, he gave an interview.

"They say Florida's a chiming stage! I've been in Florida six days, and I've been jumped six times! I got up at six AM! I had six eggs for breakfast!" Everything was six, six, six. It was great.

Boogie came off as a crazy, tough guy on TV, but in real life, he's one of the nicest, most laid back guys ever. He's the complete opposite of what you saw on TV.

Wahoo McDaniel was another third man on our team. One time, Steve and I picked up Wahoo, Boogie, and Bob at the Tampa airport. When we got to the building in Steve's van, we saw a black limo pull up behind us with the Four Horsemen: Lex Luger, Tully Blanchard, Arn Anderson, and Ric Flair. A white limo pulled up behind them, and out came Nikita Koloff, Dusty Rhodes, Jim Crockett, and the Road Warriors.

We were getting paid good money at that time, but it wasn't great. It wasn't limousine money, that's for sure. We did okay on the smaller shows, but we were getting screwed on the big shows. Wahoo knew this, and when Crockett got out of the limo, he said, "What the fuck, Jimmy? Don't starve these guys while you're riding around like the Sheiks of Arabia! Bob, Boogie, am I right?"

Bob shook his head. Boogie babyfaced him and ignored it. They didn't want to get involved, but Wahoo didn't care. He was willing to stick up for us.

We went into the dressing room, and I saw Ole talking to Jim Crockett, face to face. Dusty walked over to them and said out loud, "Hey Ole. That's my chair now," meaning he was the booker.

Dusty was joking around, and Ole played right into it. He stood up and said, "Yes, sir, Dusty Runnels, the American Dream, you can sit right there!" They were putting on a show for us, acting like they might get into it.

Wahoo egged them on, stirring the pot. "Come on, boys, let's have a little shoot here!"

That night we worked against the Mod Squad and Bill Dundee with Wahoo in our corner. Wahoo looked at all the gig marks on our foreheads and said, "Good God! It looks like a road map of Mississippi! Who told you all to do that?"

Steve and I had been blading almost every night to get color. Steve would do it one night, and I would do it the next. That's what you did to build the territory up. Bill Dundee was the man in charge, along with Kevin Sullivan, and while I didn't want to say directly, I told Wahoo, "Well, you know who's running things."

Wahoo looked at the house, which was pretty packed. Then he

looked across the ring at the Mod Squad and Bill. "Okay, I'm gonna start here. I'm going to light these mother fuckers up, and then you boys can do your thing."

Wahoo chopped all three of those boys so hard, I felt sorry for them. He really laid into them. When Bill got in the ring with him, he gave back as hard as Wahoo did. Wahoo chopped Bill, and Bill punched him. Wahoo chopped and Bill punched. Those two should have had a singles program after that, the way they worked together. It would have been great.

People don't realize how tough Bill Dundee was. He's almost 20 years older than me, still wrestling in his late 70s. He can still knock you out with that punch of his!

We did another memorable six man match around the time when the New Breed was finishing up. The two of them were in the ring with Kevin Sullivan, waiting to see who their opponents would be. Steve and I were waiting to go out, but we didn't even know up until right before our partner was going to be Barry Windham. Barry's music hit, and the place blew up. Barry told us to do that little jog he always did to the ring with him.

I looked over at Steve as we were jogging down and said, "This is cool, man! Barry fucking Windham!"

Steve said, "You mark!" Steve had known Barry all his life, so it wasn't such a big deal to him.

Say what you will about those top guys, but they earned their money. We had a spot show in Daytona, where the Four Horsemen took on Dusty Rhodes, Nikita Koloff, and the Road Warriors. They sold the place out. They were the biggest stars in the business. Arn Anderson and Tully Blanchard were a tremendous tag team, and Ric Flair was the man.

Ric Flair was not only the biggest guy in the business, he was the very best at giving back. Ric would get free T-shirts from the gyms where he worked out, and when he came into the locker room, he handed the shirts to the boys. Ric also liked to plug his favorite bars on the air. Jim Crockett gave him an expense account to buy drinks for people in the bars, and people would end up coming out to the matches because they met Ric at the bar. You can't beat that kind of free advertising.

You don't need me to tell you that all the stories you've heard about Ric and his ability to party. When Ric Flair was the champion, he lived the gimmick to the fullest. He traveled like a champion, and he partied like a champion. And if you were lucky enough to be on a show with Ric, you partied with him.

Ric would pay the shuttle drivers from our hotels a hundred bucks to track us down and give us a lift to the bars. We couldn't keep up! We'd try to hide from the drivers, but it didn't always work. "Hey, I'm getting paid," the drivers would tell us. "I have to get you to the bar."

Ric wouldn't let anyone pay for anything. He would order round after round of shots for all the boys, the fans, the waitresses, and whomever else was in the bar. Ric would get the waitresses drunk, the bartender drunk, everybody drunk.

Ric wanted everybody to have a good time, whether he was at the bar, in a hotel, or on a plane. He loved the ladies, and he loved to drop his pants. It's a damn good thing there were no cellphones back there, or else we all would have been in a whole world of trouble.

The funny thing is, Ric would drink and party all night, but Ric would also hit that gym and spend hours walking the stair stepper and doing squats. He was an absolute machine.

ON THE MOVE

Sometimes things happen in the wrestling business through hard work and effort. Sometimes things happen because of unfortunate circumstances. Such was the case with a break Steve and I caught in 1987.

Dusty Rhodes was booking for Jim Crockett, and he was a big fan of the New Breed and their gimmick. In 1987 he decided to bring them in and give them a big push by working with the Midnight Express after the 1987 Bash. Those plans fell by the wayside when the New Breed was in a car wreck. Chris was hurt pretty bad, and they were unable to start. Dusty needed a fresh tag team, and he decided to bring in Steve and me to work against the Midnights.

Our first clash with the Midnight Express took place in St. Petersburg, Florida. My old mentor Stan Lane had recently taken over for Dennis Condrey, and it was a real thrill for me to be working with the man who trained me. Steve had been in the business longer than me, so it was no big deal to him working with the Midnights, but I had a hard time containing my excitement.

Stan's partner in the Midnight was Bobby Eaton. Bobby had broken into the business when he was just sixteen years old. By the time we worked with him in 1987, he had become the best heel in the business. I mean it, no one was better than Bobby Eaton.

Outside the ring, the Midnights were managed by Jim Cornette. Jimmy was just a few years into his managing career, but he already had such a great mind for the business. Matter of fact when we worked with the Midnights, he was the one who laid out our matches. We got to work with them again in Baltimore and a few other towns in the Charlotte territory.

I remember looking out at the crowd in Crockett's territory and thinking how big the crowd was. The reaction was much different from the established boys in the locker room. They were used to sell outs, and the building, as full as it was, wasn't as full as it could have been.

We had been made a lot of promises, and the pay outs were pretty good, but we found out the Midnight Express was getting three times what we made. I'm not saying that we deserved to make what the Midnights were making, but the difference was enough to make us both pretty pissed.

Steve was missing home, and I was mad about the money. The politics were getting to me as well. We were told we'd be getting on TBS and the Midnights were going to put us over, but we decided we'd been screwed enough and walked out. We had some heat with Dusty Rhodes for not showing up for TV, but we didn't care.

As it turned out, the Rock 'n' Roll Express walked out shortly after we did. The Fantastics took their place, as they did in many places, and they went over big with the fans. We knew that could have been our spot, but who knows how things would have really turned out.

The Armstrongs and I worked some independent dates when we weren't working other places. We were down in Louisiana one night working for some outlaw promotion when one of the local boys got cut with Steve in the ring. Steve went off and then Scott went off, and they beat those guys all the way to the back.

I didn't know the guys, and I didn't want to get involved. I tried to play security and calm things down. I even dragged one guy to his car, just to get him out of harm's way.

Steve Armstrong and I wanted to go back to Tennessee and work for Southeastern Championship Wrestling out of Knoxville, which was soon to become Continental. Robert Fuller was the promoter in Knoxville, and Bob Armstrong was working for him. They brought Steve in and started using him first, and the plan was to bring me in as his tag partner.

That all changed when the Rockers got fired from WWF. Formerly known as the Midnight Rockers, Shawn Michaels and Marty Jannety had first made a name for themselves working in the AWA. They were signed by the WWF, who had big plans for them, but Shawn and Marty wore out their welcome very quickly. Despite their reputation, the Rockers were red hot, and plans for Steve and me were put on hold when Robert Fuller brought the Rockers in.

I didn't know all this at the time. I was busy working in the fields cutting tobacco and working out, just waiting for the phone call. Finally one day, the phone rang. "This is Jerry Jarrett," said the familiar voice on the other end. "What are you doing?"

"I'm down on the farm cutting tobacco," I said.

"Is that what you want to do?" he asked.

"Well, no," I said. "I'd rather be in the ring. But I should probably stick with this for a while and then go back to coaching."

It was Jerry who told me about the Rockers taking our spot in Continental. I wasn't too upset about it. I understood the Rockets were big stars, and I didn't blame Robert for bringing them in.

Jerry asked me. "How about you come back and work for me?"

I told Jerry I wasn't sure I wanted to get back into the business. In all honesty, I was fine walking away from the business. I was really ready to quit, make my family happy, and become a football coach.

"Do you want to work on a farm all your life?" Jerry asked me.

"Well no, not really," I said. "I want to get back in school, get my degree and coach."

"Well, the choice is yours," he said. "Yes or no."

I knew I wouldn't get another chance, so I said yes. Jerry told me to be at TV that Saturday. I went back to work and told them that Friday would be my last day. I was getting back into the business.

One of the tag teams we got to work with when we went back into Memphis was the Nasty Boys. Brian Knobbs and Jerry Saggs were just getting their start at that time but were on their way to WWF and WCW glory. Pat Tanaka and Paul Diamond were working as a tag team too, as were Jeff Jarrett and Billy Travis. Rocky Johnson was in there as well.

I traveled with Rocky Johnson and Bill Dundee every day. Bill was hard on me, but he also gave me my first full-time job in the business. He was always really good to me.

Rocky was a character, and he loved to drink. On the way to a town, he'd drink a 40 ounce Bud Light on the way to and on the way back from a show. He also trained hard, and he had lost a lot of weight after having let himself go for a few years.

Rocky's pride and joy was "Dewey," his then teenage son Dwayne. All he talked about was Dewey and his wife, and he always knew Dwayne was going to be someone special. Dwayne wanted to be a professional football player, and he was starting on his high school team as a freshman. He was already build like a superstar, even as a fifteen year old kid.

We saw Dwayne every now and then at shows, but he was usually busy with high school sports. He was very smart and very observant when he was around, and even though football was his first love, he loved wrestling. He was really laid back and funny, and he had that smile. He was very mature, and he was wise beyond his years even then. Dwayne knew I had played football, and whenever I got a chance to talk to him, it was always about football.

Rocky was so proud of Dwayne and all his accomplishments, but like any dad, he worried about his son. One time when Steve Armstrong was on the road with us, he was drinking his beer worrying out loud. "That fuckin' Dewey. He's jacked. I know he's on the juice! He's gotta be! There's no way a guy can look like that in the ninth grade."

People always point out that Dwayne only started one game for the University of Miami Hurricanes. What they fail to realize is that he was behind Warren Sapp, one of the greatest defensive ends of all time. Miami was in their prime back then, and their roster was absolutely loaded. Ray Lewis was on the team with Dwayne and a lot of other guys who had long careers in the NFL. He still played 39 games in his four years at Miami with 77 tackles and 4.25 sacks, and he won a national championship in his freshman year.

Rocky was very thankful Dwayne wanted to pursue football and not wrestling. Rocky didn't want Dwayne to go through all the hardships he had trying to get into the business. Wrestling was in Dwayne's blood, on his dad and mom's side, so I guess it was inevitable.

Whenever I crossed paths with Rocky, all he would talk about was Dwayne's career. He was proud of the success Dwayne had with WWE, and he was somewhat relieved when it led him to Hollywood. He never stopped worrying about his son. After the Rock got hurt at WrestleMania in his match with John Cena, Rocky told me how that injury put him behind on his movie schedule. He passed away as we were finishing this book. God bless him.

The Nasty Boys came down from Minnesota. They used to hang around with an NFL lineman named Matt Millen, who went on to become an NFL executive and announcer.

The Nasty Boys had those crazy haircuts and a look that nobody else had. Jeff Jarrett loved those guys, and he knew they were something special. They were wild, and they got kicked out of every bar in Nashville. One night they knocked a guy's hat off in a bar and started a huge brawl.

There was a kid from Arkansas working in Memphis at the time who wasn't as smart to the business as he thought he was. One day he was in the locker room talking to Paul Diamond, Pat Tanaka, and the Nasty Boys rattling off all these moves he wanted to do in the ring. The guys were ribbing him, telling him, "You can't do this move," and "That's illegal." Just messing with him.

The Nasty Boys and Rocky Johnson went on to work a huge rib on this poor guy. It all began after a female fan accused Rocky Johnson of doing something to her. It wasn't true, and they were able to squash the story quickly. Not long after that, Rocky came in on a TV day, and the Nasty Boys started riding him about the incident, throwing all sorts of racial slurs and stuff at him. It was all a work, not at all serious, because they wanted to mess with that kid from Arkansas.

Rocky played back with them and got heated, saying, "Say what you want about me, but leave my family out of this!" He ended up punching out a window or something. Jerry Lawler came into the locker room to give us all a lecture. "Guys, we're here to make money, not to break stuff."

Between TV and the show that night in Nashville, they smartened the King up to what was going on so they could take it to the next level. Rocky stormed into the heel dressing room at the Fairgrounds and went up to the Nasty Boys. "You boys want to get racial? You wanna call me the N word? Let's have it!"

The Nasty Boys started in on Rocky, and Rocky pulled out a pistol! Everybody ran out of the dressing room, and the guy from Arkansa kept going. He got in his car and left and never came back.

It was all a rib, just for that one kid! I told them afterward, I had never seen anyone put so much into a rib for one person. They were nuts.

Bill and the Nasty Boys did not get along at all. We worked Jackson, Tennessee once a month, and one night the boys actually held Bill's son Jamie hostage while Bill was in the ring. It wasn't a rib; it was real heat with Bill. But because Jeff liked them so much, they got away with a few things like that.

From my football days. Photo courtesy of Angela Evans Meadows.

Photos courtesy of Angela Evans Meadows.

Photo courtesy of Angela Evans Meadows.

With Sherri Martel. Photo courtesy of Angela Evans Meadows.

Steve Armstrong and I as the Wild Eyed Southern Boys.

Steve and I as the Young Pistols.

PWI's Top 10

Tracey Smothers

TOP 10

1. **BIG VAN VADER**
   404, Denver, CO
   (1) WCW World champion
2. **LEX LUGER**
   290, Chicago, IL
   (-) No. 2 contender: WWF World title
3. **DAVEY BOY SMITH**
   245, Leeds, England
   (-) No. 1 contender: WCW World title
4. **BARRY WINDHAM**
   263, Sweetwater, TX
   (7) NWA champion
5. **MARTY JANNETTY**
   230, Columbia, GA
   (-) WWF Intercontinental champion
6. **STING**
   260, Venice Beach, CA
   (2) No. 4 contender: WCW World title
7. **SHAWN MICHAELS**
   220, San Antonio, TX
   (5) No. 1 contender: WWF I-C title
8. **CURT HENNIG**
   235, Minneapolis, MN
   (6) No. 2 contender: WWF I-C title
9. **THE KID**
   201, Tampa, FL
   (-) No. 3 contender: WWF I-C title
10. **TRACEY SMOTHERS**
    227, Atlanta, GA
    (10) Smoky Mountain champion

The PWI Top Ten in 1993.

Japan 1993

CONTINENTAL

Just as our run in Memphis was starting to wind down, Steve and I got a call from Continental. The Midnight Rockers had just been fired, and they wanted to bring us in.

Shawn Michaels and Marty Janetty were a great tag team, but Continental was one of those territories where the people rejected wrestlers who they thought had copied off someone else. The Rock 'n' Roll Express had been on top for a long time in Tennessee, and while the Midnight Rockers had gotten over in territories like AWA and Dallas, the fans in Tennessee saw them as a rip off of Ricky Morton and Robert Gibson.

Shawn and Marty were also notorious ribbers back then, and it was one of their jokes that led to their being fired. Shawn wrote something inappropriate on the back of some kid's jacket, and as it turned out, the kid's dad was one of their top sponsors. Bob Armstrong was told to fire them, and then they called us.

I gave my two weeks' notice in Memphis, and I finished out a program I was working for them before I left. One night in Lewisburg, Tennessee, Shawn Michaels was in the locker room. I had never met him in my life, and I had no idea I had led to him and Marty being fired. I also didn't know I had heat with Shawn, who knew that Steve and I were heading to Continental to replace him and Marty.

To my mind, Shawn Michaels is one of the greatest workers in the history of the business, but back then, he wasn't the easiest guy to get along with. I was getting ready for the show that night, and Shawn sent one of the Nasty Boys after me. The Nasty Boys were brawlers but not grapplers, and when I saw him coming, I pinned him pretty quick.

I got up and said to Shawn, "You want some of this?" He just laughed it off.

I finished up my notice, tearing down the house against Pat Tanaka and Paul Diamond in my last match. It was a fitting way to end that run, and I'll never forget how much fun we had.

My first night with Continental was in Birmingham, Alabama. That night I noticed that Steve and Scott Armstrong weren't flirting with the female fans who came to the gimmick tables like the other wrestlers. They were more interested in talking to these two heavy-set girls instead. I found out later these were the pain pill girls. I never did any of that stuff and had no idea anyone else was before then, so it was an eye opener for me.

Robert Fuller had the book when we arrived in Continental, and they had some great guys working Continental when Steve and I arrived. Jonathan Boyd, one of the original Sheepherders, was in a hot program with Tom Prichard. Wildcat Wendell Cooley was working against Dutch Mantell. Robert Fuller had brought Sid into the territory working as Lord Humongous, and he was in a feud with Doug Furnas, who was the World's Strongest Man at one time.

Steve and I got into a program with Robert Fuller and Jimmy Golden, who were part of the Stud Stable with Dutch Mantell. Robert and Jimmy were two great guys with great minds for the business. Robert and his brother Ron were part of the Welch family, wrestling royalty that has unfortunately been overshadowed by other powerful families. These were the men who made this business great. They're men I would call legends. Steve and I kept swapping the belts back and forth with Robert and Jimmy.

Continental was a fun territory. Dothan was Saturday, Montgomery was Sunday, and Birmingham was Monday night with spot shows all over the place. Every two weeks we were in Florence, Alabama, up near Huntsville, but never Huntsville, which was not a big wrestling town. We also did Panama City and Pensacola in Florida once a month.

We worked Johnson City and Knoxville twice a month as well. Knoxville was absolutely on fire. I had an apartment there, and Steve, Bob and Scott Armstrong would stay with me when we were in the North end of the territory. I stayed with them at their place on the weeks when we were in Florida. The Armstrongs were really like family to me, and I had a great time making shows with all of them in Continental.

Brian Lee was a promising young wrestler I had met before moving to Continental. Most young fans today probably don't have any clue who he is unless you tell them he was once the fake Undertaker in WWF. Brian arrived in 1989, and Mark Calaway, who later became the real Undertaker, was one of his closest friends at that time. They were friends with Sid, who was based out of Memphis, but

Mark and Brian were closer because they traveled together out to Nashville.

Brian was very talented, and he had the look of a major star. Blonde hair, great body, everything. He was a good babyface, but he was a natural heel who broke out when they put him in with the Stud Stable. Brian got a few tryouts with WCW, but he didn't really get a fair shot. He was still a bit green at the time, and they didn't want to work with him.

Mark Calaway had been trained by Buzz Sawyer, who discovered Mark working as a bouncer at a bar. I worked with him a lot in USWA, and he was already doing a lot of the spots he became famous for. He did a leap frog so high, I could almost walk underneath him. He also did the top rope walk back then that later became known as Old School. We got along great back then, and I really enjoyed working with him.

One guy who didn't mesh so well with Mark was Bill Dundee. Bill and Mark were two very different wrestlers, different bodies and different styles, and they didn't see eye to eye. Mark was very expressionless when he sold, and Bill was always on him to use more facial expressions. Bill always told it like it is, and Mark, being a former bouncer at a biker bar, just didn't take guys giving him shit like that.

One night the two of them were booked together at the Nashville Fairgrounds, and Mark wouldn't really sell for Bill. The two of them went from working to shooting blows. Bill finally got angry and left the ring! Randy Hales and I were standing off to the side when Bill came to the back and kept our mouths shut, wondering what might happen next.

Bill turned and screamed at Randy, "Is he going to fucking sell for me or what??" Bill wasn't one to have a rant like that where the fans could hear him, but he was mad!

I liked both of those guys a lot and got along with both of them. Mark may not have ever taken direction from Bill, but fortunately for him, he ended up in a gimmick where he made a whole lot of money no-selling and being very expressionless. He never did come around to seeing eye to eye with Bill, though. I wasn't there, but I'm told that one night when Bill went to see WWF at the Coliseum in Nashville, Undertaker found out he was there and had him thrown out.

Bill Dundee could be hard on the young guys at times because he wanted everything to be done a certain way. When I messed up, Bill would fire on me and tell me. I was one of the guys who saw it as an opportunity to get some coaching, but not everyone did.

Bill Dundee pissed off a lot of big guys. He didn't get along with Sid very well, either. The two of them had an incident of their own at the Nashville Fairgrounds. I had been gone for a few weeks, and Sid had come in while I was away. Sid and Bill had heat from an incident in a double battle royal where Sid had supposedly pressed another guy over his head and tossed him into the other ring blind on top of some other guys.

We were in an eight man tag that night in Nashville. It was one of those where everyone tagged in and worked a few minutes each. It was a down night and a terrible house, and we were all kind of worn down. Sid ended up in the ring with Bill and started waffling him. I looked up and saw Sid throwing these stiff punches and said, "What the hell's going on?"

Sid heard me and paused to scream, "Fuck you!!" Sid took a swing at me, and I ducked under his arm, grabbing him from behind. "Sid!" I shouted. "Calm down!"

Bill took advantage and came back on Sid. Sid went off! I went flying one way, and Sid went after Bill again. Bill took off running, and Sid turned to me, taking off his weight belt.

"Whoa, Sid!" I yelled. I ducked in behind him again and grabbed him around the waist. I didn't exactly take him down, but I got him off his feet and stayed behind him, trying to calm him down. Bill took another run at him while I was hanging on and tried to punt him.

I had met Adrian Street prior to my run in Continental. I respected him a lot, but when you're looked upon as a young, pretty boy babyface, sometimes the older guys will try to take liberties with you. I was never a pretty boy. I had even boxed a little in my younger days.

Adrian's valet was his real life wife Miss Linda. I don't know what was going on between the two of them but one night she came over and flirted with me just to piss Adrian off. It worked. Adrian came after me and said, "So you're a big shooter, huh?" Next thing I knew he was on top of me!

Adrian was using all kinds of real wrestling moves, trying to shoot on me, while I'm yelling, "What's going on here?" I was doing my best just to fend him off and not hurt him, but then for some reason, he went after my eyeball. When he did that, I put him down hard. I'm not saying this to put myself over. I'm just saying that's what I did to defend myself. He crossed a line, and I let him know I wasn't going to take that shit from anybody, no matter who they were.

"I tell you what we can do, Adrian," I said. "We can go outside this door and fight. Nobody else has gotta see. Just you and me. But if you go for my eyeball again, I will kill you."

Adrian and I were cool after that. He never tried anything against me, and I never said a negative word about him until now. I hear a lot of stories about how tough Adrian was, but when he went for my eye, I went off.

I was in Continental when I wrestled the third and final bear. It was also the easiest one of the three, which is not to say it wasn't still dangerous. Dutch Mantell was working with Wildcat Wendell Cooley. Dutch was the champion at the time, and Wendell was chasing him. Wendell said he would do anything to get a title shot, so Dutch made him sign a contract without reading it before he announced the stipulation: if Wendell wanted a shot at Dutch, he would first have to wrestle a bear.

Wendell agreed to the match at first, but Wendell had a bad knee, and as the time for the match approached it seemed to get worse. I'm pretty sure Wendell didn't want to work the bear, but I also believe he really was hurt. Long story short, they didn't have anyone to wrestle the bear.

Dutch was booking things with Robert Fuller at the time. They had three big shows coming up, three nights in a row, and the fans were expecting someone to wrestle a bear in all three of those towns. They knew they had to find someone else to wrestle the bear, so who do they call? The guy who'd done it twice already. Robert Fuller called me, and we came to an arrangement where I agreed to wrestle the bear.

I was already working a tag team angle at the time with Steve Armstrong as my partner, and they didn't want to just pull me out of that angle. So every night, for three nights in a row, I'd work three matches. I'd do a tag match with Steve. I'd wrestle the bear before intermission with Dutch in its corner. Then I would wrestle Dutch later on in the night.

The bear was a Siberian grizzly bear only ten months old but weighing 550 pounds. I was told it had gained 100 pounds just in the previous month.

The Humane Society and the World Wildlife Fund showed up the first night, and they were all over us. It wasn't just that we had a bear wrestling. They were mad about the bear's front teeth being removed, mad about the claws being removed, everything.

I finished with the tag match, and when I got to the back, I started praying. I was nervous because I wasn't sure what this bear was capable of. It was young and smaller than the last bear I had faced, but it didn't have the training either the black bear or the grizzly had. The bear had never appeared in front of people, much less a wrestling crowd, and there was no way to know how he was going to react. I wasn't sure what it was going to do to me.

As I sat there praying, I felt a tap on my shoulder. I was staring face to face with a camera and a news reporter. "This is Tracy Smothers, who is wrestling the bear," the reporter said. "Mr. Smothers, don't you believe it's inhumane to do this to the bear?" The wildlife people and the Humane Society were there too, as the reporter went on. "Don't you think it's terrible that this bear has no front teeth and no claws?"

"Look," I said, "I gotta wrestle twice and shoot with this bear three nights in a row. Why are you worried about the bear?" The lady tried to go on, but my music was playing, and I excused myself to go wrestle the bear.

You can see one of the three matches I had with this bear on YouTube. The bear had no muzzle, and his handler was in the ring the whole time while Dutch Mantell "managed" the bear from outside the ring. It was a much easier match than the black bear or the grizzly had been, and I was able to get some offense in on the bear, sweeping him off his feet and even rolling him on his back. Still I spent most of the match trying to keep the bear from getting his paws on me and running for my life. You can see me on the video jumping out of the ring, which wasn't me having enough so much as it was me being blown up. I was worn out, and I still had to work Dutch after that!

The bear and I went to a time limit draw all three nights, and by the end of that run, I was spent. Watts gave me a whole week off after the bear matches, and I needed them. Working two matches a night, three nights in a row, was hard enough, but when you throw in the bear each night, I just had nothing left. I was so spent, I could barely move. I had enough strength to get out of bed and get into the whirlpool, but that was it for the first few days.

People are always impressed that I wrestled not one but three bears, but they need to understand, most of the time, I was just trying to survive. I have fans coming up saying, "Did you really pin a bear?" No, I never did. There's no pinning a bear. Bears are way stronger than we are, and all three times I faced a bear, the bears were just playing around. If the bear really wanted, and if I let him get too close, he would have hurt me as bad as that Middle Tennessee State football player in the bar back in 1982. It's a badge of honor that I wrestled those bears, but it's far more important to me that I survived those matches!

Continental was really struggling, especially on the south end, due to competition from the WWF. Ron Fuller decided to sell the south end of the territory to David Woods, a TV station owner down in Alabama. When David took over, Robert was out as the booker.

David hired Eddie Gilbert to take over the book. David also brought in Jack Curtis, the guy who had showed Steve and I the kayfabe sheets that said we were going to Japan. Jack got caught stealing from the company later on, which was no surprise. He had stolen from Watts just a few years before.

Eddie brought in a lot of guys he liked. He recruited Paul Heyman to be his assistant booker. He also brought in Shane Douglas, who he had seen and liked in the UWF before Bill Watts sold out to Jim Crockett. I remember walking into TV one day and there was Shane Douglas.

Eddie was also really high on Mick Foley and his ring persona, Cactus Jack. We worked a lot of six man tags with Cactus Jack on the other side. During a street fight in Dothan, Alabama one night, we brawled out into the chairs. Cactus grabbed me to whip me into some chairs, which nobody did back then. Cactus said, "Reverse and watch this." I reversed him, and he took that upside down bump he does and took out seven or eight rows of chairs.

Shane Douglas was working on our team that night. I remember turning to Shane and asking, "Where did you find this guy?"

Cactus would work two or three times a night and get juice at least once. Robert paid him well for it. Like the old saying goes, "Red means green." Cactus was no fool. He was a college educated guy and you could tell he was a very smart man. He saved his money wisely and did well for himself. He just happened to have a high tolerance for pain and the creativity to do the craziest shit you ever saw.

I made it a point to watch Cactus every time he wrestled. If I wasn't out there with him, I was watching him.

Eddie Gilbert pushed Shane hard as a babyface, and he pushed Sid, who was doing the *Road Warriors*-inspired Lord Humongous gimmick, as one of his top heels. It was like Beauty and the Beast with those two. Shane was great at building sympathy, and Sid was just a monster.

Steve and I had been on top as a tag team when Robert had the book, but we dropped back when Eddie took over. Eddie and I got along fine, but Steve and Eddie didn't. They were both second generation guys, and they just didn't get along.

I worked in a single match one night in Birmingham, Alabama against Afa. What a night off. He made me look great, and he was so easy to work with. Yokozuna came in later as Kokina. He did those head butts on me, and people thought I was dead. Kokina worked Shane Douglas as well with Afa in his corner. They got a lot of juice on him to build up sympathy, and then they had Sid come out and make the save.

Eddie was moving up and down the card himself while he was booking. He worked Austin Idol a lot. They did a big angle with Tom Prichard and Dirty White Boy where they hung Tom Prichard.

Steve was sure Eddie was phasing us out. Steve took it personal because they had heat, but I understood Eddie's side of it. You have to get new faces in to keep the territory fresh. I was caught in the middle of the two.

One of the last programs we did was against the Nightmares, Ken Wayne and Danny Davis. Eddie was good friends with Ken and Danny, and they were both just outstanding teachers in the ring. They booked us as a babyface vs. babyface angle, but Ken worked a little heel in there to get some heat on us. Steve wasn't really thrilled with the angle or where we were on the card, but we really had some great matches with Ken and Danny.

We did a tag match on TV one day where Stevie went for a leap frog. Ken Wayne didn't duck down far enough and caught Steve in the nuts. Kenny got a lot of heat from it and had Danny trying to pull him off of us. Steve was not happy about it at all, and it was mostly a personal thing between him and Eddie.

Steve worked a singles match against Eddie one night that tore the house down. As soon as they came back through the curtain I told them both, "You need to be in a program together because that was great. You would draw together." The crowd would sense the real heat between the two, and that just put them over even more. I certainly believed it, but neither one of them wanted to admit they had something. That's just how business heat goes.

Steve had aspirations of being a professional musician. He had been working on his music for quite some time, and he finally got some good things going. One day he decided to quit the business to focus on music. He didn't walk out, but he didn't really give notice. He just said he wanted to take a leave of absence and left.

We were still working a program with the Nightmares on the house shows, and I was left stuck in the middle. Eddie came to me and told me, "I don't want to use Steve anymore. He's been really hard to work with. I want to put you with Shane Douglas and call you the Mason-Dixon Connection."

"I really don't want to abandon Steve unless you're going to fire him," I said.

He said, "Well I'm not sure on that. However long he's gone, I want to give this a try with you and Shane. We don't have to change your attire. We'll just bill you from Tennessee and him from Pittsburgh."

Shane and I started working together against the Nightmares, the same type of matches Steve and I had had with them. We'd go 45 minutes a night.

Ken and Danny were both outstanding. One night in Dothan, Alabama, Danny had a singles match against Eddie Gilbert that went 47 minutes. It was like a clinic watching those two tell a story for that long in the ring.

I had a singles match with Danny on TV. We did a spot where we both knocked each other out. I started to get up first, but before I could take advantage, Kenny came in and hit me with a chair. Danny got up and came after me, but then he stopped and got on the mic.

"Kenny," he said. "These people are saying you hit Tracy with a chair! Is that true?"

The fans thought Danny was going to turn on Kenny right there, but they didn't. They just hinted at it. I remember thinking what a great way to start an angle.

Danny was a born teacher even then. He went on to become the founder of Ohio Valley Wrestling in Louisville where he helped to train some of the biggest stars in the business including John Cena, Randy Orton, and Brock Lesnar.

Steve came back after that match with Danny. He started going on the road with me, selling gimmicks at our table. Steve's return didn't sit well with Eddie, and Missy Hyatt, Eddie's wife, got mad about it as well. "How's somebody who isn't even booked selling gimmicks?" Eddie called Steve out on it, and Steve got mad. We could see the writing on the wall.

Before we got fired, though, I had a scary brush with death. I had a Honda 450 motorcycle that I bought for $450. Good looking bike, and I loved motorcycles. I lived 5-10 miles from the building in Birmingham and would ride it to the arena. One day, just a few weeks before our run ended, a semi truck blew a tire which came right up on me when I was on the highway. I rode that motorcycle on its side for about a hundred yards and almost went over a cliff. By the grace of God, I survived.

I took that as a sign that God wanted me to get rid of the bike. I threw the bike down off the ledge and walked the rest of the way to the building.

"Where's your bike?" Steve asked.

"I threw it over a cliff," I said.

Eddie started cutting our bookings way back. He was mad at Steve, and once again I was guilty by association. He was also upset with me for not wanting to tag with Shane. For three weeks, he kept cutting us back. You got your booking sheet every week, and on one Monday, we saw we were only booked twice in seven days.

"Well," said Steve, "What else is it gonna take? You gonna walk with me?"

"I suppose I could go back and get a job at home," I said.

"Come on," he said. "Where do you want to eat?"

I said, "Man, I don't want to eat anything."

"We're done anyway!" he said. He knew the deal. The heat between him and Eddie had gone nuclear. "When your run's up, your run's up. We're not in his clique."

I didn't say anything about Shane. I knew I wasn't going along with Eddie's plan, so I decided to walk out with Steve. Steve kept going on about getting some food. "Let's get some Chinese."

I never ate Chinese in my life before I met Steve. I always thought it was gross, but once I tried it, I decided I liked it. Steve could eat Chinese food for breakfast, lunch, and dinner every day.

We ate a lot of Chinese on the road together. We also used to eat a lot at a buffet called Quincy's that's no longer in business. It was kind of like Golden Corral but not as good. Ryan's was another place similar to Golden Corral that we liked. About every three days we'd hit Quincy's, Ryan's, and Chinese.

Steve didn't have any stress about leaving at all. All he cared about was getting something to eat. I had to watch what I ate, but Steve could eat whatever he wanted. He started every day with scrambled eggs and bacon for breakfast.

Steve was totally relaxed, but I was a bundle of nerves. Even though we weren't really wanted or being booked, we had walked out without notice which means we left on bad terms. I wasn't sure what I'd do next.

NEW JAPAN

In 1987 while working in Florida we caught the eye of Hiro Matsuda. Florida had a good working relationship with Antonio Inoki's New Japan Pro Wrestling, and in 1988, Steve Armstrong and I were offered a chance to do a tour in Japan.

There was no Internet back then, but the days of kayfabe were already numbered thanks to a wrestling writer named Dave Meltzer. Dave was really the first guy to draw back the curtain on professional wrestling, at least part way. While most of the wrestling journalists in that era still tried to protect the business, Meltzer made a name for himself as the guy who found out what was really going on.

Steve and I had a date to go to Japan, and we were going to give two weeks notice to the office at Continental because we wanted to come back. Two weeks before we planned to give notice, we were working the gimmick table in Columbus, Mississippi when Jack Curtis came up to us.

"So," he said, "You guys are going to Japan, huh?"

"No," we said, "Where did you get that idea?"

Jack showed us Meltzer's newsletter. "It says it right here in the kayfabe sheet!"

Steve and I looked at that paper, and we could not believe it! There it was, the exact starting date and everything. A day or so later, we gave a month's notice, asking if we could come back.

"Sure, that's no problem," they said. "You boys need to understand, though, it's a different era." It really was. Meltzer was an underground thing at the time, but he really did usher in a big change to the industry.

We did four tours over the next three years. I made many return visits to Japan, twenty-three in all, for New Japan, All Japan, and others.

Steve and I arrived in Japan in 1988. The *gaijin* (foreigners) crew included Buzz Sawyer, Manny Fernandez, and Scott Hall. Japan was also where I first met Vader, who was absolutely a huge star in Japan. The American guys all loved to work out daily, and they had a full set of weights they brought along for us so we could work out in all the towns.

The Japanese crew included Fujinami, Ricky Choshu, and Fujiwara. New Japan's vice president was Sagaguchi, a big 6'7" shooter, and of course the boss was the legendary Antonio Inoki, who was like a god over there.

Jushin Liger was just starting out at that time, but he wasn't yet Liger. He was called Fuji Yamada, and he didn't even have a mask yet. That came later, when New Japan had him adopt the Jushin Liger persona and mask based on a popular anime character.

My second day there was a day I can never forget. We were all working out when Sagaguchi came and found us. "Last night in Puerto Rico, Bruiser Brody died."

Shock isn't a strong enough word for how we all felt hearing those words. I've heard a lot of "brave" men tell stories about Bruiser Brody, how they beat him at something or pulled a prank on him, or got the best of him in some way. Funny how those guys waited about ten years after he was gone to tell their stories.

Take 'em with a grain of salt. Bruiser Brody was one of the biggest, toughest, realest men in the history of this business, and his death hit everyone hard. We just could not believe anyone could kill that man. It was like Superman going down.

Bruiser was stabbed in the shower by José Huertas González, who wrestled as Invader One and was Brody's top rival in Puerto Rico. There was a joke of an investigation into the incident after, and González got away with murder. The story we heard was that Bruiser laid on the floor in the shower for 90 minutes before they took him to the hospital. The whole time, all he kept talking about was his wife and son. They finally took him to the hospital, and he died there.

We were not the only ones feeling the pain of Bruiser's untimely death. Bruiser was one of the biggest stars in the history of Japanese wrestling. He had actually had a falling out with Inoki after the two of them had done a contest in the ring during a show. Inoki and Bruiser squared off to see who could do the most Hindu squats. Bruiser had been told to put Inoki over, but Bruiser ignored that and beat him. After that Bruiser jumped to All Japan and went to work for Inoki's rival Giant Baba.

The night after we learned about Bruiser's death, I walked into the locker room and saw the Great Muta. Muta was in Puerto Rico on the same tour with Brody when we arrived in Japan. As soon as the story broke, New Japan got Muta on a plane and back home right away. Muta was their guy, and the management at New Japan was not going to take any chances.

Everyone knew why Muta was there and what he had supposedly witnessed. When Steve and I saw him standing there, we went over and asked, "Hey, man, what happened?"

Muta just looked at me and exhaled. "Very bad. Very bad. So sad." He shook his head. He didn't even want to talk about it. I never got to work with Muta unfortunately, but I'll never forget the somewhat unfortunate circumstances of how we met.

Muta did work with Brad Armstrong when I was at WCW, and he got Brad booked in New Japan. The two of them had a hell of a match one night, and afterwards, Muta went up to Brad and said, "You are best wrestler in America."

You hear a lot of stories about top guys using their influence to push other guys down the card they perceive as a threat. Muta did not do that. Muta used his to bring guys up, and Brad got a great opportunity in New Japan because of Muta's generosity.

Stan Hansen took Bruiser's death very hard. He and Bruiser had been tag team partners in Japan, and they were best friends. No steroids in either one of them; they were just two romping, stomping Texans.

Stan was in All Japan working for Baba at the time, and one night during a match with Tenryu, he took a shot that he didn't like. All the emotions of losing Brody came to the surface, and Stan went off. He beat the crap out of Tenryu. There was blood everywhere, and Stan had tears in his eyes.

We got off to a sad start, but overall, my first tour with New Japan was a great learning experience. We were told to watch the Japanese workers, to see how they got their spots in and how they put together a match. Steve and I worked a lot of tag matches against Manny Fernandez and Buzz Sawyer. We called the whole thing in the ring, and it was such a pleasure to work with them.

I got to work with Antonio Inoki in some four man and six man tags. One of those nights I got to work against him in a singles match. He was so great, it was an easy night in the ring.

The Japanese crowd is very different than what I was used to. They don't cheer and boo like an American crowd. They go, "Whoa!" and they clap when they see something they like. They see wrestling as a contest rather than a show, and that's how they react.

The Japanese style took some getting used to as well. They go a lot harder and a lot stiffer, which is both good and bad. They're going to hit you a lot harder, but they expect you to hit them as well.

We returned to Continental for a few months and then went back on a second tour of Japan. Scott Hall, Dick Murdoch, Bob Orton, Jr., and Mark Rocco, who was the original Black Tiger, were on this tour for Inoki as well.

Bob Orton, Jr. was only working Japan tours at that time. He's one of the great workers of all time, and I learned so much from him. One thing I remember about Bob is if he was on a tour with a bunch of younger guys, he wouldn't drink all that much, but if he and Dick Murdoch were on the road together, it was on.

This was a tag tour, and we worked a lot against Murdoch and Orton, who were a great tag team. Sometime during the tour the Grappler Len Denton came in to join the tour. Murdoch and Orton were excited to see their old friend from Portland, who was a great guy. We were also joined by two guys they weren't so excited to work with: Kerry and Kevin Von Erich from Dallas.

Kerry and Kevin had a reputation for partying, ribbing, and talking trash. There was also heat between their dad, Fritz Von Erich, and both Murdoch and Orton. Both of the boys had refused to job for Murdoch and Orton back in the states, probably at their dad's insistence. I think there was even heat between Fritz and Bob Orton's dad.

I don't like to talk money, but here are a few figures I heard at that time. Bruiser was making $18,000 a week at the time of his death working for Baba. Stan Hansen was making $15,000. Inoki didn't pay as well as Baba, so over on our side, Murdoch was making $8000, Buzz was getting $5000, Manny was getting $3000, and Steve, Scott Hall, and I were getting $2500.

Word had it the Von Erichs were getting $20,000 total for working a week and a half. Again, this is just what I heard, but it was enough to stir up even more heat with Murdoch and Orton.

When the Von Erichs showed up, the first thing Kerry did was call Murdoch an old man. Murdoch clammed up, didn't say a word, which we all knew meant trouble. Then Kerry turned to Bob Orton. "Hey, looks like you're getting a little gray on you! Getting a little old, huh?"

"Uh huh," said Bob, real calm and quiet. "It's just wisdom, kid. You'll find out."

I turned to Steve and said, "Oh Lord, those boys are in trouble."

Kerry and Kevin were very cocky, talking a lot of trash about settling a few scores with some of the Japanese guys. They were also tossing beer bottles out the windows of the bus, which was a big no no and very disrespectful. Manny wanted to do something about it, but he didn't. He knew the Von Erichs were in for it.

The second night, Steve and I set to wrestle Manny and Buzz, while Murdoch and Orton were booked against the Von Erichs. Murdoch was known to go out for a drink after a match, even if he was wrestling the next night. The night before this match up, Murdoch did not go out drinking. He went back to his hotel and rested. That's when we knew shit was going to hit the fan.

We were on the bus on the way to the Arena. Orton was at the front of the bus, and Murdoch was in the back. I think Kerry sensed something was up because he went up to see Orton and try to be a peace maker. He started to talk to Bob, but Bob told him, "Hey, I'm trying to fucking sleep. You wouldn't put me over in St. Louis, mother fucker, but you won't have any choice tonight. Your daddy ain't here tonight."

Kerry went to the back of the bus and tried to talk to Murdoch, who wasn't open to negotiating, either. "I don't like you," Murdock said. "I don't like your brothers. I don't like your dad. I don't like your mom. I don't like any fucking one of you, so get out of my face."

The bus made a stop at a rest area, and Kevin found a pay phone. He was on for a very long time, talking to the New Japan office, telling them that they refused to work with Orton and Murdoch. We were all sitting on the bus waiting, and we knew what Kevin was up to. Steve and I kept quiet, but Manny, Buzz, Dick, and Bob were shouting, "Fuck these guys, leave 'em!"

When we got to the building, the card had been changed. Murdoch and Orton worked against Manny and Buzz. It was an absolute classic. Murdoch actually did a flying head scissors on Manny. It was unreal. Those four guys were great.

Steve and I worked the Von Erichs, and we had a great match. We made those boys look good and got them over, which made the Von Erichs happy but not the other guys. We got back on the bus, and Bob, Dick, Manny, and Buzz were all saying, "Why didn't you fight them?"

We weren't in any position to take advantage of those guys, and that's exactly what we said. Orton and Murdoch could have gotten away with some shit, but not us. We did our jobs. The boys were pissed at first, but they understood and it was all cool.

Steve and I worked a lot with Hashimoto and Chono in four man tags. This was right about the time they decided to partner them up with the Great Muta as the Three Musketeers. Chono and Hashimoto were a great team. Hashimoto's passed away now, and I heard it was because he had gotten himself in debt to the wrong people. The mob is heavily tied to pro wrestling over there, and you do not want to mess with those people.

Of all the foreigners working in Japan back then, no one was over more than Vader. He had just started doing the gimmick with the large, metallic mastodon mask that had smoke pouring out of it at that time, and he was over big time. Vader was a big man who could move like a smaller guy. Fans had never seen anything like him, and he was a huge star. Vader was working 30-35 weeks a year in Japan, and he was selling out buildings everywhere.

During either our first or second tour, there was an incident during one of the shows. We boarded the bus after the show, and the New Japan crew kept us on the bus at the venue for two hours. Nobody knew what was going on at the time, and it wasn't until the tour was over we found out.

Vader was brawling out into the audience during his match. A young guy got in the way, and Vader slapped him. Some of the Japanese fans want to get hit. They're crazy. But this kid's father was Yakuza, the Japanese Mafia. The Yakuza was tied closely to New Japan and had sponsored the shows. One thing you never do is put your hands on one of those guys or their families.

The two hours while we were sitting on the bus, New Japan was in talks with the Yakuza. The mob wanted to kill Vader! Fortunately for him, the New Japan crew was able to smooth things over.

Vader didn't know about this at the time, and neither did we. In fact they didn't tell Vader about the situation until the end of the tour. Vader came to us and told us. "Guys, whatever you do, don't do anything with that kid. That's all over with now."

Of course that wasn't the last time Vader got in trouble slapping someone in a foreign country. I'll get to that story later.

Steve and I were treated to a number of dinners by the "sponsors," the big money wrestling fans who love to be seen with the wrestlers. We all knew that a lot of these guys were Yakuza. In fact you could tell some of those guys because they had part or all of some fingers cut off. The veterans always made sure us young guys knew the rules for going out with the sponsors.

First, never refuse food. If they buy you something you eat it. I couldn't believe some of the things that got put on my plate, but I ate it all because I knew it was disrespectful to say no. I ate all kinds of things I'd never eaten before including oysters and squid.

Second, never refuse a drink. I had never really drunk alcohol in my life prior to my trips to Japan, but when the sponsors were buying, I couldn't refuse. They got me drunker than Cootie Brown, but I didn't have a choice. If they wanted you to drink, you had to drink!

Third, never touch the ladies, especially if you are a *gaijin*, a foreigner. A lot of the clubs we went to had these pretty Filipino girls who would come, sit on our laps, and dance for us. We had to keep our hands to our sides, and we were not allowed to touch them. Once again, it was disrespectful to break the rules.

One night we were taken out with Masa Saito. Saito was a bad dude, a former Olympic silver medalist who worked in New Japan, Florida, and AWA for Verne Gagne. This wasn't too long after he and Ken Patera tore up a restaurant and beat up some cops. Saito and Patera served a little time in the States, but that incident made the former Olympian even more of a national hero in Japan than he already was.

Saito was a cool guy, but he was still a tough dude, not one you wanted to mess with. One of the men with our sponsors was getting kind of cocky with Saito. Saito was older, and he was pretty worn out from the tour. He growled at the guy, which was kind of his way of saying, "Get this guy the fuck off me."

The guy took offense to it and made a move to attack Saito. Saito beat the fuck out of him. Saito tossed the guy through a table like it was nothing and then tore him up!

We looked over at the other guys, wondering what they were going to do. The head dude got up and came over to his guy, who was knocked goofy on the floor. He was mad at his guy for disrespecting Saito, and he gave the guy a second ass whooping! His own men had to pull him off the guy. The head guy composed himself, and his men dragged the guy who had messed with Saito outside.

We weren't sure what happened to that guy. We really didn't want to know.

The promoters took good care of us, providing lodging and transportation on these trips. We would all board a bus at the hotel, travel to the show, and then ride back to the hotel or wherever we went after the show in transportation they provided.

There was a guy named Hiro Hase, an Olympic hero who was a big star for New Japan. Hiro had been out of the country and made his triumphant return at Korakuen Hall against Steve and me in a tag team. We came out to the ring waving our rebel flag, and Hiro shoved it away.

I turned to Steve and said, "He's not gonna sell for us tonight."

Hiro got in with Steve first and wasn't really working with him. He summoned me in, so I took the tag from Steve and got into the ring. Sure enough he shot on me. He double-egged me, and I grabbed the ropes, refusing to let him take me down.

"Steve! Come get this muther fucker!" I shouted. Steve came in, and we wailed on him, beating him down. We got him back up and set ourselves up to take a double clothesline, which he hit. Then I called for him to suplex us both, which he did. We were in there to put him over, and once he saw we intended to do just that, he started working with us.

MEXICO

The tours Steve and I took in Japan opened the door for us to visit another country. Vader liked us a lot and asked if we wanted to go to Mexico. He made a few calls for us and got us booked.

Our first tour of Mexico was a two week trip. We worked a lot of six man tags with guys like El Canek and the Fishman against teams like the Brazo Brothers and the Villano Brothers. That was the tip of the iceberg as far as the talent we saw on that tour.

There was a sixteen year old kid working the same tour by the name of Rey Mysterio, Jr. Rey wasn't wearing the mask yet, and he looked like a little kid he was so small. You could still see the talent in him, and you knew he had potential to be a star one day.

There was also a young Japanese kid named Yoshihiro Asai. Asai had tried to train in New Japan but was told he was too short, so he traveled to Mexico to break into the business. Years later, when Inoki came over to do a tour of Mexico, he took a liking to Asai. He offered Asai a chance to go back to Japan with him.

This same situation had already happened with Jushin Liger. New Japan told Liger he was too short to make it as a star. Liger traveled to Mexico and trained, and when Inoki spotted him in Mexico, he took him back to Japan that same night.

Inoki wanted to do the same thing with Asai, but Asai said, "No. Fuck you. You didn't want me then. I'm going to come back and stick it up your ass and run against you."

Asai did return to Japan as Ultimo Dragon, and he worked for Inoki's competition when he did.

Asai was a tough kid, a great worker, and a cool guy. I saw him not too long ago at WrestleCon for the first time in about thirty years. He had a lot of trouble in Mexico being Japanese, with people trying to rob him or kill him. He beat the shit out of a few guys who tried him. Tough guy.

Steve and I had a driver from El Paso named Johnny who lived in the same hotel with us. He was half-Mexican and was also our translator. He couldn't return to the States because he owed a lot on child support in San Antonio, but he was making good money in

Mexico.

Mexico was strange because there were certain days of the week you couldn't drive. We got pulled over one time while Johnny was driving. He had Texas plates, too, which was added trouble. We listened while Johnny and the cop argued back and forth for quite a while. We knew there was something bigger going on than just a traffic violation.

Johnny finally reached into his pocket and pulled out a badge that he flashed at the cop. Johnny had a friend who lived in our hotel that worked for the Mexican equivalent of the FBI, and Johnny's friend had given him the badge to help him get out of trouble. Johnny ended up having to bribe the police officer to let us go. There was a lot of corruption like that in Mexico.

The federal agents like Johnny's friend really stood out with their suits down there. Thankfully, they were all cool with us. They looked out for us too, and it was good to know we had someone watching over us.

Being a cop in Mexico was a pretty rough job. Some of the cops who worked as bank guards carried machine guns, and even that wasn't enough to stop people from trying to rob the banks. We really didn't see or hear much about the drug cartels. We knew they were there, of course, but we just never saw much of it.

There were a lot of homeless and beggars in the streets. Some of them used to throw mud at our cars as we drove by. You can't imagine the level of poverty down there. We were told the richest man in Mexico was a beggar who had a bunch of other beggars working for him. He took a little of each man's take, and he lived in a mansion.

One time in the middle of a traffic jam, we saw a kid try to steal a car. The cops raced out and beat the shit out of him. Then they handcuffed him and threw him in the back of a police car.

We saw a dead body in the street once, probably someone who was hit by a car. Nobody stopped to check or help or anything. They all just drove around and left it for the authorities to take care of whenever they got to it.

There were a few times the office put us on a bus with Johnny to get us from one town to the next. When we were on the bus, we kept our wrestling bags and our money close. You never left anything in the hotel rooms, except maybe a few items of clothes. You always kept an eye on everything. We actually got our draw, our big pay out, at the end of the tour, but you kept your day to day money on you.

We ate at a Fuddruckers one time down there. We had been warned not to drink the water, but Steve for some reason ordered water. He told me later he thought he saw the waiter getting the water out of a water fountain. Steve got really sick that night and had to sit out the next show with food poisoning, but he worked the day after that even though he was still sick.

We watched a lot of soccer and bullfighting on TV down in Mexico. Bullfighting was fascinating, but they don't show you everything in America that happens in a bull fight. They kill the bulls! They butcher those poor animals with like twenty knives until they finally go down. The Mexican fans loved that part of the match, but as an animal lover, it was really hard for me to watch. There was plenty of soccer on TV as well, but bullfighting was their number one sport.

We worked Mexico City every Sunday at the El Terrero. The roof wasn't very well sealed, and when it rained, it leaked inside the building. No matter the weather, they always drew really well in Mexico City. We also worked in towns like Pachuca, Taluca, and Cuernavaca.

La Minez, the promoter, owned all the buildings, and he really had it going. These venues were crowded, and it felt like the fans were right on top of you, but they were great places to work.

There was a lot of talk and worry in the locker room because of a new promotion generating some buzz called AAA. Word had it that AAA was going to run an hour of live television every week. The boys were really worried how that one hour of television might hurt the attendance at their shows.

In Mexico, Steve and I were *rudos*, the Mexican term for heels. We were the ugly Americans who not only waved the American flag but the Confederate flag. I get a lot of heat with the Confederate flag these days, but it was even worse back then in Mexico. You don't have to be African American to hate that flag. The Mexican fans saw it as racist back then, and they hated us for waving it.

There's a goofy little dance I'm known for where I hump the air. I picked it up in Mexico. I actually stole it from Steve, who created the dance to rile up the marks when we were working heel down there. One night we were the last ones out of the building. We were headed toward Johnny and our car, and we spotted a crowd of about three or four hundred fans still in the parking lot. Steve and I did that little dance at the fans, and they took off after us. Johnny had the doors open for us, and we sped out of there with fans spitting and pounding on the car trying to get at us.

The Mexican style was different than American. We worked two out of three falls most nights. Tag teams didn't actually tag, either. They just got in and out of the ring without tagging.

All of the Mexican guys took really hard bumps like you wouldn't believe. They all took shots of tequila before they went to the ring to get themselves pumped up. I didn't like taking those shots, but I did it because it would have been disrespectful not to drink with them.

The Mexican guys brought beer and liquor to the shows, and every night after their matches, the boys got wasted, every one of them. They cut loose and have a great time with each other, and after that they'd all drive back home, drunker than hell. Nobody stayed over in the towns. It was like working night shift to them, and those boys were incredibly hard workers. They'd drive to the town, wrestle, drink, and drive back home in the same night.

On Saturdays the guys liked to have Pina Colada parties. We all gathered at someone's house where everyone would drink a lot of beer and liquor. Some guys even smoked a little pot. All before we went to a show that night.

My first Mexican tour came right on the heels of a run Steve and I had in Japan. In Japan everyone works really stiff and hits hard, but Mexico wasn't like that. On our first night in Mexico, Steve and I worked against a popular *tecnico* (babyface) named Dos Caras. I grabbed Dos Caras in a belly to belly suplex and flipped him as I would anyone in Japan.

The Mexican rings were really hard, much stiffer than the ones we were used to in Japan. To put it in perspective, a flat back bump on an American ring is like being hit by a car doing 20 miles an hour. Hitting that Mexican ring was like being hit by a car driving 40 miles an hour. Dos Caras let me know he did not appreciate that, and we learned to adjust our style pretty quick.

Dos Caras had a young son who would follow him into the business. He was always classy looking in the way he dressed, but he was a tough kid in the ring. He started out as Dos Caras, Jr., and adopted a new name when he reached the WWE: Alberto Del Rio.

La Parka, known in the US as L.A. Park, was around at the time, too, but this was way before he became known by either of those monikers. He was just starting out the same as Rey Mysterio.

Perro Aguayo was a part of a lot of six man tags Steve and I worked. He was a legend in Mexico who looked a lot like Gypsy Joe. He was a hard-nosed, tough son of a gun. I remember meeting his son, Perro, Jr., who was just a boy back then. He died in the ring tragically just a few years ago in a match with Rey Mysterio, Jr.

One of the great guys we met was El Cigno. He was good friends with Johnny, and he always knew where the best places were to get really good burritos.

The Brazo Brothers were two huge guys I had met a few years earlier in Japan. They would load up about eight people in their pickup truck with beer. They drank all the way to the town, hit a shot of tequila before their match, wrestle, hang around in the dressing room a while, and then drink all the way back home. Every day!

One of the big draws when we were in Mexico was Vampiro. Vampiro started out as a hockey player, and he was also a musician. He went to Mexico to pursue music, but he ended up training to become a wrestler. He had a great look and he became a huge star down there. He even made a lot of movies like Blue Demon and El Santo before him. We didn't meet him on those tours, but we heard a lot about him from guys like Johnny. Word was he was making huge money too, $10,000 to $15,000 a week. That would be more than double that in today's money.

We were in McDonalds down there when we ran into Ken Timbs, who I had first met in my earliest days in the business. Ken Timbs was a great guy who had taught me a lot about the business. He worked under a lot of names including El Gringo Loco and Mr. Class. He was in Mexico working for another promoter and doing hot shots in different towns.

The thing I remember about seeing Ken in Mexico is how he talked about his kids. He had eight of them, all of whom he helped deliver, and they all had blonde hair like their dad. Even though he was in another country, he was trying his hardest to keep up with all eight of them and what they were doing back home.

Ken's one stipulation with promoters was his kids had to get in free - all eight of them, plus his wife Juanita. Juanita was a great lady, strong and tough but not a wrestler. She used to work concessions, and I think she's still doing it last I heard. We lost Ken in 2004, God rest his soul, but from what I've heard all eight of his and Juanita's kids are grown up and doing great. I always liked him a lot.

One night we were booked in an eight man tag, and one of the Mexican guys was going off before the show in the locker room. I can't remember the guy's name, as he only worked that one show, but he was pretty pissed off. I didn't speak any Spanish, so I had no idea what he was saying, but Steve leaned in and said, "He's talking about us."

When we went out to the ring, the guy would work with everyone except us. We couldn't figure out why. Steve ended up in the ring with him, and to our surprise, the guy sucker punched Steve. Steve wasn't going to take that. He laid into him and beat his ass.

Dos Caras was the guy's tag partner, and when he saw Steve going off, he jumped in the ring to pull Steve off the guy. "Work with me!" he said, trying to calm Steve. "Work with me!" Steve started working with him, and the match continued.

When I got into the ring, the guy wouldn't work with me either, so I took him down. I had him in a grapevine with my elbow in his throat, and I said, "Do you want to work with me or not?"

"It's okay, amigo," he said. I let him up, and he started working with me.

After the match, he came over to us in the locker room to apologize. Steve didn't want to talk to him, but I was cool with him and accepted his apology. I was a little worried we might find ourselves in some kind of fight with the boys in the back, but everything was cool.

You always had to be ready for something like that. You wanted everyone to get along, and for the most part we did, but you needed to be in shape and be able to take care of yourself if any shit went down.

In the locker room, you wanted to get along with everyone, but you knew there were just some guys you didn't get along with. At the end of the day, whether you liked them or not, you remembered you were all in it together. If you saw a guy you didn't get along with stranded on the side of the road, you stopped, you helped them change their tire. You did whatever it took to get them going. No-shows were a big deal, and the next day, it could be you broken down on the side of the road in need of a hand. Whether you got along or not, you took up for one another. We had each other's backs.

You had to be on guard against the marks as well. The fans in Mexico would throw pesos at us. One time a fan in the balcony beaned me right in the Adam's apple. I never saw it coming, and it hurt bad. I went down and struggled to breathe for a minute.

It was different for Steve and me playing the heels, but they liked us because we were really good at getting heat. Like Jerry Jarrett told me, a knight needs a dragon to slay. We were the dragons, and the fans treated us as such. We got pelted with a lot of pesos as a result.

Every night after the show, Johnny made sure we got something good to eat. He had a little help from the ladies who hung around after the shows. There were girls who were there for the sex, but most of them just liked to hang around and lend a hand. The girls were always ready to cook for us or run and get whatever we needed.

Steve was always uncomfortable with that. He had a wife and a couple of kids already, and he grew up with his dad always being on the road. He really didn't like being on the road like his father and brothers did. The years were starting to catch up on him as well, with the injuries, and more and more he wanted to be home.

On the last night of that tour, Dos Caras got me back for the suplex I gave him on our first night. I tagged in and came face to face with him in the ring. Dos Caras picked me up in a belly to belly and suplexed me right out of my boots onto that stiff ring.

"Receipto," he said.

He was right. I had it coming.

After that first Mexican tour, we returned to Tennessee and did another tour of Japan. A year later we were invited to do a second tour. Steve had contracted an infection in his foot when we were in Japan, so I went back by myself.

It was a two week tour like the one before. Remembering how they treated me on my first tour, the second tour was another story. Mr. Minez liked me and was paying me really well, but the other guys on the tour were getting screwed over. They knew I was getting paid better than them, and they didn't like that.

I did a lot of four and six man tags working as a heel like I did before. The guys didn't tag me into matches or want to work with me. I stayed out of their way and didn't make waves, but when I got in the ring, I busted my ass and got myself over, just to get back at them. The *tecnicos* didn't have any problem with me because I made them look great, but the heels wanted nothing to do with me.

Even Johnny, who was so nice to Steve and me on my first visit, had a different attitude. Johnny would promise to pick me up at six and then show up at eight. When we were in the car, he never talked to me. He didn't hang out with me like he did before, and I never saw his federal agent friends.

I was alone a lot, so I filled the time by training and tanning. I had a nice little balcony at the place where I was staying, and I loved to watch people. I kept myself out of sight, though, just to be cautious. You never knew if there might be a fan with a few pesos in hand a few stories up.

I got to know Konnan on that tour. He was a pretty big deal then, even before he went to WCW.

About a week into the tour, we were in a town called Nessa, which was a very dangerous area with a lot of illegal drug activity. We were warned going in that most of the fans in the crowd were probably involved with gangs or drugs or both. I was working a six man match with Fishman and El Canek against Dos Caras and a couple of other guys. During the show, someone killed the electricity, and when it went dark, we knew the fans were going to riot.

Riots like that are more dangerous for the *rudos* than the *tecnicos*. I knew the marks were scared of Fishman and El Canek, so I hid behind them, but I knew those guys were looking out for each other and not for me. It was like I wasn't even there.

I made a run for the back, and as I got there, someone grabbed me. I drew back to hit the guy, but then I saw it was Minez.

"Whoa, whoa, whoa," he said. "Come with me!" I followed him the rest of the way to the back.

Fishman and El Canek made it to the back as well, but as soon as they got there, Fishman remembered he had left his necklace out behind. It was part of his gimmick, something he wore to the ring and left in the corner during his matches. He went back into the arena to get it, and as soon as the marks saw him, they were all over him! Fishman climbed on top of a table, and he was fighting for his life.

I had my flag hooked up to a metal pipe, taped really tight. I grabbed it and raced toward the arena. Minez grabbed me. "No, no, what are you doing? Leave him! Leave him! He take care of himself! He okay!"

El Canek said, "No go! No go!"

"You're gonna leave him out there and not help?" I said. "Fuck you!"

I've been in a lot of fights in my life, going back to my days with the Thugs in Springfield, but that night was the scariest fight I've ever witnessed. I raced out into the arena, swinging that pipe like a baseball bat, knocking people down left and right. They were all so focused on Fishman, they never saw me coming, and I was fucking people up left and right. I baseballed them in the head, in the nuts, whatever I could hit, working my way to the table. It wasn't just trying to help a brother out of a bad spot. It was all the pent up frustration of the way everyone had treated me on that tour.

Fishman was fighting like a mother fucker when he looked up and saw me. "What the fuck are you doing?" he yelled. "You take care of yourself!" I ignored him and just kept swinging that pipe. Fishman got to the back and I followed him out.

I so was furious with El Canek when we got to the back. I had thought he and Fishman were friends, and I couldn't believe he had left him in that position. Fishman had treated me poorly, but he was one of the boys. We protected each other. When El Canek came over, I started cussing him out. "Get the fuck away from me. I've got nothing to say to you!" Most of the other guys couldn't understand a word I was saying, but they could tell I was mad. Some of them translated for the other guys. They all enjoyed it because they hated Canek too.

Minez came over to talk me down. I was mad at him and the other boys too, including Johnny. None of them went out to help Fishman. Not one.

Fishman didn't say anything at first when he got to the back, but after a few moments he came over to where Minez and I were standing. He didn't speak English very well, but with someone translating for him, he thanked me.

"Look," I said. "You don't like me, and I don't like you, either. That's cool. I get it. But I'm from the old school. We take care of our own. I'm from that same mold. I can't help that I'm making what I'm making. That has nothing to do with me. All I know is I'm here by myself, but I didn't hesitate to come help you. I'd have done it for anybody."

My words were translated back for Fishman and all the boys to hear. Fishman hugged me and thanked me again right in front of everyone.

The tension finally broke, not just from that moment but from the whole tour. It felt good to have all that frustration out. "Fuck it, I had fun out there," I said. "Now you guys love me! Now we're amigos!"

I never hit so many people in my life as I did that night. It was a huge release for me, getting all that frustration out on all those marks. I carried that stick with me everywhere with me the rest of the tour. I'd even take the flag off and take the pipe to the pub with me.

Fishman never said a word to El Canek about it. They were the top two heels in the company, and they went on with business as usual. I don't know if they liked each other before or after that, but most of the guys didn't like El Canek and respected me for going out to rescue Fishman. El Canek never said a word to me after that, but the rest of the boys stopped mistreating me.

Things didn't change with Johnny, who still picked me up late for the shows. Johnny had become an office stooge and was always playing politics. One of the Brazos brothers told me at the show one day, "Johnny not your friend. He always talk bad about you. He stooge. He get me in trouble for saying, but he's bad mother fucker!"

Johnny overheard and started turning red, but I told the guy, "I don't have any problem with Johnny. It's cool, man." I knew Johnny was jealous of my spot and the money I was making, but I really didn't take it personal.

Not long after the riot, I was eating a buffet lunch at the place where I was staying. In walks this gorgeous woman about 5'10" who sits down at my table.

"How are you doing, Tracy?" she said in better English than I spoke.

"Who are you?" I asked.

She introduced herself, and we started talking. She was half-Mexican, half-American, born and raised in Los Angeles, and she told me she was in Mexico doing some modeling.

Every day, for the rest of the week, we'd meet up after she was done shooting and then go up to my room for a few hours. We were both adults, so you can figure it out from there. She was very sharp, well-educated, and she was great company.

On the last night of the tour, Fishman came up to me in the locker room. "So, you've been seeing my niece's friend."

"What?" I said, a little nervous and playing dumb. "Not me! I don't know what you're talking about. I've been working out and looking at the walls."

Fishman smiled. "It's okay, amigo. My niece's friend, she watch some things you do in the States. She research you and want to meet you."

I was dumbfounded. "Are you serious? She never told me who she was. She never said a word to me about you!"

"I have big family and many nieces," he said. "You have her phone number, right?"

I did have her number in Los Angeles. She had given it to me that day. "Yeah, I got it right here."

"Thank you," he said. "She like you. She no rat. She like you and she want to stay in touch."

"I will," I said.

"Much thankful my family for helping me," he said.

"I'd help anybody. That's who I am," I said. Then I kidded him a little. "Now you're talking to me! We could have been hanging out this whole time!"

I had every intention of calling out with that girl. We spent six wonderful days together, and when I left for Japan, I had the piece of paper with her phone number in my gimmick bag.

I lost it on the plane.

BACK TO NEW JAPAN

Steve and I took one final tour of Japan together in 1989. Our tour mates that time around included Brad Rheingans, a big time shooter who trained a lot of guys including Vader. Vader was on the tour as well, along with Buzz Sawyer and a new guy from Cincinnati, Ohio named Brian Pillman.

Brian got his start working for Stu Hart in Calgary, and he was preparing to go to WCW. There were some badass shooters on that tour, including some former Olympians from Russia. Brad, Vader, and Buzz would have meetings in their hotel rooms to strategize how to handle these guys in the ring, just to make sure they survived. I got to work out with one of those guys, but for the most part, Steve, Brian, and I didn't get to work with the Russians.

Steve and I hung out with Brian and Brad a lot on that tour. Brian Pillman had that great look and was a high flier. He lived life to the fullest, and he was a lot of fun to be around. He was always focused on staying on his diet. That was easier said than done in Japan, and he really struggled to find anything he could eat.

There was a big show scheduled at the Tokyo Dome at the end of this three week tour, and for some reason, Brian, Steve, and I were not booked for the show. As a matter of fact, something happened with the scheduling, and we ended up with five days off before the show. The New Japan office paid us for that full week, even though we were off and wouldn't be wrestling at the Dome. They even told us that they might send us home early.

We were pretty excited to hear that. Japan was great money, but you missed the comforts of home. We thanked them for the money, and as soon as they were out of the room, we jumped up and down and cheered. We went back home, and I went back to working in Tennessee.

By the end of the 1980s the growth of the WWF was forcing the old territories out of business. World Class Championship Wrestling down in Dallas was feeling the pressure, which led Fritz von Erich to reach out to Jerry Jarrett. The two promotions created a working partnership that ultimately led to them merging into USWA.

In 1989 I went down to Texas to work a big joint show between the two promotions. Jerry Lawler worked on the show as a heel against Eric Embry. Jeff Jarrett, Matte Bourne, and Billy Travis were on the show as well, and the Von Erichs worked against Brickhouse Brown and Iceman Parsons. The Simpson brothers, two huge babyfaces in WCCW from South Africa, were on the show as well.

I was in a tag team match with Jesse Barr against Gary Young and a very young Mick Foley, who was then going by the name Cactus Jack. It was a hell of a match. Gary and Cactus had been working a program with Jesse, who was a great babyface. Gary and Cactus got the heat on me, and Jesse took the hot tag to come in and clean house.

The next day they put me on TV as a babyface, and I got a good win. I was excited, because I could see myself getting in as one of the big babyfaces alongside the Von Erichs and the Simpsons.

Just as things were looking good in Dallas, I got an offer to go back to Continental. Eddie Gilbert was gone, and Robert Fuller had returned to take the book. Robert wanted me to come back. I told him the one way I would go to Continental and not stay in Dallas was if I could tag up with Steve Armstrong again.

I've never told anyone this, not even Steve, but it's the truth. Robert told me he didn't want Steve. It wasn't personal as much as it was business. The Armstrongs had been in and out of Continental quite a bit, not just Steve but his dad and his brothers. Robert didn't want to bring Steve in again. I told Robert thank you, but I was going to stay in Dallas.

Robert didn't give up. He kept calling for a few weeks, asking me to come in as a single, but I told him I wasn't coming back without Steve. "The Von Erichs will hold you back," he warned me. "They won't let you take the top spot." I already knew I wasn't going to replace the Von Erichs. I'd be underneath them in that sympathetic babyface role, and I was cool with that. It was still a great spot.

Robert Fuller kept calling and inviting me to join Continental. My position stayed firm. I would come back if I could have Steve as my partner.

"Steve is a hell of a worker, and I love him. I want you back in here, and if I have to bring Steve in to get you, that's what we'll do. We can do our angle again. Are you down for it?"

"Yes, I'm down," I said. And that's what I did. I turned down

Dallas and went back to Continental.

It was one of the few moments I've looked back on and wondered what would have happened if I had done the opposite. Steve was great in the ring, but he was not as into the business as I was. He was a homebody and a good family man, but I was single and free. A big push in Dallas could have opened big doors for me. I didn't regret it then, and I don't really regret it now, but you just never know.

Business was way down for Continental when Steve and I returned. We were still drawing okay on the north end, but the south end in Alabama was pretty much dead. We worked the circuit for a few months, but then one day, Continental just shut down.

Right after Continental closed down, I spoke to Cactus Jack. He had made the trek down to Atlanta and just showed up to try and get a job with WCW. He suggested we come down and do the same.

There was just one problem with that idea. "Eddie Gilbert is in Atlanta," I said. "We've got heat with him."

"That's okay," said Cactus. "Let bygones be bygones."

I spoke to Cactus and Shane a lot before trying to go to WCW. We knew Kevin Sullivan was there as well as Jim Cornette and the original Assassin, Jody Hamilton, so we knew we had some friends.

I started talking to Jim Cornette as well, trying to find out if we had a chance to get in. Meantime, I went back to Memphis and worked with John Paul where we became the Mason-Dixon Connection. I also did a trip to Mexico, a tour through Singapore and Malaysia, and my fourth tour with New Japan.

I made my fourth trip to Japan without Steve Armstrong, who was injured at the time. The tour was set to begin with a show at Korakuen Hall, but one of the ladies in the New Japan office messed up on getting my visa. I checked my mailbox every day, waiting for my papers so I could hop on a plane to Japan.

Without a visa, I could not travel, and when the visa finally arrived, I was a day late. Through no fault of my own, I had missed the Korakuen Hall show, which was a pretty big deal. It wasn't my fault, and it was probably an honest mistake, but the lady in the office put the heat on me saying I had missed my plane. I told them the truth, that my paperwork didn't arrive on time, but they did not believe it.

There were a lot of Russians on this tour as well. The Japanese office was using more and more Russians and fewer Americans at that time. Inoki was working the Three Musketeers gimmick with Hashimoto and Chono. Muta was in Atlanta at the time, but Fujinami, Sacaguchi, Fujiwara, and Masa Saito were on the road with us. The Americans on the tour included Bob Orton, Jr., Scott Hall, Mark "Rollerball" Rocco, Beef Wellington, Vader, Owen Hart, and Kokina. Kokina was a big Samoan guy whose real name was Rodney Anoa'i. You probably know him best as Yokozuna.

Yokozuna was touring all over Mexico the same time I made my two trips down that way. He was a big star down there, and he even made a few movies. He was a great worker in the ring, and everyone loved getting in the ring with him.

Vader was a different story. He was a huge star, but not everyone liked working Vader the way they liked working Yoko. Vader was a big old teddy bear away from the ring, but he could snap in a second. He was pretty spoiled after all his runs in Japan and used to getting his way. They took good care of Vader, though. He made them a lot of money, and he made a lot of money himself.

This will give you an idea how well Vader did in the business. When Vader got divorced, he told me his wife got three and a half million dollars. His wife got the big house they were living in, and he got a little bitty house down the street. It was just like that old Jerry Reed song. She got the goldmine. Vader got the shaft!

Owen Hart was the cruiserweight champion at that time, and he was working a program against Liger. They had one match in particular with a lot of false finishes where Owen really put Liger over. Liger also worked with Ultimo Dragon on that tour and had some great matches with him.

I spent a lot of time hanging out with Owen. He was a true artist in the ring and a man who loved life. I never heard the man cuss, and he was a model citizen on the road, except of course when he was pulling ribs. He always liked to laugh, and he would do anything to get a laugh out of us.

One time one of the young boys came up to Owen and was telling him a problem he had with someone else on the tour. "Well, I tell you what," said Owen, "If he gives you any more trouble, Tracy and I will be there to back you up."

"Ah," said the young boy, "But this guy, he had Road Warrior as friends."

"Ah, well, we're cool with the Road Warriors," said Owen, backing off, "So we don't want any part of that."

Owen was also one of the most dedicated family men I ever knew in the wrestling business. He was very frugal, and he saved his money to take care of his family. The biggest expense he had on the road was for calling cards so he could talk to his wife and kids. He was a perfect husband and a loving father, and as much as he enjoyed wrestling, he was always eager to get home and see his family.

The same time we were on that tour, Mike Tyson was in Japan preparing to defend his world championship against an unknown named Buster Douglas. Tyson was just destroying guys so quickly, no one would give odds on him in the States. The Douglas fight was scheduled in Japan, 30 to 1 odds. We had some time off one day, and Owen decided to make a trip to watch Tyson work out. Owen knew Japan really well and knew how to navigate the trains to get from one place to another. Owen wanted me to go with him, but I was really banged up and just wanted to rest.

Owen went by himself and even got a picture with Buster. When he came back, he made a very bold prediction. "Listen to me," he said, "Tyson is going to get beat."

We thought he was ribbing us. No one believed Douglas stood a chance in the match. Tyson was killing people so bad in the ring, Vegas wouldn't even give odds on the fight. In Japan the odds were set at 30 to 1 for him to win. Owen loved a good rib, but he said he was dead serious. "Tyson's not training hard. He's not taking the guy seriously. This is his first time in Japan. They're wearing him out. They've got him out partying every night. He's going to get beat!"

The fight didn't take place until after our tour, and I went out to the bar that evening with some friends to watch the fight. As soon as the fight started, though, I could see Owen was telling the truth. Tyson wasn't his usual self at all, and sure enough, Buster Douglas beat him.

From what I was told later on, it was the Japanese Mafia that had Tyson out every night partying rather than training. The mob runs everything when it comes to sports over there: boxing, sumo wrestling, professional wrestling, you name it. When they saw those 30 to 1 odds, and they saw a chance to make some serious money. It went down just the way Owen called it, with Douglas knocking out Tyson and stunning the world.

Because I was by myself without Steve, and because of my late arrival, I had heat with some of the Japanese guys. They would have sold more for Steve because of the Armstrong name, but without Steve being there, it got rough. A couple of guys even tried to shoot on me, but I was able to take care of myself. I had to! If you want them to respect you, you have to be able to defend yourself, and I did.

I got a couple of days off mid-tour, just before I was scheduled to work against Masa Saito. With all the heat I had on the tour, I was pretty nervous about stepping in the ring with the former Olympian. I remembered a few tours back, Hashimoto had gotten cocky with Saito and tried to shoot with him. Hashimoto was a kickboxer, but Saito beat the shit out of him. I figured if I was going to go down, I would go down swinging. I didn't figure I could beat him, but I was going to be ready for anything. I got good rest and trained like a mad man.

The night of the fight, I must have looked a little anxious. One of the guys asked Vader, "What's wrong with your buddy? Nobody's talking to him tonight."

Vader said, "He's got Saito tonight. He's ready for anything. He's just a little crazy."

I said, "Hey man, I'm just trying to survive. If he don't start none, there won't be none. But I ain't taking no shit from him."

As luck would have it, I had no heat with Saito. He actually liked me. He worked with me that night, and he made me look like a million dollars. I put him over with his suplex move, and the fans went wild.

When we got back to the locker room, I overheard Saito talking to one of the other Japanese guys. "Tracy's a good kid. Been working for a few years and is better. He can work with these guys and teach the young guys. I wanted to show you all that he can work." That meant so much to me, hearing him say that. Later that evening, we hit the bar and did a bunch of shots on Saito.

There were other guys who were always good to me and great in the ring. I always loved working with guys like Riki Choshu, Fujinami, Sagaguchi, Fujiwara, and Ultimo Dragon. Inoki was always a pleasure, too. It was like having a night off, being in the ring with him.

Right after that, maybe even that night, someone drugged me

with Halcion. It may have been Buzz or Vader. I don't know for sure. But they got me. One of the side effects of Halcion is memory loss. They gave me two or three as a rib, not trying to be mean. We left the bar and went back to the hotel.

Later that night, I left my room and went down to the hotel lobby. I went to the desk and asked them if they could let me back in my room. I did it all completely stark naked.

I barely remember the old man at the desk looking at me funny, but I don't remember anything else. I really don't remember how I ended up naked. I don't even sleep naked.

The next morning I came down to breakfast. Everything I said was funny and made everyone laugh hysterically. Tiger Hattori took care of me and told me what had happened. I was so embarrassed.

To make things worse, the incident got me more heat with the New Japan office. They weren't too happy that one of the *gaijin* had taken a naked stroll through the hotel lobby in the wee hours of the morning.

At the end of the tour, it was New Japan's VP Sagaguchi who paid me. They paid me what was promised, but I could tell the big man wasn't too happy with me.

"Next time," he said. "Maybe we tag. Keep you out of trouble."

I said okay.

"But for now," he said, "Russians."

That was the last time I toured with New Japan. The Russian thing didn't last much longer, but I was ready to move on.

BIG TROUBLE IN SINGAPORE (AND MALAYSIA)

Before we move on to Atlanta, I have to tell you about another wild trip in Asia.

I thought Japan was a long trip until I made the journey to Singapore. It's seven hours by plane from Japan! It's also one of the most beautiful places I have ever visited in my life. If you've seen the movie *Crazy Rich Asians*, you've seen what it looks like now. It was a popular vacation destination even then for people from all over Asia and Europe.

In addition to myself, the tour included Bob Orton, Jr., the Magnificent Muraco, the Iron Sheik, Tony Torrez, Kamala, Jr., and Tiger Conway, Jr. When we arrived, we were directed to some signs in the airport warning us that there was serious punishment for drug possession in Singapore. While we were there, a girl from a prominent Swiss family was caught with an eight ball of cocaine. She was sentenced to life in prison in Singapore.

They don't mess around over there. As a matter of fact, just four years after we were there, a kid from America was convicted of spray painting graffiti and sentenced to a beating with a cane. We drove by one of their big prisons, and we all knew from the look of it that it was no place we wanted to be.

All this to say we all attempted to be on our best behavior on this trip. Everyone, that is, except the Iron Sheik. One night I opened the hotel room door and saw him walking down the hall smoking a joint. Matter of fact several of us opened the doors, spotted the Sheik, and slammed our doors shut. None of us wanted to be nearby if the Sheik got busted. The Sheik obviously didn't care.

I suffered an elbow injury on that tour. I hurt it in the ring and didn't think anything of it, just icing it down, but I later discovered I had chipped a bone. It still bothers me to this day.

A few nights after hurting my elbow, we went out to a popular underground bar in Singapore City. There were a lot of foreigners in the bar that night from Europe and other places in addition to us. I still wasn't much for drinking at the time, but Tiger Conway and Tony Torres started buying me Singapore Slings. The drink itself doesn't have that much alcohol in it, but before they handed me my third, Tiger and Tony slipped some Valium into it. I'm not one for taking pills, so the Valium hit me hard. "I thought you guys said these drinks didn't have much alcohol," I said. They just laughed at me. I didn't think anything of them laughing, either. I just thought everything I said was funny.

Needless to say, I was feeling pretty good and found myself standing on the edge of the dance floor watching this really cute girl dance. The local girls really took to the foreign guys, and this girl was starting to give me the look. The girl would dance with some of the guys when they came out on the dance floor, but she kept looking over at me.

I started waving my hand, nodding my head, sipping on my Singapore Sling. I played it cool, chilling on the sidelines. I knew she was flirting, but I could also tell she was trouble. I was more right than I knew. There was a group of German guys in the bar, and one of them had a jealous eye on me. He was a big dude, maybe 6'7" tall. He looked like Bruiser Brody without the long hair. Germans didn't like Americans anyway, and this guy had either come in with the local girl or set his sights on her.

I saw the girl flirting with him as well, and I noticed she was flirting with other guys just to piss him off. She came over to me and took my hand, leading me out on the dance floor. I followed her out there, but when she let go, I backed off a bit. Like I said, we had been warned about the laws in Singapore, and I had no desire to get into trouble.

The first sign of trouble was when I heard a gruff voice with a German accent growl, "Fucking American!" The big guy comes in between us and looks down at me.

"I'm sorry, man," I said politely. "I didn't know this was your girl."

I was ready to leave it at that, but the German snarled, "I'm not your man!" He straightened his arm as stiff as he could and WHAM! He hit me right in the nuts! I did my best to no-sell it, but it fucking hurt! I started to fall down, and the German knocked me down hard.

The guy came right at me, screaming and throwing punches. "Mother fucker get off me!" I yelled, getting behind him to tie him up. As buzzed as I was, my high school wrestling skills instinctively kicked in. The guy kept yelling at me, throwing homophobic slurs at me and everything, which really pissed me off. I kept trying to tell him to calm down, but he kept resisting. "Let me up!" he yelled.

The guy started to stand up, and when he did, I came up with him. I grapevined him with my left leg and tripped him up, jumping on top of him. I put my knee in his crotch and my left elbow in his throat, hooking him.

Tiger and Tony saw the bouncers moving in and came racing in to break it up. Lucky for me, the guy already had a bad reputation with the bouncers for causing trouble, so they didn't give me any grief. They escorted the dude out of the bar while Tiger and Tony checked on me.

"Dude, you just kicked that guy's ass!" said Tiger, laughing.

The bouncers kicked the guy out of the bar with an assist from the police. I stayed in the bar, drinking and hanging out for another two hours with the boys. I was pretty drunk by the time we left, but fortunately, the guys didn't drop any more Valium in my Singapore Slings.

I had hoped that the German guy would be long gone, but when we came out, I heard a loud growl.

"What was that?" I said.

Torres said, "Oh, fuck, look who's been waiting on you!"

Sure enough, I looked and spotted him. He was still pissed, and he had waited two hours for me to come out. The club being underground, we had to get to an elevator and take it up to ground level before we could get a cab to our hotel.

"Don't say anything," I said. "Let's just get out of here." We were flying out of Singapore the next morning for a three day stint in Malaysia. After that we would fly back to Singapore and stay the night before flying on to Japan. I was too drunk to fight, and I just wanted to get to the hotel and get the fuck out of Singapore, never to see that guy again.

We got to the elevator ahead of the German, and as soon as he saw us get on, he started running. He made a beeline straight toward me while I'm pressing the door close button, but the doors weren't faster than the German. He crashed into me and grabbed me in a bear hug. His head was digging into my chest, but my arms were free so I could swing at him from above.

The guy was slamming me around in the elevator while I kept throwing rabbit punches into the back of his head and his back. Torrez was hitting him too, but neither of us could get a good shot on him. "You ain't gotta hit him!" I said to Torrez. "I got him!"

"You got nothing!" shouted Torrez. "He's kicking your fucking ass!"

Finally, I got my opening. As the guy reared back to slam into me again, I side-stepped him and clotheslined him in the back of his neck, as hard as I could. He went head first into the steel arm rail in the elevator and fell to the ground, busted open. I got on top of him and went after him, throwing punches and knees and headbutts as hard as I could, fighting for my life.

The guy finally went down, and Torrez said, "What's that smell?" We both sniffed the air, and Torrez said, "He shit his pants. I think the mother fucker might be dead!"

The guy wasn't moving, and when I smelled the shit, I got nervous. We both had heard that people shit themselves when they died, and I was scared to death I might have killed him.

I'm not proud of what happened next, but again, I was drunk and I was scared. The elevator opened at ground level, and a security guard looked inside the elevator. "Hey, what did you do to this guy?" he shouted.

The guy grabbed me and tried to restrain me. I threw him into the wall and beat his ass. Like I said, I'm not real proud, but I was scared and my blood was up. Torrez and I got out of the elevator, and we took off running. I didn't even look back, but Torrez turned around and saw the German and the security guard moving. It was a relief to know the guy wasn't dead, but I knew we could still be in a lot of trouble.

We got into a cab and asked the driver to take us to the hotel. The driver sensed that something was up, and he didn't want to take us. I reached into my pocket and threw about a hundred and fifty dollars of American bills at him. The ride back to the hotel probably would have cost us twenty bucks, but I was scared. The driver took us and didn't say another word.

As soon as I got to my room, I packed my bag. I was spooked, scared shitless that the police would come and knock my door down in the night so they could drag me off to jail. The next morning, I was so relieved to get to the airport and board a plane for Malaysia.

Torrez and I didn't tell anyone what happened the whole rest of the tour. We knew the boys loved to talk, and we didn't want anyone saying anything that might incriminate either one of us.

Malaysia was not as nice a place as Singapore, but the hotel where we stayed and the ballroom where we wrestled were nice. I was told that there was a tribe of headhunters who lived not too far from where we were wrestling.

There was some drama in Malaysia as well, but thankfully, I wasn't involved this time. The Iron Sheik wrestled against Mark Lewin one night. The Sheik didn't like Mark at all, but Mark was over big in that region, having wrestled there a long time. The Sheik put him over, even though he didn't want to do it. After the match, Sheik tore up the ballroom, just trashing the place.

We were all worried what the repercussions would be, but the press ate it up. They made a big deal out of the Sheik trashing the hotel and even showed it on the news.

I worked a six man tag match with Don Muraco and Tiger Conway against Kamala, Kamala, Jr., and Bob Orton, Jr. Bob was getting some good heat on me outside the ring, and he picked up a chair to use on me. One of the fans nearby grabbed the chair and tried to stop Bob. I heard a loud WHAP and looked up to see Bob had slapped him hard.

The guy turned out to be a very powerful government official. All of a sudden we saw the man's bodyguards with their guns drawn, moving in on Bob. I remember hearing Muraco say in a low voice, "Somebody cut me off so I can sell!"

The guy wasn't mad at Muraco or me or anyone else in the match. Bob was the one in trouble, and he's lucky he didn't get shot. We were told we could not leave until Bob went out and publicly apologized to the man, which he did.

The guy was a big wrestling fan, so it wasn't near as bad as pissing off the Yakuza in Japan. Bob even smartened the guy up a bit, letting him in that it was all a work and he wasn't actually trying to hurt me or anyone. I think that played to the guy's ego, making him feel privileged to be on the inside.

When our two days in Malaysia were up, my nerves came back

as we boarded another plane to fly back to Singapore. The whole way, I was on pins and needles. I was sure as soon as I stepped off the plane, the police would be there waiting to arrest me. I knew if it happened, I would never, ever come back home.

There was no one waiting for me at the airport, and when we got to the hotel, there was no one waiting to arrest me there, either. I didn't sleep much that night. I got up early the next morning to wait in the hotel lobby for our ride to the airport - or the police. I figured if it was going to happen, I'd just let it happen and face the music. I was so relieved when everyone came down that morning. We headed to the airport, we went through security, and we boarded the six hour flight to Japan.

Even in Japan, I couldn't relax. I was still watching and waiting for the police to show up. I couldn't get home to America soon enough. It wasn't until I was in Nashville, out of the airport, and in my car in the extended stay parking lot that I finally breathed a sigh of relief.

I had dreams about that incident in Singapore for the longest time afterward. It was one of the scariest experiences I ever had in my life.

WCW

I went back to Tennessee when I moved back to the States, but I also resumed talking to everyone I knew down at WCW. After a lot of time and a lot of phone calls, Steve and I got a tryout. We went down to WCW and worked a dark match in Philadelphia against DOOM. DOOM was made up of Ron Simmons and Butch Reed with Teddy Long as their manager. Butch was really gifted, and he should have gone a lot further than he did in the business. He trained Ron Simmons, and they had really good heat as heels.

DOOM turned the crowd in our favor. Between Teddy's promo before the match and their work in the crowd, they put us over as babyfaces. We got to work with them a few times in WCW, and they were always great.

WCW paid their wrestlers monthly, and at the end of that month, Steve and I each received a check for eight thousand dollars. I couldn't believe it. I called Steve and said, "Did you get the check I did?"

He said, "Yes!" We only worked that one show, and we got eight grand!

We came to find out at WCW that you got paid whether you worked or not. We were thrilled to death with those checks, and we were even more excited the next day when we were told we were officially hired on a verbal deal.

I got a call from Jerry Jarrett while all this was going on asking me to come back in to Memphis. Jerry had brought back the Fabulous Ones, and he needed a babyface tag team to use as the stepping stone to the Fabs. Jerry wanted to pair me up with his son Jeff, and the heel tag teams would work a program with us while they were being built up to wrestle the Fabulous Ones.

I loved Jerry and I was glad he offered me the opportunity, but I had been tagging with Steve Armstrong for three years at that point. The Armstrongs were like family to me, and I couldn't turn down the opportunity.

Jerry had been working with the Atlanta office a little bit, and he had an inside knowledge of some of the disfunction already going on there. He tried to convince me to walk away from the deal, but I told him I was going to stay with Steve in WCW. Jerry wished me luck, and I thanked him for the opportunity. I could tell he was disappointed, but he understood why we wanted to go to Atlanta.

Jim Herd was in charge when Steve and I started in WCW. Later on it was Ole Anderson, then Dusty Rhodes, then Kip Frey, then Bill Watts. Even back then, it was a revolving door in the booker's office, one of the long-standing hallmarks of WCW.

Jim Herd's booking committee included Kevin Sullivan, Jim Cornette, Jody Hamilton, Eddie Gilbert, and to some extent, Ric Flair. Eddie ended up quitting after his then-wife Missy Hyatt got caught cheating on him with a pro football player.

At the time we went in, WCW had a tag team scene which was second to none in the history of the business. We were brought in as a mid-card babyface tag team, as the Rock 'n' Roll Express held the number one spot. The other teams in the division included DOOM, the Midnight Express with Jim Cornette, the Road Warriors, the Steiner Brothers, the Samoan SWAT Team, the Wrecking Crew, and the Freebirds. Brian Pillman and Tom Zenk were working as a tag team during that time, and Sid and Mark Calaway, the future Undertaker, were tagging up as the Skyscrapers.

Sid and Mark were bound for stardom as singles, but the Skyscrapers were a formidable tag team. They made the Road Warriors look small, and that didn't sit well with Hawk and Animal. Sid and Mark were both much taller than the Warriors, and they were both in great shape.

We appeared on Clash of the Champions 1990 in Charleston, South Carolina working against the Freebirds. We opened the show that night, with both teams doing interviews before we hit the ring. I remember one of the guys telling us, "There's 20,000 people in the crowd and 8 million watching on TV!" Those numbers were nothing to what they'd get a few years later, but any promotion today would kill to have those numbers.

When our music hit and the crowd popped, it got us so jacked up. Then "Badstreet USA" started playing and the Freebirds made their entrance. We had a good match and got a surprise win over them, which really popped the crowd. We played up the babyface angle after our win like we had just won the World Series. I even gave a big babyface "Hi Mom!" to the camera.

At the 1990 Great American Bash, we got to work with the Midnight Express. We spent the two weeks leading up to the Bash working against the Midnights every night on a loop. Jim Cornette laid out the matches, and we just followed Bobby and Stan. We had the match down pat by the time of the pay-per-view.

We were on the mid-card, and while we didn't get a big pop coming out, we had a lot of false finishes that really got us and the match over. The Midnights got a big pop when they beat us, and we all got a standing ovation. Most people said it was the best match of the night.

The 1990 Bash was when Sting faced Flair for the title in the main event. Sting came into WCW with Lex Luger, and they were both pretty difficult to deal with in the early days. I've gotten to know Larry Pfohl pretty well since he left the wrestling business, and he's a really good guy, but back when he was Lex Luger, he was all business, and he could be a real prick.

Sting took his lumps for a time, but he not only learned the ropes, he became the face of WCW. His big break came on a night when Flair was supposed to work a title match against Michael Hayes. For some reason, Michael was a no-show, and Ric was left without a challenger.

Flair was the champion at that time, and he was going into all the different territories defending the belt against the top babyface in hour-long matches. When it was clear Michael Hayes was not going to make the show, they asked Ric what he wanted to do.

Sting was still fairly new to the business, but he had the look and the charisma of a star. Brad Armstrong was the guy who gave Sting the idea to beat his chest as part of his gimmick. Ric had seen Sting work, so when he was given the choice, he said, "Let me work with Sting."

Ric loved the match, and at the following TV taping, Ric and Sting worked together on TV. They went on to work forty minutes at the next Clash of the Champions. I knew then Sting that was a made man.

Ric lost the title to Sting in the main event of Clash of the Champions. Two days later a bunch of us were at catering, and Larry Zbyszko walked in. Larry was working some commentary at the time for WCW. He was a guy I always respected and loved to work with in the ring, but he and Flair had heat going way back.

"Guys, you ain't gonna believe what your boy Naitch did," he said, referring to the Nature Boy Ric Flair. "When he lost the belt, he had to go to a shrink! He had to go see a psychiatrist because he wasn't the world champion." We couldn't believe it when we heard it. Nobody really put it over because we all had such respect for Flair.

When Ric Flair was in WCW and the champion, he lived the gimmick to the fullest. As I mentioned earlier, he traveled like a champion, and he partied like a champion. And if you were lucky enough to be on a show with Ric, you partied with him. Ric would hire cars to pick up all the boys and take us to and from the hotel. He would order round after round of shots for all the boys, the fans, the waitresses, and whomever else was in the bar.

As for Steve and me, we were worn the day after the Clash, especially me since most of the heat in our match with the Midnights fell on me. There was no time for rest, though as the very next night we were working with the Samoan Swat Team, featuring Fatu and Little Sam, aka Tonga Kid, Jr.

The Samoans hadn't been on Clash of the Champions, so unlike us, they were well-rested. They had just finished a program with the Road Warriors, who were leaving to go to WWF, and they were about to go into a program with the Steiners. The bookers wanted us to put them over. Steve was never a fan of doing a job, but I didn't mind. I agreed to take the pin and said, "Steve, do you mind if they get the heat on you? I'm worn out." Everyone died laughing.

Steve took the heat, and I took the pin. The match went well, and the Samoans made us look good. I was exhausted, though. We had worked fifteen straight days, and I was tired!

I remember Brad Armstrong wrestled Arn Anderson that night. They weren't really pushing Brad, which I never understood because he was so great. That night, though, Brad and Arn had an unforgettable match. I can still remember the finish. Brad went for a Russian leg sweep, and Arn grabbed the rope. Brad took a bump, Arn hit him with a DDT, and Arn pinned him with his feet on the ropes.

The next big show coming up was Halloween Havoc. Steve and I were booked against the Master Blasters, Kevin Nash and Al Green. This was Kevin's second or third match, and they wanted us to put them over.

Ricky Morton was tagging with Tommy Rich at the time because Robert Gibson had blown his knee out. Ricky and Tommy were working against the Midnight Express. Their match went on before ours, and the finish for that match included Steve and I hitting the ring dressed up as Jim Cornette. Tommy and Ricky were going to go over the Midnights, and afterwards, Ole Anderson wanted Ricky and Tommy to bash a pumpkin over Cornette's head. After that finish, the Midnights would come out and distract us, allowing the Master Blasters to beat us and setting us up for another run with the Midnights. Ricky and Tommy, meanwhile, would go into a feud with the Freebirds.

Ole and Cornette weren't getting along, and while Cornette didn't mind doing the job, he wasn't happy about the pumpkin. Steve and I were sitting in the cafeteria with Ricky and Tommy listening in as Ole and Cornette tried to talk things out.

"First of all you're beating us with a team that isn't established. Nothing against Tommy," said Jim. "You're beating us to death as it is, and you've already taken the titles off us!"

It wasn't uncommon to see Ole and Jim nose to nose in those days, but Ole wasn't really fighting with him. The pumpkin was actually Jim Herd's idea, not Ole's. It was supposed to tie in to the Halloween gimmick, just like Steve and I dressing up as Cornette. Ole tried to coax Cornette into going along with it, but Cornette wasn't giving in.

We did the finish where we came out dressed as Cornette, but we did not do the pumpkin. Our match with the Master Blasters went well, too. Kevin Nash had been discovered working as a bouncer at a bar, and he was a student of the Power Plant, WCW's training school. They really wanted us to get him over, and we made him look strong.

The next night I arrived at TV by myself. Steve was sick and unable to work, and when I got in, I was shocked to see whose name was next to mine on the match list: Bobby Eaton.

I was late getting to TV that day, and I just missed a huge scene. Jim Cornette and the Midnight Express had not been getting along with Ole for some time, and it all came to a head. Jim and Stan Lane decided to walk, and they asked Bobby if he wanted to do the same. Bobby chose to stay for reasons Jim and Stan understood. They shook hands with Bobby, grabbed their bags, and walked out.

I was so excited to be wrestling Bobby Eaton one on one. I didn't know if there were plans for us beyond that, but I was thrilled. Bobby and I had a great match, and I put him over. They then decided to push Bobby as a singles star and eventually put him into the Dangerous Alliance with Paul Heyman. Bobby also tagged with Arn Anderson in a tag and later Steve Austin.

Six months to a year later, I found out Ric Flair liked my match with Bobby Eaton so much, he had asked to work with me. Ole said no because he had different plans for Steve and me. He put us into another program with the Freebirds, Michael Hayes and Jimmy Garvin. We did some six man and eight man matches with them, with Bob Armstrong at ring side in our corner. Steve Austin was involved in some of those matches as well.

There was a bit of a dust up one night when we were booked in a six man match. Buddy Roberts was going to join the Freebirds, and Bob Armstrong was supposed to be on our side. Jim Herd said no, letting it be known he thought Bob looked old. He didn't want Bob in the ring. Bob was about 50 at the time, but he still looked great. He and Buddy were both ready to go before Herd put the brakes on the match. Bob walked around all day before the match with his shirt off, strutting around and showing off a physique that was better than most of the young guys in the back. People would stop and ask him if he was working that night, and Bob told them, "Nope! I'm too old."

Bob did get in at the end of the match to throw one punch, and boy, did he make it count. The boys gave us a standing ovation when we got to the back.

Most of the other tag teams loved working with us. They knew we wouldn't hurt them, and they knew we'd take their bumps. But a few guys, like Killer Kyle, didn't like us.

Killer Kyle was an African American from the country who was 6'3" weighing about 245 pounds. I always enjoyed working with him, but for some reason he and Joe Cazana became resentful of us. "You only got your spot because of us! If it wasn't for us, you wouldn't be where you are!"

One night in Montgomery, Alabama, they started in on us. I was worn out and tired, so I just said, "Yeah, yeah, I know we suck. We should be fired." Never mind that we were getting a push and traveling to all the house shows while they were just doing jobs on TV.

Next thing I know, Killer Kyle charged after me while I was trying to eat at catering. We brawled all over the cafeteria, and I ended up beating him down. Joe Cazana tried to blow it off afterward. "That wasn't nothing but technique!" I ignored him and went over to Kyle.

"If you want to finish this, we can take it outside. I've never been anything but nice to you, but if you want to fight, I will put you down!"

In the fall of 1990 Mark Calaway signed a deal with the WWF and gave his two weeks' notice. There was never any doubt that Mark had a lot of potential, but I don't think any of us would have guessed just how big he was about to become as The Undertaker.

Mark and Ole did not get along well. Ole liked Mark, but he wasn't really Ole's type of guy. Mark didn't suck up to Ole, and he wasn't a shooter, but he was still a tough, tough guy. When Mark was working out his two weeks' notice, Ole gave him a lot of shit every night. This did not put Mark in a good mood.

Mark was not a guy to fuck around with. Back in 1989 in USWA, Mark got mad and sucker punched manager Ronnie Gossett. I didn't see him punch Ronnie, but when we heard about it, we went racing to see what was going on. Four guys had jumped Mark, and Mark was beating the hell out of every one of them.

One evening in the locker room in Frankfort, Kentucky, I was on the floor stretching out, and Mark jumped on top of me. "I hear you're a pretty good shooter," he said. Mark tried to shoot on me, but he had never wrestled before. He grabbed me high, I got leverage on him, and I pinned him quick. I'm not trying to put myself over here, but Mark had never wrestled before, and that's what happened.

Mark went on to Knoxville after the show that night. Steve and I headed back toward Nashville, and Dutch Mantell hitched a ride with us. Dutch filled us in on how pissed off Mark was at the time. Mark had an appearance in the Hulk Hogan movie *Suburban Commando* lined up as well as his WWF debut, and Ole was still pushing his buttons.

Dutch was really close with Mark. He had even helped Mark get his first car. He put Mark over as to how tough he was. After we dropped him off, Steve turned to me.

"Look, we both know Mark is tough," he said. "But you

pinned him tonight! I saw that!"

"Yeah," I said. "But I don't want to say anything against him. He's going through a rough time, and he's going to get a good break." I honestly wasn't going to brag about what happened because he'd never wrestled before. I loved the guy, and I was hoping the best for him.

The next night in Knoxville, Mark finally hit his breaking point. He was in a bar talking to a girl, and some guy who was with the girl came up to Mark. Mark was a big guy even then, and the guy got in his face. Mark told the guy, "Man, get away from me. I'm not having a good night."

The man took a swing and missed. Mark knocked him the fuck out. Mark then punched out another guy, who might have been the bouncer, and walked out of the bar. He went home, called the office, and quit.

Mark and I got along in USWA and WCW, but after that night, things were never the same between us. I tried talking to him and tell him things were cool, and he acted okay about it. He was a basketball player in high school, not a wrestler. He had nothing to be ashamed of.

Things might have been different had he tried to shoot with me several years later. Between when I knew him in WCW and when I was in the WWF locker room with him, Mark learned how to wrestle. He pinned Henry Godwin in the WWF locker room, and I saw him pin Ahmed Johnson with my own eyes.

"Brother," I said, "Who have you been throwing with, Karl Gotch?"

"I learned how to grapple," he said.

"I wouldn't want to grapple with you now," I said. He just glared at me with that intimidating look. I'm proud to say I pinned 'Taker back in his early days, but I would not have tangled with him after seeing how easily he handled Ahmed Johnson.

THE YOUNG PISTOLS

In early 1991 Steve and I had to change our tag team name. The Wild Eyed Southern Boys the Confederate gimmick had served us well as babyfaces in the smaller territory days, but when TBS got involved with their national broadcast on cable, they wanted to see us lose the Confederate flag. This was around the time of the Rodney King incident as well, so the TV network began pressuring Dusty Rhodes to change our image.

Dusty brought us in to let us know TBS wanted us to explain the situation. Steve and I had never played the Confederate thing as a racist gimmick, but after hearing what Dusty had to say, we were okay making the change. Dusty came up with the idea of calling us the Young Pistols, a pair of cowboys from Wyoming, and that's who we became. We got new robes and hats to go with the new name.

At Super Brawl I in St. Petersburg, Florida, Steve and I had a title match against the Freebirds for the vacant tag team championships. We were sitting down in the back going over the match when all of a sudden, a wooden board fell out of the ceiling and hit me right in the head.

I was in a bad spot. I was knocked goofy, and I had ten minutes to recover and get to the ring. I was wondering how in the world I would get through all the spots we had planned for the match.

There was a lot to get through that night in St. Pete. Michael Hayes and Jimmy Garvin had been teasing a new third member to the Freebirds, a masked man named Arachnaman (later changed to Badstreet to avoid any copyright issue with Spider-man). During the match, Brad Armstrong came out to cause interference on our behalf to try and help us beat the Freebirds. Then after Brad left, Arachnaman appeared to help the Freebirds.

It was never revealed on television but Brad Armstrong and Badstreet were one and the same: Brad was the third, mysterious member of the Freebirds.

At Clash of the Champions XV on June 12, 1991 in Knoxville, Tennessee, Steve Armstrong and I teamed up with Tom Zenk to open the show taking on the Fabulous Freebirds, Michael Hayes, Jimmy

Garvin, and the newly renamed "Badstreet" Brad Armstrong. Jimmy and Michael were both great minds for the business, and Steve and I learned a lot working with those guys. Bill Alfonso worked as the referee for the match that ended with Steve, Tom, and I pinning Jimmy, Michael, and Brad.

Salt-N-Pepa, the female rap group, was on the show that same night. They were just starting to get hot, and Steve had just put out an album of his own. Steve got to talking music with the girls, and later on in the evening, Steve pulled me aside.

"Salt-N-Pepa has invited us to the bar after the show to party with them," he said.

"Really?" I said.

"Yeah! They listened to my music, and they liked it," he said. "They like our gimmick as well."

We went over to talk to them for a bit, and just as Steve said, they were into us. One of them had her eye on Steve, and the other was very interested in me.

"You wanna come with us?" she asked.

"I'd love to," I said. "But…"

"But what?" she said.

The "but" was my son Kyle. I had just won full custody of him, and I was planning to drive back to Springfield that night to be with him. I told her I couldn't go party.

She asked me, "Is it because I'm black?"

"No," I said. I told her about my son and how I had to get home to see him.

"I never heard that from a man before," she said, really sweet. "But I respect that so much." She gave me a big hug and a kiss on the cheek and said, "Go on home and see your boy."

I told Steve he could get a ride with someone else if he wanted to stay, but he chose to go home with me. The girls were hinting that if he hung around, they'd help him with his music. Steve wasn't really into that idea. He wanted to make it on his own. He also didn't want to fool around because he was married.

In spite of all that, the whole way home, we just kept going back to it. "Man, Salt-N-Pepa were into us!"

A month later at the Great American Bash, we worked a six-man elimination against the Freebirds. This time our partner against Michael Hayes, Jimmy Garvin, and Brad Armstrong as Badstreet was young Dustin Runnels, Dusty Rhodes' son who later shot to fame as Goldust. Steve was the first guy eliminated by Michael Hayes, who was disqualified shortly after for backdropping me over the top rope. Jimmy and Badstreet double-teamed me to eliminate me from the match, leaving Dustin in a two-on-one situation. Dustin beat Jimmy with a lariat and Badstreet with a bulldog, which really got him over.

There was some jealously from the boys because Dustin was Dusty's son, but he was a good worker and cool with us. Dustin traveled with Steve and me, and Steve understood him better than most because they were both second generation guys.

Terri Runnels, who came into WCW as a makeup artist, started working ringside as Miss Alexandra York. She became the leader of the York Foundation, recruiting guys like Terrance (Terry) Taylor, Richard (Ricky) Morton, and Thomas (Tommy) Rich to join her stable. Dustin Runnels was Terri's real-life husband and in-ring rival, and we did some six-man tags against the York Foundation.

We worked some tags with the Desperadoes, a faction they put together with Deadeye Dick (aka Randy Colley), Dutch Mantell, and Black Bart. They were going to have Stan Hansen come in from Japan and have the Desperadoes trying to hook up with him. Steve and I worked Bart and Dutch in a lot in tags.

The Young Pistols turned heel in 1991, and we got into a feud with the Patriots, the tag team of Ron Simmons and Big Josh. We beat them for the US Tag Team Championship in the fall on *WCW Main Event*, and in early 1992 we dropped them back to the Patriots, also on *Main Event*.

There was a big reason why Steve and I worked so much with the Midnight Express and Freebirds. Both of those tag teams would much rather work with us than get pummeled by the Road Warriors or get suplexed from pillar to post by the Steiners. The Steiners were killing guys back then with their raw power and strength, the Midnights and the Freebirds knew they'd have an easier night working with us.

We never minded working with the Steiners. I got to know Rick before I met Scott when I was working for Bill Watts, and I met

Scott in 1989. Steve and I had some great matches with the Steiners. Scott wasn't as bulky as he later became as Big Poppa Pump, but he was much more athletic back then and could move. It was a great match up. We would take their suplexes, and they would take our double teams.

Rick could take some great bumps when he wanted to, but he didn't always show everything he could do in the ring. He often told us to put the heat on Scott so he could get the sympathy and Rick could get the hot tag. The Steiners were good about putting us over and making each other look good. We never had any issues working with them at all.

I see the Steiners every now and then at autograph shows. Both of those boys really saved their money and did well. Scott owns a Shoney's restaurant down in Georgia, and he spends a lot of time working there. Rick is a principal in a school!

Rick Rude came into WCW around the time we ended our run with the Steiners. He had left WWF during a feud with the Ultimate Warrior. He found out how much more Warrior was getting paid than he was, and he quit. WCW brought him in and put him in a program with Sting and then Ricky Steamboat. The two of them had some tremendous matches

I worked with Ricky Steamboat once in a singles match. Ricky let me lay out some of the things we did in the match, and it went really well. We later did a tag match with Ricky Morton as my partner and Nikita Koloff as his. I learned a lot about cardio and conditioning from him. Without a doubt, he's one of the greatest ever.

I worked with Nikita in a number of singles matches as well. He was great to work with. We built most of our matches around Nikita trying to hit me with his finishing move, the Sickle. We kept teasing and teasing him hitting that move on me every match. It was fun working with him.

Dick Slater and Dick Murdoch paired up to become a tag team called the Hardliners. Steve and I worked with them a lot, and we had a lot of fun in the ring with those guys. We learned a lot from those matches.

One unique character Steve and I got to know was El Gigante, a seven and a half foot tall giant from Argentina. El Gigante had started out as a basketball player, and he once told us he could easily feed his family making $700 a week playing ball down there.

The weakness in his game was getting up and down the court. He couldn't move very well with his immense size, and when he signed with the Atlanta Hawks of the NBA, that started to catch up to him. Ted Turner owned the Hawks as well as WCW, and when basketball didn't work out. Ted made him finish out his contract as a professional wrestler. He achieved his biggest fame when he moved to WWF and became Giant Gonzalez.

Steve and I played a lot of two-on-one with El Gigante when we had down time. I'd love to say we beat him, but he dusted us, dunking on us forty times a game. He was a really nice guy who passed away too young in 2010.

Scott Hall was working for WCW in those days, and he was such a fun guy to run around with. He had just started doing the Diamond Studd gimmick, which was partly inspired by the movie *Scarface* and partly crafted by his friend Diamond Dallas Page. That character became Razor Ramon when he moved to WWF and really launched his career.

Steve Austin was in WCW back then as well. He was a long way from becoming Stone Cold, but he was a really great heel even then. Nobody could have predicted how big he would become, but looking back, there were signs of a superstar in his early work. The two of us had a great singles match for the World TV Title that you can find on YouTube.

I got to work Mike Graham a lot in WCW. I knew Mike from my earlier days in Florida, and it was always a pleasure to be in the ring with him, whether in a singles match or tagging with Steve.

Another young guy I got to work with at WCW was Buff Bagwell. I first got to know Buff down in Dallas, when I would see him and Raven working out at the gym. Buff had "the look," meaning he had that heartthrob type look and a great physique. Dusty loved him. Buff was a good Georgia boy, and he was eager to learn and wanted to learn everything he could. We worked a few pay-per-views and a lot of house shows together, and I always thought it was great.

Buff and I have worked together hundreds of time on the independents since WCW went under. When I have a match with Buff, that's an easy night off. I told him once I wanted to be his designated opponent any time he wrestled an independent show!

One night Buff was scheduled to work against Harley Race. Buff was still pretty new to the business, and Harley had already cemented his legacy as a legend. Buff got on the mic in the ring to call Harley out, and to our shock, he really went after Harley, calling him an old man. Harley went out to the ring to wrestle Buff. He didn't shoot on him, but he made Buff work his ass off. Buff probably learned more from that one match than he ever had in his life.

No one left the locker room after the match was over. We all wanted to see what would happen next. Buff came back, and then Harley came back. He walked right up to Buff and spoke.

"If I didn't like you, we would have a problem. We don't have a problem because I know you don't know better. Now I'm going to explain this to you, and I want everybody to hear this."

We were all ears now, leaning in to listen to the former champ. "When you're out there with someone in my position, working these opening matches, I'm going out there to put you over. When you call me old or a has-been or washed up, here's what happens. Who put heat on you? An old man. Who put a shine on you? An old man. Who did you put over? An old man. Who put you over? An old man. You should be putting me over as a seven time world champion because then when I put you over, you're being put over by a seven time world champion. You're not hurting me when you call me an old man. You're killing yourself by calling me an old man."

It was the best explanation I ever heard for why younger guys should still put over the veterans in the locker room. When I was coming up, we never, ever would have called a Jos LeDuc or a Harley Race or anyone like that an old man. For one thing, they would have beat our asses. For another it's disrespectful. Most important, you're only hurting yourself if the fans see you beating up an "old man." You don't get over by beating a has-been. You get over by beating the best!

I wish today's young guys could understand that. I get called old, which I am, a has-been, which I am, broke down, which I am. I roll with it because I know they don't know better, but they could put themselves over more by putting me over. It's much better to go over a man who wrestled three bears than a broken down old man. When I explain that to them, they get it, and they thank me for it. They end up being better for it, too.

Butch Reed was in WCW at the time. Most fans don't know

how good Butch really was. As part of the tag team Doom, he was working a program with the Rock 'n' Roll Express. Ricky Morton, who got most of the heat in the Rock 'n' Roll matches, had separated his shoulder during their previous feud. He worked every night with Butch Reed with that separated shoulder, taking all the heat like he usually did, and never got worse. That's how good Butch was. Ricky trusted him, and Butch took care of him for five months.

Stan Hansen spent most of his career as a top guy for Baba in Japan, but I got to share the locker room with him for a time when he worked for WCW. Stan was the kind of guy who, even if he liked you, he was going to beat the shit out of you in the ring.

Being a top guy from All-Japan meant nobody could get over on him. He could be disqualified, but nobody ever got the best of him in the ring. Lex Luger, Sting, and Junkyard Dog were all working with him at the time, and they started taking exception to this. They decided they didn't want Stan to be around.

Ole was the booker when Stan was in WCW, and Luger and Sting didn't like him, either. They were trying to get Ole fired. Ole caught on that the boys were after him and Stan, so Ole responded by bringing in Dan Spivey. Dan was 6'8", 290 pounds. He was a big guy who had previously tagged with Mark Calaway and Sid.

Ole put Dan and Stan in the ring against Sting and Luger to teach them a lesson. All the boys enjoyed watching those matches a lot. Vader was riding with Steve Armstrong and me at the time, and he wouldn't leave until Stan and Dan had their match with Sting and Luger. The matches ended up being pretty good, mainly because Lex and Sting were fighting for their lives.

One guy I never got to work one on one was Ric Flair. The closest I ever came was in a six-man tag when Steve and I partnered with Iron Eagle to take on three of the Four Horsemen: Ric, Arn Anderson, and their then stablemate Sid. Ric and I wound up in the ring together only once during that match and not for very long.

Earlier that evening 'before the match, Sid was 'roid raging and came over to see Steve and me. "Guys, when we get out there tonight, watch out. These guys are messing with me, and my head's not right."

"What are you saying, Sid?" we asked. "We're here to work with you. Don't mess around with us, man."

Sid was fine when he got into the ring, but there was some real animosity brewing between him and the other guys who really didn't want him in the group. The Horsemen gimmick was big money, and they really protected it.

I was in WCW when the famous incident took place between Sid and Arn Anderson. An argument in a hotel bar during a European trip spilled over into hotel rooms and led to broken chairs and scissors being used for real. It was an ugly scene.

Here's what I know about what happened. The travel schedule on that trip was brutal, and those guys were all burned out. When the guys are that worn out and alcohol gets involved, some guys are going to be at each other's throats. I know both guys felt bad about the incident, and I'll almost guarantee you they were so tired and drunk, neither one remembers exactly how it happened. It wouldn't shock me if both of them were blacked out that night. I've been that drunk myself where you can't remember what you've done, and I don't like that one bit.

Bill Watts was the boss for the last six to nine months I was in WCW. The company was in some rough shape financially with a lot of guys' contracts bleeding the company of money. Watts was brought in to try and trim the fat, and over those few months he was in charge, he let a lot of guys go. Some were fired, but most were simply let go when their contracts expired.

WCW came to Steve and me asking to sign us to new contracts. Steve didn't like the terms of his agreement, and if memory serves me right, he was wanting more time off to work on his music. Steve asked me if I wanted to go with him and work some independents. I couldn't leave because I had my son Kyle to care for, so I told Steve I was going to stay.

For the next nine months or so, WCW used me mostly on TV shows but not the house shows. It wasn't a lot of work, and they kept jobbing me out, but I got to spend a lot of time with Kyle, which was more important.

Bill was an old school promoter who fined guys for leaving early and wanted everyone to stay through the main event. He told us straight out he was brought in to save the company money, and he told a lot of us our contracts would not be renewed. I have to say that Bill was always good to me, and he never lied to us, but he was an asshole to a lot of people.

There were a lot of people who wanted to see Bill gone. One day, Mark Madden, who later became a commentator for WCW, gave a copy of an old interview Bill had given to a wrestling magazine to Hank Aaron, who was working for the Atlanta Braves at the time. In fairness to Bill, he was the man who made Junkyard Dog a star and put the belt on Ron Simmons, but Bill was quoted saying some terribly racist things in that interview. Hank Aaron was pretty disgusted, and he demanded Ted Turner fire him.

I was seeing two different girls during that time: one was working in the WCW office in Atlanta named Janie, and one named Roxy who was living in Knoxville. I was getting some heat, not just for dating two girls but dating one who was in the office. Our relationship had nothing to do with her job. She was a cool person, and I enjoyed hanging out with her.

The beginning of the end for me in WCW started when Janie told me Dusty wanted me to go to a party. A lot of the office brass and some of the boys who lived in Atlanta were at the party, and Janie, who was Dusty's secretary, was expected to bring me as her date.

I told Janie I'd love to, but I couldn't make it because I needed to be home with Kyle. "My parents have been keeping him while I'm on the road, and I haven't been home to see him much."

Janie understood, but she made it clear Dusty wanted me there. It was a political thing more than a social thing, and I ruffled a few feathers by not going to that party. If I could go back, I'd have made the same choice. It was more important to be a Dad.

I was finally sent home to finish out my contract, which ended up being a blessing in disguise for me and my son. My mom and dad kept Kyle when I was on the road, but when I was let go, I was able to spend a lot of great time home with my boy. Kyle was only a year old, and I was raising him as a single father. I was grateful to have that time and to have guaranteed money coming in. I was also once again thinking about quitting the business, going back to school, and becoming a high school football coach.

I wasn't in a hurry to give up wrestling, though. In late 1992 I got a call from Greg Price who booked me on a series of shows with Pez Whatley, Scotty the Body (who later became Raven), Disco Inferno, and a young kid named Rob Van Dam. Rob was originally a kick boxer who trained with Sabu and the Sheik up in Detroit. He wrestled barefoot back then, and in the tag matches we worked the first few nights, he was really impressive.

I told Pez and Greg how impressed I was with Rob, and I asked if I could work a singles match with him. He was so impressive back then with his footwork and all the stuff that he could do. You could tell he really had something special.

SMOKY MOUNTAIN

Jim Cornette was one of two men I thought had the best minds I ever saw for the wrestling business. The other was Paul Heyman. Jimmy was old school, and Paul was new school. I always thought if you could get those two together and manage to keep them from killing one another, you'd have one hell of a wrestling promotion.

During my last year with WCW, I spoke to Jim every now and then as we crossed paths on the road. He would ask me how I was doing and whether or not I still had all the stuff from my rebel flag gimmick. I knew he was up to something, but it wasn't until one night in Columbia, South Carolina, that Jimmy told me he had started his own promotion: Smoky Mountain Wrestling. He was running a weekly loop of towns and doing TV tapings, based out of the Knoxville area, and he told me if I wanted a job, I could have one.

I was honestly pretty down on the business at that time. I was working for a company called Rock Solid Security, mostly providing protection for a lot of country music stars. It was a pretty good job for a while, but eventually, Jim persuaded me to get back into the ring. In November of 1992, about a year after the promotion had begun, I started with Smoky Mountain.

Smoky Mountain was Jim Cornette's baby, and Jim had assembled a great crew. Ricky Morton had finished up with WCW before me, and he had reunited with Robert Gibson. Jim also had Nightmare Danny Davis, the Fantastics, the Heavenly Bodies (Tom Prichard and Stan Lane), Dirty White Boy, Brian Lee, Tim Horner, and Kevin Sullivan. Smoky Mountain was not only one of the last of its kind and school territories but an early developmental territory for the WWF.

Business as a whole was pretty slow in the early 1990s. Atlanta wasn't doing very well, and even WWF was struggling. Jim picked a difficult time to start up a new promotion, but he had a lot of guys who worked hard to try and build up a new territory.

I have to give Jim Cornette a lot of credit for turning me into a singles wrestler. Prior to Smoky Mountain, I had worked almost exclusively as a tag team wrestler. Jimmy taught me how to be a top babyface and how to get over as a singles star. He taught me all the little things I needed to do in interviews that would help to draw money. This is no exaggeration: I honestly would have quit the business in 1992 had Jim Cornette not put so much faith in me!

Jim started bringing me in and giving me wins. He filmed some interviews with me that aired on TV. It was really the first time I had done interviews like that as a single, and Jim taught me a lot during those filming sessions.

My first few matches in Smoky Mountain were with Dutch Mantell, and he put me over big time when I arrived. Dutch had such a great mind for the business. It was his idea to put me over quick in the Knoxville Coliseum a few times, and that really built me up in the eyes of the fans.

I worked some matches with Kevin Sullivan when he came into Smoky Mountain. Kevin had done some deathmatches over in Japan prior to his run in Tennessee, and while we didn't do deathmatches, we did some hardcore stuff to get him over with the fans.

My first real program in Smoky Mountain was working against the Dirty White Boy. That feud kicked off in 1993 in Jellico, Tennessee, right near the Kentucky border, when Dirty White Boy committed an unspeakable crime in the eyes of the fans by burning the Confederate flag. Today that would be a babyface move just about anywhere you work, but back then in Eastern Tennessee, West Virginia, and Western Virginia, that was some major heat.

The whole promotion was red hot at that time. The Rock 'n' Roll Express had a hot angle going with the Heavenly Bodies. Brian Lee was working with Kevin Sullivan. Dirty White Boy's desecration of the Rebel flag got some crazy heat, and our program took off just like the others. We ran that feud for a good six months, drawing big money in places like Johnson, Tennessee and Knoxville.

After my feud with Dirty White Boy ran its course, I did a program with Brian Lee. Brian was one of many bright young talents Jim Cornette gave a chance to thrive at Smoky Mountain. Jim signed Brian in 1992 and started him out as a babyface, but he never felt comfortable in that role. When Jim turned him heel to put him in a program with me in late 1993, that was when he really took off. Jim also put Tammy Sytch with Brian as his manager, and the two of them clicked not only personally but in the ring.

Tammy was a pre-med student at the University of Tennessee who was not only brilliant but drop-dead gorgeous. It was Jim Cornette who saw potential in her to become a heel manager, and when he handed her the mic, she ran with it. Tammy became one of the most hated people in the territory with her attitude and that mouth. Tammy adopted a Hillary Clinton type persona in Smoky Mountain, and she really helped Brian get over big as a man the people hated.

Brian went on to feud with the Dirty White Boy, with Brian working as a heel. Dirty White Boy's wife Kim, aka Dirty White Girl, was working in his corner opposite Sunny, who was with Brian. The guys worked great together in the ring, but the ladies were another story. Kim hated Sunny, and Sunny didn't care too much for Kim, either. Kim was a good Southern girl, Sunny was a Jersey girl, and the two just didn't mix. One night in Johnson City they got into a fight backstage, and the guys had to pull them apart.

Brian's biggest moment in the spotlight came in WWF, when he was brought in to work as the fake Undertaker for Summerslam 1994. Brian and Taker went way back to their early days in the business, and they had been great friends at the start. Brian wasn't as tall as Mark, but Taker was the one who recommended Brian to do the character.

There's a lot of mystery surrounding the fake Undertaker match and what went wrong with that angle. The blow off match itself didn't live up to the hype, and that's probably because it got cut short. The story I was told was that a match between Owen and Bret Hart had gone on too long, and Brian and Mark had their time slashed. They had laid out a hell of a match, but they couldn't tell the story they wanted to tell in one quarter of the time they'd planned for. Taker pinned Fake Taker, who was rolled into a casket, never to appear on WWF television again.

Brian and Taker remained friends, in spite of the way things panned out with the Fake Undertaker gimmick. Brian got another run in WWF as Chainz in 1997 that lasted about a year. He went to work for ECW, and Tommy Dreamer took a liking to him there.

The road eventually got to Brian, and his love of booze and drugs became his undoing. Mark tried to step in and help him out, but Brian was out of control. He also spent a little bit of time in TNA when they were starting out, and Vince Russo became an advocate for him there. Mark's demons just wouldn't leave him alone, though, and he finally had to leave the business.

After several years away from the business, Brian made a brief return on the indies in 2014. I was glad to see him again, and he looked great. He's making good money in the construction business down in Florida, and he's taking care of his family. He could have been a bigger star, had it not been for all his vices, but I love Brian and I'm glad to see he's happy.

Shortly after my feud with Brian ended, I found myself needing a new program. We were in Newport, Tennessee, doing a fair show. Jim Cornette had booked Tony Atlas, planning to put him with Tammy, but Tony didn't come.

Ricky Morton was telling me about it when I asked him if I could go out and do something. "How about that kid over there?"

"Who?" said Ricky.

I pointed to a young, good looking, blonde-headed kid. "Suicide Blonde. That kid works his ass off. I think I can get him over."

"You know, he's got a lot of heat on him," said Ricky. The new kid had been working a lot with Tim Horner and Bobby Blaze at that time, putting both those guys over, but they were really good matches, every one of them.

"It's up to y'all," I said.

Ricky said something to Jimmy, and Jimmy was all for it. That's how I got my first match with my favorite opponent of all time, Chris Candido.

God bless him, Chris Candido was a phenomenal talent and as good a wrestler as you'd ever find anywhere. Chris had a great mind, and even though he was the younger guy, he laid a lot of our matches out. His cardio was off the charts, too, and some nights it was all I could do to keep up with him. Some of the best matches I ever had were singles matches against Chris. We did some ladder matches around the same time Razor Ramon and Shawn Michaels were having theirs in WWF.

One night Ricky got food poisoning in Harlan, Kentucky. I worked a 30 minute ladder match with Candido and then did a sixty minute tag match. Robert Gibson was my partner against the Heavenly

Bodies, who were now Tom Prichard and Jimmy Del Ray. That was a hard night, but that's just what you did back then.

Chris was dating Tammy Sytch. In fact Chris was the reason Jim Cornette discovered her. Chris really loved Tammy. He would have done anything for her. Back then you heard a lot of stories that seemed to indicate Tammy wasn't quite as dedicated to him. Maybe they had an open relationship. Maybe he was fine with her dalliances. Maybe he got a kick out of it. I don't know. I will say I was one of the few guys she didn't sleep with in Smoky Mountain.

Years later I crossed paths with them in ECW. Thanks to their run as The Bodydonnas in WWF, Tammy had become a huge star known to most wrestling fans as Sunny. Tammy looked amazing, as she always had, and one night in the locker room, she came and sat on my lap. It didn't take long for nature to do what it does. I'm a man, and she could definitely tell I was aroused, but I didn't let it get anywhere. I picked her up off my lap and said, "I'm sorry, you can't do that with me." I loved Chris, and I was a firm believer in not messing with another man's girl.

One of my favorite stories about Candido was the time I introduced him to natural spring water. We were on a road trip, and I was riding with someone while Candido and Tammy were following us. I saw a waterfall coming down the rocks along the side of the highway, so I stopped to get some of the water. Candido and Tammy stopped, and I tried to get Candido to drink the water.

Being a country boy, I knew that the water was purified coming down the rock like that, but city boy Candido wouldn't touch it at first. I finally got him to take a sip, and he loved it so much, he started stopping on trips to get that fresh spring water himself.

I went into a program with Brian Anderson, Ole's son, for about six months, and that was a great run. Brian was right out of college, and he was a real shooter. We used to do 20 minute Broadways with no spots - just wrestling each other. We didn't call anything in the ring. Brian was in incredible shape, and he was wearing me out every night. I wasn't that old, but I realized pretty quickly I needed to work on my cardio to keep up with the kid.

I worked with Bruiser Bedlam after Brian and Chris. He was a crazy kid who hung around with his fellow Canadians, Lance Storm and Chris Jericho. Bruiser was a powerlifter and a big guy weighing about 300 pounds. He did a lot of enhancement matches for WWF, and they really liked him. He had a great heel persona, and he was very strong!

I worked against Bedlam in his first television match. I called it in the ring with him, using all strong man spots. He was so strong, didn't even know his own strength, but he had a lot of potential. I let Bruiser kick out of my finish, which was really rare back then, and put him over.

Bruiser Bedlam was a good guy to work with and a great guy to be around, but he had a lot of demons. He belonged to a few gangs over the years and had legal problems, everything from smuggling cigarettes into Canada to conspiracy to commit murder. He passed away in 2017.

There was a crazy incident one night in Wise, West Virginia back in 1994. Jim Cornette got into a verbal tirade with a football player. Jimmy Del Ray was working against the Harris Twins, Ron and Don, and did something where the Harris boys shot Jimmy into the football player, knocking him down. Security got the guy out of the building, but that wasn't the end of it.

After intermission I went out to the ring to work against Killer Kyle. The crowd was really hot and cheering, and I said to Kyle, "Hey, we're over!"

Kyle told me the cheers weren't for us. "There's a fight in the hallway!"

The football player had gone out and rounded up about thirty of his teammates and come back looking for Jimmy Del Ray. The locker room came out to Jimmy's defense, and Kyle and I raced out to help.

Ricky Morton had just been arrested for assault prior to that show. I remember specifically watching him knock some guy's front teeth out, thinking Ricky was going back to jail again.

About that time Ron and Don Harris came out of the locker room. Those boys were 6'5" and about 300 pounds each, both reminding you of Bruiser Brody. Fans probably remember them best as Jacob and Eli Blu from their WWF run with Dutch Mantell as Uncle Zebekiah. They laid into those football players, romping and stomping and kicking ass all over that building.

Ron and Don had to go to court over the fight, but it got tossed out because the other boys never showed up. Ricky Morton went back to jail, just as I feared, and we had to bail him out. We never went back to Wise, West Virginia again.

Mick Foley came in a few times in between his WCW and WWF runs. He was still working as Cactus Jack at that time. A very young Al Snow came in and worked for Jimmy as well. I didn't know who he was at the time, he was so new.

The first time I ever saw Al was in a match against Bobby Blaze, when Al was working a ninja gimmick. What a match. On Eddie Gibert and Dutch's recommendation he also brought in Glenn Jacobs, who after a few false starts (Dr. Isaac Yankem, DDS and fake Diesel) became Kane.

I got to work with a sixteen year old North Carolina boy named Jeff Hardy at Smoky Mountain. Jeff and his brother Matt were part of a group of kids from the Carolinas including Shane Helms and Shannon Moore who would all go on to become huge stars in WWF and WCW.

I worked Jeff as a dark match on a day when we were taping three TV shows. The Hardys were all over the independents and already doing some extra work for WWF even though they were still underage. I had a concussion at the time from working a ladder match the night before, and I wasn't happy when Jimmy asked me to work a dark match.

"Jimmy, you know what happened last night," I said. "I've been throwing up all day. I can hardly remember my own name right now."

"You've gotta work with this kid," said Jim. "He's fucking great."

I went over and introduced myself to Jeff and asked him, "What can you do?"

Jeff shrugged and said, "Whatever you want me to do."

I knew from the way he said it, this kid was going to be special. We went out and had a hell of a match - so I am told. I don't remember much of it because like I said, I had a concussion.

Given what we know today about concussions, it's crazy to think I would not only work with one back then, but do three TV matches, including another ladder match, and a dark match all in one day! It wasn't like I got paid extra, either. I was drawing a weekly salary from Jimmy. Wrestlers have always had to walk a fine line between protecting their health and keeping their spot. Wrestlers today have a lot more knowledge of science and medicine to back them up today, but it's still a pretty cutthroat business when it comes to promoters asking you to work injured.

One thing I do recall is talking to referee Mark Curtis afterwards. Mark called my match with Jeff, and he asked me how good I thought Jeff was. I said exactly what Jimmy had told me. "He's fucking great."

That's when Mark told me, "He trained himself in the backyard."

The Hardys were part of that first generation of "backyard wrestlers" who ever made it in the business. It was unheard of at the time, and I couldn't believe a kid that good could have trained himself. Jeff was confident but he was not at all cocky. I knew right away he was going to make it.

D-Lo Brown was the same way. The first time I worked with him was one night when I had just arrived back from a trip to Japan. He was fantastic. Once again, Mark Curtis is the one who told me he had trained himself in the backyard.

Of all the young stars who got their break in Smoky Mountain, none would become as big as Chris Jericho. Chris came in with Lance Storm out of Canada as a tag team called the Thrillseekers. Jim Cornette helped them to get their work visas, and they moved to Tennessee.

Jim took them into Pigeon Forge to shoot some video vignettes to introduce them on Smoky Mountain TV. It was a lot like the old videos they did for the Fabulous Ones in Memphis.

Lance wasn't a terribly vocal guy on promos, but that was never his thing. He was a very serious wrestler, and that's how he came across on promos as well.

Chris had more charisma, but he was still a long way from becoming the best in the world. I remember telling Chris all the time, "Just be yourself." I think it's safe to say Chris finally got more comfortable on the mic, considering all he's done in the business.

Their promos might have been a work in progress, but their in-ring work was way ahead of its time. The first time I saw them work in 1994, their finish was a double dropkick off the top ropes. That may seem common today, but nobody was doing that in 1994!

Ricky and Robert got a little upset when they saw the move. "That's our finish!" one of them said.

"Guys," I told them. "Y'all do it from the mat, but they did it from the top rope." They couldn't argue with that. Lance could jump over the building back in those days, and Jericho was already working for Tenryu in Japan.

The Thrillseekers could have made a ton of money at the gimmick tables, but they were too busy working out what to do in their next match with Well and Dunn to acknowledge all the girls who came up to see them. Lance was married, and his wife worked the gimmick table for them. Chris had just gotten out of a relationship and wasn't really interested. Meanwhile, Ricky and Robert and I would be hustling and selling out gimmicks. It always drove Cornette crazy that Chris and Lance never showed any interest in the girls, but as Chris said later, Ricky and Robert were more than happy to pick up the slack.

Ricky and Robert were the masters of the gimmick table, and they still are today. Wherever you are, sitting and reading this book, Ricky and Robert are probably some place hustling 8 x 10s or T-shirts. I've seen them work their magic in McDonalds, in a 7-11, you name it. I've never seen anyone work the gimmick table better than them, with the possible exception of Jimmy Valiant.

One of the real legends I got to work with at Smoky Mountain and later ECW was Terry Funk. What you see when you watch Terry Funk is no act. He is crazier than a rainbow trout in a damn car wash, but he's one of the greatest, and I love him. Everybody does.

Terry, Bruiser Bedlam, and Terry's brother Dory Funk, Jr., were put in a three-on-three against Bob Armstrong, Road Warrior Hawk, and me. Bob and Hawk were the big guys who had to be booked strong, so it fell to me to take all the heat from the Funks. Terry and Dory suplexed me all over the ring that night. Between the two of them and Bruiser, they damn near wore me out.

Terry and I worked together later at ECW and also at IWA Mid-South for Ian Rotten. IWA Mid-South is known as a hardcore, deathmatch territory, which was right up Terry's alley, but the two of us had some straight-forward wrestling matches for Ian. It was more classic wrestling, which was different than the normal IWA-MS, but they were classic matches. There was no pre-planning the matches because there was no need. Terry is so good at calling things on the fly.

One of the craziest incidents that happened in Smoky Mountain was a fight between myself and Dr. Tom Prichard. Some of the boys had been stirring up shit between the two of us. Guys would say one thing to Tom and another to me, and we both got a little heated at one another. We should probably have just talked it out between us, which we did - the day after the incident.

We were on our way back to Knoxville from a show in Paintsville, Kentucky. We had stopped somewhere around Hazzard, and the two of us got into a real scuffle on the side of the road one day. A bunch of guys jumped in to pull us apart, and some marks who saw the fight start up between the two of us called the police.

The fight was over before the cops arrived, but we still had to explain what happened. "We weren't actually fighting," we said. "We were just practicing some wrestling moves."

It was a total lie, but they bought it. A real shoot fight, and we convinced the cops it was a work!

Dr. Tom and I had one of the damnedest spots you ever saw one night. We were juiced up, with blood dripping everywhere, and I pulled him up on a table for a piledriver. I set him up correctly and dropped straight down. When I did, my bottom broke a hole in the table, and instead of snapping the table in half, we both fell through the hole! I protected Tom as best as I could as we fell, and as soon as I hit the ground, I was sure I had broken my back and was paralyzed. We were both okay, other than having a ton of splinters in our bodies, but I was sure I had messed my back up when I fell through that table.

Steve Armstrong didn't come into Smoky Mountain at the same time I did, but when he finally did, Jim opted to put him in a tag team with his brother Scott instead of me, knowing it would mean more to have the Armstrong boys paired up.

Jim also put Dirty White Boy and me together after our feud was done. They called us the Thugs, and we had a good run with Scott and Steve. We worked with the Heavenly Bodies after the Armstrongs and were then slated to work with the Rock 'n' Roll Express.

One night at a bar there was an incident involving my then-girlfriend Angela and Ricky Morton's wife. Ricky's wife accused

Angela and I of beating her up, which we didn't, but that brought a halt to any plans of a run with Ricky and Robert.

Dirty White Boy and I did end up working with the Gangstas, D-Lo Brown, New Jack, and Mustafa Saed. This is no exaggeration, Dirty White Boy and I had to fight for our lives every night against them. Those kids were young and hungry, and we fought them around the arena almost every night.

Probably the biggest angle that took place in Smoky Mountain was when Smoky Mountain invaded and took on the USWA. One of the first shots fired in that way happened when I did a run-in on Memphis TV and attacked PG-13.

Randy Hales

I was booking Nashville in 1994 when Jim Cornette was booking Smoky Mountain in Eastern Tennessee. I started a program between PG-13 - Jamie Dundee and Wolfie D - against the Rock 'n' Roll Express. The Rock 'n' Roll were working for Jimmy, as was Tracy, and I brought Tracy in as a surprise. Tracy had never worked as a heel in Nashville, but when he came out and broke a beer bottle over Jamie Dundee's head, I didn't think Tracy was going to get out of town or even to the dressing room alive.

Tracy fought his way back to the locker room, and we had to escort him to his car. Tracy had parked in the alley near Arthur Street behind a liquor store, and we hid him in the backseat of another car on the floor to drive him there.

Tracy Smothers

The USWA/ Smoky Mountain angle turned out to be good business. I got to work with my old friend Pat Tanaka a bit as well as Brian Lee. We split our time during the week between the two territories, working the Memphis circuit Monday through Wednesday and Cornette's Smoky Mountain circuit Thursday through Sunday. It drew well, and we did a lot of six man, eight man, and bunkhouse brawl matches. Rumor had it that Eric Bischoff was a fan and followed the feud on TV.

I didn't get to work much with Jerry Lawler during the USWA feud, but the two of us were finally on good terms. I had a bad falling out with Jerry in 1989, and we didn't speak again until 1993, when I ran into him at a show for Dennis Coraluzzo.

I had spoken to another wrestler who had had a falling out with Jerry, and he gave me some advice on how to handle it. I went up to Jerry in the locker room and said, "Hey, I said some things about you, and you said some things about me. I apologize, and I respect you." Jerry shook my hand, and that was that. We never had a problem between us again.

By mid 1995 it was clear Smoky Mountain wasn't going to make it. We were drawing okay, but we weren't drawing enough on the big shows to justify keeping the promotion going. Jim Cornette was already working for WWF both as a manager and as a hand in the office. We tried to get Vince McMahon to help us, but WWF was still having problems of their own. Smoky Mountain finally shut down before the holidays in 1995.

Smoky Mountain Wrestling has seen a resurgence of interest in recent years, thanks to YouTube. It was a great time and truly one of the last of the old school territories.

American Kickboxer

I met Tracy Smothers when he was working for Smoky Mountain Wrestling. Les Thatcher, who was my original trainer, was working with Jim Cornette to expand the territory, and they started running shows at a place called Peal's Palace in Erlanger, Kentucky.

I was allowed to hang out backstage, keeping my mouth shut and my ears open. I got to work some opening matches with Tarek the Great, but Cornette saw us as being too small to use in any significant way. Tracy, on the other hand, was into the high fliers and Lucha style wrestling, and he really liked us. When Tracy traveled to other promotions from that point on, he'd tell them, "You need to see Tarek and Kickboxer!" We'd end up getting to visit new promotions based on Tracy's word alone.

Steve C. Branam

Mike Samples came up to Indianapolis in the mid 1990s to start a wrestling promotion called Circle City Wrestling. They began at the Tyndall Armory, which was a popular boxing venue, and later moved to the Stout Field Armory. I volunteered to help Mike wherever I could, and he told me he was looking for an announcer. I had some experience being on stage playing in a band, and Mike said that would do.

Tracy Smothers was on the first show that I worked, and he was teamed up with Ricky Morton of the Rock 'n' Roll Express at the time. Mike introduced me to both of them, and he warned me that if I messed anything up, Tracy and Ricky would kick my ass.

The promotion moved to an old, abandoned machine shop closer to downtown. I had become a full-time announcer by that point, and I sat at a table near the wrestlers' entrance. Early in the show, Ricky and Tracy came out to sit behind me, one on either side of me. All through the show, Tracy was reaching up trying to stick his finger in my ear while Ricky did the same from the other side, doing everything they could to mess me up.

I got back at Tracy a little bit. When Tracy made his entrance, I called him the Wide Eyed Southern Boy, which is how I knew him from TV. Tracy, I had found out, didn't care for that moniker, and after he heard that, he shook his head and gave me the dirtiest look. He came over after his match and said, "Now I'm gonna sit with you the rest of the show, and you're in trouble!"

Tracy and Ricky really were helpful to me that first night and every night. They gave me a lot of good advice and gave me the confidence to stick with it.

FREDDIE JOE FLOYD

When Smoky Mountain shut down, I went back to work with in Memphis. The promotion once known as the CWA was now the USWA, having absorbed Fritz Von Erich's WCCW territory in a merger. Just like Smoky Mountain, USWA was used as a developmental territory for the WWF, and some big time stars came through during those days including Dr. Isaac Yankem D.D.S, who became "Fake" Diesel and then Kane, and Flex Kavana, who became Rocky Maivia and then The Rock. I worked whatever shows I could for them and filled the rest of my dates with engagements on the independents that were just beginning to spring up.

I tagged with Brian Armstrong, aka Road Dogg, a lot during that time. Road Dogg and Jeff Jarrett had become national stars thanks to their run on WWF television, but the two of them left the company abruptly in 1995 following an In Your House pay-per-view in Nashville. Dogg was known as Jesse James Armstrong during that time, and we won and lost the USWA tag team championship twice feuding with PG-13 (Jamie Dundee and Wolfie D) as well as Tommy Rich and Doug Gilbert.

Thanks to Doug Gilbert, I got to go on another tour of Japan. I injured my groin on that tour, but as soon as I got back to the States, I went right back to working the independents without taking time to let it heal properly. That's one of the reasons I walk with a limp to this day.

I worked some more with USWA, but their days were numbered as well. They managed to limp along until 1997 when they finally shut down. Before that ever happened, Jim Cornette reached out to me with an offer to join the WWF.

Bruce Prichard was the Head of Talent Relations at the time I went to WWF, and he and Jimmy were the main ones responsible for getting me hired. He had been with the company for about thirteen years at that time, and he was best known to the fans as the "televangelist" character Brother Love. He stayed with them until 2008 and had a brief run with TNA before becoming the co-host of one of the most popular wrestling podcasts in the world.

Bruce and Tom started out with the legendary Paul Boesch in

Houston. Tom is easily the greatest trainer I've ever seen. Bruce has a great mind for the business, too. He's a lot more laid back these days, just being on-air talent, but he was in a very high stress position back then.

Dirty White Boy and I were invited to Titan Towers together, where they interviewed us and tried out some different gimmicks on us until they decided what to do with us. My first day, I sat at a table with Gerry Briscoe, Vince McMahon. and Jim Ross. Gerry mentioned something about a wrestler who worked down in Florida using the name Briscoe, and how he wasn't very good. Vince's eyes got real big, and he said, "Ohhhh, I bet Jack wasn't real happy about that."

Vince looked over at me, and I thought to myself, "Fuck. I haven't got a chance here."

They gave me green wristbands, green tights, and banjo music as my entrance theme. Vince gave me the name Freddie Joe Floyd from Bowlegs, Oklahoma. I only found out later that was an indirect rib on the Briscoes, most likely inspired by the fake Briscoe down in Florida.

Five of us were offered contracts at the same time, and we were all given new identities: myself, Dirty White Boy (who became T.L. Hopper), Tom Brandi (Salvatore Sincere), Alex Porteau (Pug), and Bill Irwin (The Goon). We were essentially offered the chance to be job guys, but we could still work independent dates, so long as we didn't work for any of the bigger federations. They called us the Kiss of Death Five. Tom Prichard was already in WWF, having worked as part of the Heavenly Bodies and later as one of the Bodydonnas with Tammy Sytch and Chris Candido.

I'll never forget my first time wrestling for WWF. I know many of you have read Chris Jericho describe his first entrance with WWF and many others and how amazing it was, and it should be a special moment. This is what we work for, to reach the top of the business, and the WWF is without question the top.

I was standing at the Gorilla position in my new green ring gear, waiting for my music to play when I heard that banjo music start up. I looked down at my gear and thought to myself, "Fuck, this is what I worked fifteen years for?"

I was already starting to break down even then. My groin was shot. My hip was bothering me. I looked over at Bruce Prichard and wanted to say, "Can we back this up and start over?"

I worked Bradshaw, who later became known as JBL in that first match, and I got the victory with a quick pin to put me over. Bradshaw didn't want to put me over when we were given the finish, but that decision had nothing to do with me.

"I'm going to kick out," he warned me. "If you don't pin me, I will kick out!" If you watch the tape, he kicked just like he said he would so I made sure I had him good and hooked to get us to the finish they wanted. Bradshaw came back to beat me the next time around, and after that, I really didn't have any problems with him.

Bradshaw had been in the company about a year at that point. He was working hard to move up, and I'm sure he had some people whispering in his ear about me. I worked with Bradshaw as an extra for WWF in 1999-2000, that time as Tracy Smothers, and we got along great.

Following those first few matches with Bradshaw, they put me with Dutch Mantell. I scored three wins in a row over him. Dutch knew how to put me over big. Every time we went out there, Dutch told me, "When you win, get up and celebrate as much as you can. Really make a big thing of it!"

After that third victory, Bradshaw hit the ring to get some heat on me before Savio Vega came out to make the save. That set up a tag match for the next TV taping with me and Savio versus Bradshaw and Dutch.

The plan was to have the four of us work a program on a loop. At that time most of the tag teams in the WWF were guys who looked alike. The exceptions to that were the Bubba Ray and D-Von Dudley. Savio and I had the potential to be another unique tag team, but for some reason, they canceled our tag program.

Jim Cornette was on the booking committee at that time, but he didn't have much pull because he was starting to phase himself out. Jim also had some heat with Shawn Michaels, who was the top guy at the time, and with me being one of Jim's Smoky Mountain guys, I was guilty by association. I don't know exactly why plans got changed, but when the tag feud with Dutch and Bradshaw stalled, they started beating me down every week.

Mark Calaway was becoming one of the biggest names in the business as The Undertaker. Mark and I used to get along well, but I could sense a change in him in WWF. Sometimes guys who achieve success in this business start to get a little paranoid and insecure about keeping their spots. Mark used to have a smile on his face all the time, but he definitely had withdrawn into himself to protect his spot when I reached WWF. I heard stories about him getting guys fired, and he wasn't the only one who did such things.

Shawn Michaels and I never met before WWF, but I soon discovered I had heat with him not only for being one of Cornette's guys, but for his firing from Continental years earlier. There was definitely heat with Bob Armstrong, and he said some things about Steve and I as well.

It didn't help things that I was hanging out with Chris Candido. Chris and Tammy had come in before me as The Bodydonnas, Skip and Sunny, and I was unaware that there were things going on between Sunny and Shawn that had caused a lot of heat between Shawn and Chris. It wouldn't have mattered to me. Chris was my friend, and I would have hung out with him anyways.

One day I was sitting with Candido in the dressing room, and Dirty White Boy was over talking to Shawn, who suddenly spoke up really loud. "Yeah, Ronny West told Bob Armstrong to fire me because of something I wrote on a kid's back, and he hired Tracy Smothers and his son to take our place!"

The dressing room got real quiet after that. Shawn was the man backstage, and when he spoke, everybody listened. I didn't know Shawn before I got to WWF, and I had nothing against him. Everything that happened in Continental was completely out of my control. I didn't appreciate what he said, not because he was trashing me, but because he spoke out against Bob.

This was the same night The Godwinns threw slop on Sunny, which was televised. The Godwinns came in right after that and announced what was going on and invited the guys to contribute whatever they wanted to the slop bucket. Sunny had a lot of heat with a lot of people backstage, so the guys were lining up to add spit, piss, cigarettes, and all kinds of shit to the bucket.

I walked over to talk Shawn as all that was going on. "Hey Shawn," I said, "Whatever happened was years ago. I had nothing to do with it. I was just working."

Shawn blew me off. "Aw stop it!" And he just walked off. That's when I knew for sure I had heat with him.

Make no mistake about it, Shawn Michaels and The Undertaker were two of the best of all time. Shawn's supposed to be a changed man these days, and I think that's legit, but back during that time he could be really difficult. They were sharks protecting their waters. Sometimes you have to be a shark in this business. You have to fight if you want to survive the politics.

For my part, I was just trying to survive. I was jobbing out to Brian Adams, Vader, and other guys night after night. I did what I was told because I really had no other choice.

Wolfie D and Jamie Dundee got a shot in WWF at the time I was there, and they were doing well as part of the Nation of Domination. They even made an appearance at WrestleMania. They could have been huge stars, but their vices took them down. Drinking got Wolfie, and cocaine got Jamie. They were great workers, but they had too much fame too soon, and they couldn't handle it.

One guy who didn't change with success was Steve Austin. I remember seeing him for the first time back in 1989 when he was starting out in Texas. I loved watching him, and I kept telling Grizzly Smith to check him out. When Austin got to Memphis, they put him with Tom Prichard to teach him how to work. Prichard also trained the Rock when he was working in Memphis and a bunch of other guys. It amazes me he doesn't have a job in Orlando at the WWE Performance Center. When I was in WCW, Steve was the TV Champion. I got to work with him there and put him over, as did Steve Armstrong, Dustin Runnels, and Ricky Morton.

It was when Steve started talking about Bret Hart on television that the WWF fans started to rally behind him. We were at a TV taping for Raw, and at that time, they would actually shoot four Raws in one night! Bret had been out for a while, and he came back specifically to work with Steve. You could sense during that time the fans were starting to get behind Austin.

We taped four Superstars episodes in a day as well. At the next Superstars taping, Austin had a TV match that didn't end right because whomever he was working didn't take the finisher properly. I was supposed to have had a dark match, but Jake Roberts, who was booking at the time, came up to me and changed plans.

"I want you to have a match with Steve," said Jake. "A competitive match, but you're still going to put Steve over."

Steve and I went about eight minutes in that TV match. Steve was a great heel, and we had a really good match. Afterwards, Steve got on the mic. As soon as they heard him say Bret's name, that crowd popped. I was like, "Wow, this guy is really taking off."

Steve remained a heel up to WrestleMania, when he worked with Bret. That was the day the fans turned him babyface, and he became the top star in the business. People today don't appreciate how hard he worked to get there. He worked his ass off and overcame some bad injuries to reach the top.

Fame and success can change people, but Steve was a guy who stayed true to himself. He was always down to Earth, and the guy he was in the ring was very much an extension of that. People connected with Stone Cold Steve Austin because they could relate. People didn't cuss on TV like Austin did at that time. They loved the "Hell yeah," drinking beer, flipping the bird, and telling the boss to kiss their ass.

One of the biggest wins I had in the ring back then came against the heir to the throne, Triple H, on Monday Night Raw. It was a DQ, but a win is a win, right?

Hunter was always good to me, and we got to wrestle each other on a few occasions. I worked with him one time at a house show in Madison Square Garden. They put us on after intermission, and right before intermission was Sid versus Vader. They had Steve Austin come in to interfere so Sid would lose to Vader. They wanted Hunter to look strong because he was starting to get a push again, post Curtain Call, so they had Sid choke slam him from the apron into the ring. We had a really competitive match that night.

The night I beat Triple H was one of those evenings where they were taping four episodes of Monday Night Raw at once. Hunter was shooting a big angle that same night with Mr. Perfect, Curt Hennig, so we didn't have a lot of time to talk over the match outside of being given the finish. Hunter trusted me, so I told him I would call it in the ring.

We were given the finish, in which Hunter would Pedigree me but lose in a disqualification. It wasn't my finish, but even that got me some heat from certain parties in the back. Not Hunter, though. He was following orders like I was, and as frantic as he was that night he was grateful I made his night a little easier. "You're a hell of a worker," he told me after the match, "I really appreciate what you did out there."

THINGS GET EXTREME

Chris Candido got the boot from WWF before I did. Chris, who was such a tough kid, worked a pay-per-view with a broken neck, and right after that, Shawn Michaels got him fired. Shawn even admitted it to Sunny, who stayed in WWF and was messing around with Shawn behind Chris's back.

Chris went to work for Paul Heyman, who was running the newly-renamed Extreme Championship Wrestling in Philadelphia. Chris loved the place from the moment he got there, and he started calling and telling me about it while I was still on the WWF roster. I learned even then that Paul was a guy who did things on the spur of the moment, booking people at the very last minute. He had an incredible mind for the business.

ECW had a working relationship with WWF at that time, and I got a last minute call from Chris, who was also working in the office along with Tommy Dreamer, Taz, and Bubba Ray Dudley.

"Paul wants to book you for a show," said Chris. "You will be working in New Haven that afternoon for WWF, and you can hitch a ride with Tammy to the Arena that night. Paul wants you to come in as Tracy Smothers, not Freddie Joe Floyd, and put over Terry Funk."

Terry Funk? "Hell yes," I said. "I'm there!"

I did the afternoon show and then hopped in a car with Tammy Sytch to drive to the Arena. Things had changed a lot for Tammy thanks to the success she had as Sunny. She was staying at the Marriott while I was still at the Day's Inn. She was the most downloaded woman on the Internet at that time according to America Online, and she was one of the biggest stars in WWF.

When we got to the Arena, plans had changed a bit. Paul was unable to get Lance Storm a flight in from Canada, so he had to shuffle the card. I remember being in Paul's office and noticing how very differently organized he was than WWF. WWF would have all these nice bulletin boards and booking sheets. Paul sometimes might have the card written on the back of a napkin.

"We're going to have Brian Lee work Terry tonight," said Paul. "Would you mind working against Rob Van Dam?"

"Not at all," I said. I knew Rob and had worked with him when he was 19 years old wrestling for Greg Price. He was great even then.

They came back later and changed things again. "We'd like you to put Taz over instead. He's going into a big program with Sabu for our first big pay-per-view, and we need someone to put him over."

"Cool," I said again. I ended up working with Taz, and the match went great. Taz put me over to Paul after I put him over in the ring. Paul let me know he wanted to use me more often. In fact he offered me a spot on the pay-per-view.

"Paul," I said, "I've got a tour to Kuwait coming up for a week and a ten day loop after that. I know I can make some money there, but I know I'm on my way out."

Paul was very supportive and understanding. "Go make your money. You have a job here when you need it."

The tour of Kuwait was one of my last loops with WWF and one of the most memorable. It was only a few years earlier that Operation Desert Storm had happened, when the US led a coalition of nations into Kuwait to liberate them from Saddam Hussein and Iraq. I remember flying into Kuwait seeing fighter jets in the air as we were coming in to the airport and thinking, "Whoa, this is the real deal."

This was also the rather infamous trip when Vader pulled a Dr. D David Schultz maneuver, slapping a TV host and cussing him out for saying wrestling was fake. Vader was just doing what he thought he was supposed to do, but it ended up becoming a pretty tense situation for him and the WWF at that time.

I worked a short match with Vader one night around the time of the incident. He was suffering from food poisoning at that time, and we worked a very short match. Vader slipped out of the ring afterwards, and as he headed to the back, one of the fans in the crowd tripped him. He went off! Vader destroyed everything in sight except the fan in an absolute rage.

The next morning we all got up and had breakfast. We had to eat quickly before heading to the military base at 9 am to work out at the gym and spend some time with the troops. Vader was still hot, and he went off on some of the locals who had helped to organize the tour at breakfast.

Later on that morning, some of the troops we were working out with started talking about the incident. "He really shouldn't have done that, you know."

"What do you mean?" we said. "Hit the guy?"

"Not just that," they said. "The cussing. He shouldn't have cussed like that on TV."

We went back to the place where we were wrestling that night, and a bunch of us went up on top of the building to lay out in the sun. All of a sudden Davey Boy Smith came running up on the roof toward us.

"Oh my gosh, you're not gonna fucking believe this!' he said. "Vader's been arrested! These guys came and took him back to the hotel!"

I don't recall all the details now, but Vader was sort of put on house arrest at the hotel. He had one of those security anklets on his leg, and he wasn't allowed to go anywhere, not even to wrestle. The government was mad at him for attacking the guy on TV, but the major offense was cussing, just as the soldiers had told us.

What made things worse for Vader was it was Ramadan, a holy time for Muslims when they don't eat meat. Since the whole country was Muslim, there was no meat to be had, and poor Vader was going nuts being stuck in a room and not being able to get any meat.

Vader spent a lot of time pacing the halls and drinking. He was an absolute mess. I remember him coming to a group of us and saying, "I'm not much of a religious man, but please, pray for me." Leon White was a big, tough man, but he was really scared to death. He didn't think he was ever gonna see his kids again.

Vince was working hard with the U.S. government to convince the Kuwaitis to drop the charges. The TV host was the man pressing charges, and he was not about to let it go. He was getting a ton of free publicity, and the ratings for his TV show were up.

When our tour was over, Vader was not allowed to leave with us. I remember us all getting on the plane, and the mood was really somber. We were all thinking about poor Leon back at the hotel.

"You guys, let's all say a prayer for Vader," said Paul Bearer. He then yelled out, "What time is it?"

We all answered, "Vader Time!"

We were all glad when the plane left the ground and the wheels went up, and we were thrilled when we got back on U.S. soil. You would not believe the military presence that surrounded us as soon as we were out of there. There were helicopters and tanks and all sorts of military personnel providing security for our arrival.

It was still a while until Vader was able to come home. Ten days he waited, with no meat, until the US sent Delta Force into the hotel to bring him out. Delta Force had no jurisdiction there, but they went right in, grabbed Vader, and brought him out without firing a shot. Then the poor guy didn't get any breaks when he got back. They put him right into a program with Ken Shamrock.

Here's the really scary ending. We were later told that the TV show host who was pressing charges against Vader disappeared. One day he was gone, and he was never heard from again. He's probably buried in the sand somewhere in the desert over there. It gave us all chills to even think about what had happened to him.

I did a ten day loop with one of The Head Bangers, whom I had known since Smoky Mountain. I got some really good reviews on those matches. They started talking like they were going to give me a push, but I was getting impatient.

The Road Warriors had just come into the company, and they were building them up as the Legion of Doom. They paired me up with Barry Horowitz, and we got to tag with them a few times, putting them over.

One Monday night after we had worked the Road Warriors, I was watching Ken Shamrock in the ring. Ken was doing an open challenge gimmick at that time, where they would bring in guys from his dojo to shoot with him in the ring. I was talking to Jim Cornette one day and I told him, "I'll fight that mother fucker. I'm not scared of him. Five grand to fight him, and ten if I beat him."

I was pretty vocal about fighting Shamrock. I didn't care if he beat me or not. I just wanted a chance. "I'll fight Shamrock! Hell, bring Mike Tyson in! I'll fight him too. He might knock me out, but at least I'll still get paid for it!"

I was dead serious about a shoot with Shamrock. I wanted a real fight, but I wasn't going to fight fair. I was going to get a pair of steel-toed boots and take his knees out. I had it all planned out.

Jim Cornette took my idea to Vince, and Vince told me he loved it. A week later, I was psyched up for the bout myself. I didn't know if it would actually happen, but I was doing everything I could to prepare for it.

Raw was in Albany, New York that week, about three hours' drive from where Candido lived. I had a few beers with Candido, Bubba Ray Dudley, and Guido before making the drive. I turned to Guido at one point and said, "What do you say, Guido? You wanna come down here and fight him?"

"Uh, Trace," he said, "I'd rather not."

I rode with Candido and Sunny to Raw, trying to rest as much as I could. Candido was teasing me the whole way. "What's the matter? You tired or something, Tracy?"

When I got to the building I spotted Ken Shamrock. That's when the reality of having a shoot fight with him started to sink in. I did ask myself, "What am I getting into?" I should have known, though, that it was never meant to be. Vince might have liked my idea, but he had other plans for me personally.

Jim Cornette spotted me in the hall and hollered, "Hey Tracy. Wait a second." I thought, "Is this it? Am I really going to have to fight Shamrock?" I knew I was probably going to get knocked out, but at least I'd make five grand.

"Would you really fight Shamrock?" asked Jim.

"Hell yeah," I said. I wasn't really prepared for a shoot fight, but I wasn't going to back down if they gave me the opportunity.

"Vince was really impressed with that," said Jim. "He said you've got a lot of guts."

"I'm not trying to impress anybody," I said. "I just want to make some money."

"That's what I want to talk to you about," said Jim. Jim told me that Vince wanted to put masks on me, Bart Gunn, and Bull Buchannan, and build us up as a faction. In spite of the fact I was going to be under a mask, I was thrilled they were finally going to give me something to do.

As for my idea of the fight challenge, Vince later did something similar called the Brawl for All that led to Bart Gunn getting knocked out by Butterbean. I couldn't help but laugh. I popped even harder when I saw Mike Tyson come into the WWF. I'm not saying it was all my idea and Vince stole it. I'm just saying, that's what happened.

I later found out word had gotten around to Shamrock about my challenge. Some people tried to stir up some shit over it, but Shamrock was cool with me. He understood why I did it.

Shamrock had trained to become a wrestler with Buzz Sawyer. One time I got to talking with Shamrock and told Buzz how he used to bring pictures of Shamrock to show the guys in New Japan to try to get him booked, telling them how Shamrock was beating guys up.

"Yeah," said Ken. "He used to pay me $50 a fight."

"That's Buzz," I said. "But he also set you up to make a lot of money in the pro wrestling and the UFC." Shamrock couldn't deny that.

The Truth Commission never came to be for me either, and it was probably my fault. I made the mistake of opening my mouth and talking about it in the car that night. I was riding home with Chris and Sunny, and when Chris told me what happened, I told him what Jim had offered me.

Sunny caught just a little of the story and turned around. "What did he say?" Sunny asked. Chris repeated what I had just told him, and Sunny replied, "So they can find a spot for him, but not for you."

Right then and there, I knew I was done.

My last match in WWF was a dark match against Dirty White Boy in Evansville, Indiana. Jerry Lawler was backstage that night ranting about me being there. He was mad at me because I had been working with Bert Prentice.

Dirty White Boy and I were first on that night in the dark match, and they planned to have Doug Furnas and Phil LaFon go on after us with Bradshaw and Barry Windham. The powers that be in the WWF/WWE love to mess with the boys. That night we had guys coming and telling us all sorts of different things. One would tell us to go five minutes. One said ten minutes. One said three minutes.

Bruce Prichard was working gorilla and told us to keep it short so the tag match would have time before Raw went on the air. They told referee Mike Chioda something different, and while I kept telling Chioda to let us go home, he kept telling us to go longer.

"We can't go home yet," he said. "We'll get heat!"

"What are they going to do?" I said. "Fire me? Fuck with me? That's all they've done for a year."

Chioda finally gave us the cue, and we finished the match. As soon as we reached the back, Bruce was screaming at us. "Hey! Why didn't you go home?"

"I went when I got the cue, man," I said and walked away.

I went down the ramp and saw Jimmy talking to Cactus Jack. I went by him and sounded off. "Hey, Jimmy. I've done everything you've asked me to do. Y'all have done nothing but beat me like a drum, fucked with me the whole time. I get it. The snakes and the sharks. I know this is my last day, and I'm out of here."

The Undertaker was standing close by too, so I spoke up for his benefit. "All these guys I know and I've helped, they've put the knife to me too. That goes for you too!" I pointed straight at 'Taker when I said it.

When I got into the locker room, I saw Furnas, LaFon, Bradshaw, and Windham staring daggers at us. I knew they were all mad at me, and I didn't care. Owen Hart came in behind us raving about us. "These guys just had a hell of a match out there! You should have seen it!" We did, too. I beat Dirty White Boy out of nowhere, ending my WWF run with a rare, surprise win.

The guys didn't care. They were all pissed. "Hey guys, it's my last night. I went home when they gave us the cue."

"Hey, man, go as long as you want," said Ron Simmons, tongue in cheek. He got it. He'd been there long enough, he knew how things were. They all knew.

That's the way it is in the WWE. They love to mess with the boys. Roger Ruffin once put it this way. "If you were on your death bed, dying, they'd love to be there and say the words, "You're fired!" just to see your face in that moment. It's sick.

It was my last night, and I was thrilled to be done with them. I lived 150 miles from there, and I had a job waiting for me with Paul Heyman. I was headed home as soon as I could.

FULL BLOODED ITALIAN

The next time I went back to ECW, I lived the wrestler's version of the actor's nightmare. Actors sometimes have a recurring dream, where they are about to go on stage but they don't know their lines or even what play they are in. That night, it was ten minutes until the eight o'clock curtain, and I still didn't know what I was doing or who I was wrestling. I was used to knowing weeks or at the least days ahead, so I was starting to panic.

It was ten 'til eight when I went up to Sabu and asked if he knew who I was working with.

"Hang on, I'll go ask," said Sabu. He went over to Paul and asked, "Who is Tracy with tonight?"

Paul said, "Do you want to work with him?"

"I can't," said Sabu. "I'm already working with Spike." Sabu was in a program with Taz at the time, and he was scheduled to work against Spike Dudley because Taz had trained Spike.

"Oh yeah," said Paul.

Dreamer was standing beside them at the time. "Where's Tracy?" he asked. Sabu pointed in my direction, and Dreamer walked over to me.

"Do you have your Confederate flag?"

I said yes.

"I'm going to put you in a tag with Chris Chetti against the FBI."

FBI in ECW stood for Full Blooded Italians. At that time it was a tag team consisting of Guido, who was very Italian, and Tommy Rich, who was as far from Italian as you could get. It was a gimmick that made me laugh when I first saw them together, but things got really interesting when Dreamer told me the plan for that night.

"You and Tommy won't get in the ring together until the end, and when you do, you're going to turn on Chris and join the FBI."

It was 7:57 pm when he told me this, and we went on first right at 8 pm. I didn't know it at the time, but it was just another typical night at ECW!

The match went off as planned. Chris Chetti and Guido worked the whole match up until the end. Chetti hit me with the hot tag, and Guido tagged Tommy. I came into the ring, but instead of leveling Tommy, I went after Chris. Tommy and Guido joined in with me, and the FBI was officially reborn as a trio.

I was no more Italian than Tommy Rich was, but they billed me as being from Nashville, Italy. It was kind of goofy, but ECW had a lot of factions that didn't make sense. Have a look at the Dudley clan and tell me how many of them you honestly think are related!

Twenty years later, I'm still doing the FBI gimmick with Guido and others on the independent circuit. If you only know Guido from his run in WWF as Nunzio, you haven't seen how great he can be. He was trained by Billy Robinson, and he's a hell of a wrestler.

ECW was a great place to be in a trio because there were so many threesomes and factions to feud with. We had a lot of fun working against the Blue World Order of Nova, Stevie Richards, and the Blue Meanie as well as the trio of 2 Cold Scorpio, Sandman, and Tommy Dreamer. We also worked a lot with the Eliminators, the Pit Bulls, Axl Rotten, Balls Mahoney, and Shane Douglas.

ECW had a completely different culture in the locker room than WWF. Vince had a dress code we all had to follow when we traveled. He didn't smoke, and he would not allow smoking in the locker rooms. There was also no drinking and no drugs. At least, not out in the open.

ECW was the total opposite of WWF in so many ways. It was a zoo. I loved that there was no dress code, and it felt good to be working in a place where I totally fit in.

In November 1997 we were scheduled to do an eight-man tag match on the November to Remember pay-per-view in Monaca, Pennsylvania against the Dudleys, The Ganstanators (John Kronus and New Jack), and the Hardcore Chair Swingin' Freaks (Axl Rotten with Balls Mahoney). Something had happened just before that night in town in Morristown, Tennessee involving New Jack, and there was a warrant out for his arrest. Two serious looking guys in suits showed up outside of Pittsburgh with that warrant, looking to take New Jack back with them to Tennessee.

Paul Heyman stepped in and started talking to the suits, who explained what New Jack had done and showed Paul the warrant. Paul told the guys he understood but that New Jack was needed for the pay-per-view that evening. He asked if it would be all right for New Jack to work his match, after which Paul would make sure he went back with the men to Tennessee. The men agreed.

Paul gave his usual "state of the union" speech before the show that evening, declaring this to be the biggest crowd we'd ever had and hyping us up for the occasion. We all knew there were two men waiting to take New Jack back to Tennessee as soon as our match was over. We also knew that some way, somehow, whether through his own plan of Paul's, New Jack was going to get out of the building without being taken into custody.

We went out and had our match, with all eight guys getting in on the action and doing our brawl. As soon as the match was over, New Jack vanished. Not a trace of him! He was just gone. Those guys from Tennessee were mad, but after searching the building, they finally gave up and left.

About a week later, the story finally got out. Kronus and the Dudley Boys had stationed a van outside the building, and as soon as the match was over, they got New Jack out the side of the building and into a van. New Jack did not go back to Tennessee. There were rumors that Paul had paid the bond for him or Paul's attorney father got the charges dismissed. Whatever the case, it was soon behind him.

While we were getting our big push in ECW, Goldberg was starting to take off on his winning streak in WCW. Guido started kidding Dreamer about having us go on a winning streak like Goldberg's.

Goldberg was known for a spectacular ring entrance involving smoke and pyrotechnics. One day, Dreamer came up with the idea of having Guido sport a Fu Manchu mustache while Tommy Rich and I carried sparklers when we came out to the ring. It was kind of a rib on Guido, but we were excited to try it out.

The "Guido-berg" spoof was killed off before we ever got a chance to try it. I remember Tommy coming into the Arena, mad as hell. Tommy never cussed, but that night he was cussing and throwing things, just as mad as he could be.

"What's wrong with Tommy?" we asked.

We found out later why Tommy was upset and why our

sparkler gimmick never happened. ECW had a working relationship with WWF at that time. We came to find out that Paul had liked the idea so much, he told Vince about it. Before we could unleash Guidoberg, the WWF introduced Gillberg, doing the same gimmick with the sparklers as a rib on Goldberg.

This was during the ratings wars, and Vince was looking for every idea he could to combat WCW. I saw it and laughed my ass off, but Tommy definitely didn't think it was funny.

"They stole your idea," I said.

"You're damn right they did!!" Tommy is a good Christian man, easily the nicest office guy I ever worked with. But he was mad that night.

Tommy Dreamer was really the meat and potatoes booker for ECW. He handled all the details so that Paul could just create. Paul gave Dreamer a lot of leeway to work out the mid card, and he came up with a lot of the gags we did. They had a good thing going when Paul was allowing Tommy to worry about the little stuff. Part of me feels if they had kept that balance, they would still be in business today, but who knows?

Going to ECW was like traveling to a different world. WWF even then had some pretty strict rules for travel and discipline. They had a dress code. You had to be on time or they would fine you. You were expected to act like a professional at all times. ECW? It was the land of the misfits compared to that. The guys were drinking and partying in the back, wearing whatever the hell they wanted. They had a pretty good time, but they also did their job.

Rob Van Dam

I love Tracy to death. He was a hot head, and he was one of the guys we knew would fight. We had some of the toughest people in the world in ECW, and Tracy fit right in that environment.

I saw him get mad and punch a few lockers back in the day, but I never saw him in a real fight myself. Tracy used to tell us stories about when he was growing up, when he and his friends on the farm would pick a guy to fight a kid from another farm. I'm not sure what they were fighting for, but we were all pretty entertained by those stories.

Tracy and I had a match together at a TV taping in late 1999, where I defended my TV title against him. Tracy and I were a clash of styles. He's a classic Southern wrestler compared to my style, but Tracy really cared about the match and wanted to make sure we both looked great. He didn't always know where I was or what I was doing, but he made sure he was in the right place to catch me when I landed.

Joel Gertner

There was an incident once when someone tried to call out Fonzie at our hotel. The situation started at the hotel bar and escalated when the fan pulled his van up to the front of the hotel and called out Fonzie, wanting to fight him. About five or six of us left the bar to go out and take a stand for Fonzie.

I was outside the van banging a blackjack on the windshield as hard as I could without breaking it. I wanted the guy to hear the windshield was being hit while he himself was being hit inside the car. I didn't want to break the glass because I didn't want to hurt our guy who was inside the van handing the guy his ass. It was Tracy, of course, giving him the business in the front seat to teach the guy a lesson.

I had a red drink in my hand that I took out of the bar with me. I remember because as the capper of the evening, after we were sure the guy would never mess with another wrestler again, I threw my red drink on his white shirt, just to put a point on it.

Tracy was a prince. He's a man's man, a guy who would always back up the boys. He's just a great guy. He can also be very intense.

One Saturday afternoon we were at the hotel before an ECW show watching a college football game. I'll never forget how intense Tracy was just watching the game. He never said anything, but you could just tell, by his body language, how focused he was. As soon as the commercial came on, his posture relaxed and you could see the wheels turning. He shook his head and said, "War. War, man, war." Then as soon as the commercial was over he was right back into it.

Rick Brady

Tommy Dreamer once told me a story about Tracy's ECW days. One night at the ECW Arena, they had a riot where the cops were called in. The cops brought in K-9 units, and one of the cops was about to let the dog go on Tommy Dreamer.

Tracy had wrestled earlier in the night, and he was in the shower when the situation got out of hand. Hearing the commotion, out in the main part of the building, Tracy came flying out of the locker room. He still had shampoo in his hair, and he wore nothing but a towel around his waist.

Tracy Smothers

When that riot broke out, I raced out of the shower in just a towel and tried to assess the situation as quickly as I could. It was total chaos, and there were 70-80 cops including K-9 units and SWAT units. I remember seeing one guy get in Roadkill's face, and Roadkill just beat the hell out of him, right in front of the cops.

I had a lot of adrenaline going as I was trying to size up the situation. I spotted a K-9 unit right in front of Tommy Dreamer and me, turned to Dreamer and said, "You get the cop, I'll get the dog!"

Please don't get me wrong. I'm the biggest animal lover in the world, especially dogs. But something snapped in me when I saw all that commotion, and when I laid eyes on a police dog that night, something snapped. I wanted to kick its ass.

In Allentown, Pennsylvania, a fan went after Francine at ringside. The whole dressing room emptied chasing after the guy, but it was Perry Saturn, who had blown his knee out the night before, who got to him first. They beat the hell out of that guy.

Any night a fight broke out was a good night for Atlas Security, the company that worked security for ECW. Whenever people ask me who the toughest people were in ECW, I tell them it was Atlas Security. They were all big and tough, and they loved a fight. They loved any excuse to rough people up. They used to tell Tommy and me to try and start something with the fans. Anything for an excuse to get into it.

Paul Heyman gave Rick Rude a job working in the ECW office. Rude had taken Paul under his wing when he was first breaking in to WCW, so when Rude got hurt and WCW let him go, Paul had a chance to pay him back. Rick was there every weekend helping the guys in the back and managing on occasion.

The Pit Bulls had been busted for drugs in real life. Paul kept them on the payroll and let them continue working out and train with the other guys. There was real heat backstage between New Jack and Anthony Durante, aka Pit Bull #2, at that same time, and we could all see it was coming to a head.

One night in Queens the two of them finally came to blows. New Jack and Anthony went at it hard like they wanted to kill each other. We were all exhausted, having been on the road for a while, and it took the entire locker room to pull those guys apart.

The next night we were at the ECW Arena in Philadelphia. Tommy Rich and I had a tradition back then. Once we were finished with our matches, we went out back and split a case of beer. Our job was done for the night, and it was time to kick back and party. Some of the other guys would occasionally come out and join us. I once told Tommy he was the bartender of ECW because he loved to sit down and counsel guys. He was the guy who would gladly listen while you spill your guts.

Tommy and I were already out back drinking beers with Shane Douglas when a riot broke out in the Arena. A fan sucker punched Mikey Whipwreck, and once again, the whole dressing room hit the ring, mowing fans down left and right.

I was out back when the melee broke out, and I was one of the last ones to walk out into the fray. Tommy and I strolled in with Shane to get the lay of the land. One thing caught my eye, and I climbed up on a table to get a better look.

"Tommy!" I said. "Look over there! Look who's working together!" The two men who were ready to kill each other the night before, New Jack and Anthony, were side by side, back to back, beating the fuck out of the fans!

"Last night we were pulling them apart!" I said. "Look at them now!"

When the fighting was over and everyone came back into the dressing room, Tommy let them have it. "Last night it took all of us to pull you apart! Now look at you two! You boys gonna get married now? Get a room! Get a room!"

We were in either Long Island or Staten Island one night. I wrestled somewhere in the middle of the card, and afterwards, Tommy Rich, Tommy Rogers, Guido and I went and find a spot to watch the main event. I want to say we were sitting on top of a bus, but I don't remember.

The Dudleys were in the main event that night, and nobody knew how to get the crowd riled up like them. They got the fans going good that night, and a fan threw a chair into the ring that hit Big Dick Dudley. Big Dick went off, and when he did, so did Bubba and D-Von and Atlas Security. They were mowing the fans down left and right.

Tommy Rogers said, "Do you think we need to go help them?"

Tommy Rich said, "I don't think they need our damn help. Look at 'em! They're whipping every son of a bitch in the crowd!"

The ECW Arena riot with the SWAT and the K-9s was a pretty big fiasco, but what I saw that night made the Arena riot look like a minor skirmish. All of a sudden, the NYPD was everywhere. They came streaming in every door, every hall, every nook and cranny of that building! They arrested Big Dick, took him to jail, and shut the show down. Nobody touched Big Dick's bag, as everyone was worried what might be in there. We all got to our cars and got the hell out while Paul arranged to get Big Dick out of jail.

That's the way it was in ECW. It was fucking crazy every night.

Big Dick Dudley was a monster, and ironically, a full blooded Italian in real life. He had done time in prison for manslaughter. He had turned his life around, but he was still a tough man. In fact the only person he was afraid of in the whole world was his wife, a former model who was 6'3" and a beautiful lady. He was a good guy, God bless him.

A few months into my tenure with ECW, I started working and training some of the boys. I got into the ring one day with Spike Dudley and just started chain wrestling with him. Paul liked what he saw, and he started sending more guys in to workout with me. Paul tossed me a little more money, and I became the trainer for ECW. I worked out with a lot of the guys when we had the time, and I'd help some of them put together matches including Tommy Dreamer, Bubba Ray, and Candido.

Paul kept a close eye on those training sessions, especially when guys who weren't signed with ECW came in. I remember working with Shane Helms and Roadkill one night, and I was stunned Paul didn't sign them both on the spot.

One of the top guys in ECW who helped launch them to national prominence was Shane Douglas. I had known Shane since 1988. As a matter of fact we were roommates at one time. We played many intense rounds of putt putt together, talking trash and doing commentary for one another.

Of all the guys in the ECW locker room, if I had to pick one who was the very best, it was Jerry Lynn. Jerry probably worked himself out of more jobs in the business because he was just that good. The matches he had with RVD in ECW were game changers. Jerry lost to RVD almost every time, but Jerry was so good, he was getting over by losing every night! Everybody wanted to work with Jerry because he was just so damn good!

Sabu was a game changer too. He was a guy who was pretty much made as an independent when Paul brought him into ECW. Sabu wasn't a very political guy in the locker room, but the things he did in the ring were revolutionary.

The ECW fans were the pioneers of today's hardcore fans. ECW fans got there the night before and tailgated in the parking lot. They started bonfires in the middle of the city the night before shows, and the police didn't mess with them. The only fans I can say are more hardcore than that ECW crowd are the Juggalos. I'll get to those crazy mother fuckers later on.

Paul Heyman said the ECW fans were just as important as the wrestlers in the ring, and he was right. They made thousands of dollars selling those black T-shirts and really changed the business as far as selling gimmicks.

I left ECW about six months before they closed and were bought out by WWF. I had had a solid run for two and a half years tagging with Guido, and I knew it was time to move on when they started having us put a lot of the other guys over. They wanted to move in a different direction with cruiserweights like Super Crazy and Tajiri, and they saw Guido working into that scene as well.

Steve Carroll came into the company around the same time, and he and Paul were bringing in a lot of younger guys they could pay less. They were still paying me and some of the older guys to fly in to the shows, and they started letting guys like Tommy Rich and One Man Gang go. One weekend, when I thought I was booked on some shows, they didn't send me a ticket. I knew I was going to be fired, and that didn't bother me. I've been fired from everywhere at least once.

One of the kids who came in for a tryout was a guy out of Detroit called Rhino. The moment I laid eyes on him, I knew he was a beast. I let Rhino into the ring for his tryout match, and it was there that I suggested to him the move that would become his signature. Goldberg and Edge were already working for WCW and WWF, and they both used the spear.

Before we got started, I asked Rhino if he could do a spear. "Yeah, but I also do this tackle thing in the corner. Can I do that?"

"Yeah," I said.

"Really?" he said. "I don't want to get in any trouble."

"Just put the heat on me," I told him. "Tell them I told you to do it. Tackle me into the corner, and when I stagger out, hit me with the spear."

Man, when he hit me in that corner, he about broke me in half! Then I staggered out and he hit that spear, which looked great. I told Rhino he needed to use that as his finish, and the move became known as the Gore when Rhino did it. Before he agreed to use it, though, Rhino got in touch with Edge and asked his permission to use it. The two of them were tight, and Rhino showed a lot of character doing that.

As it turned out, my letting Rhino do that tackle move on me was one of the reasons given for my firing a few weeks later. I knew the writing was on the wall, even before that match, but I didn't know for sure when it was coming until I got a phone call from Ian Rotten. "They're about to fire you," he said. "Why don't you come in and work with me on such and such a date?" Ian was dead on about the dates, and I was glad to know I had a place to go after Paul fired me.

I finally got a call from a lady in the office. She told me Paul wasn't planning to bring me in anymore, and that was really the only notice I got.

There's never been a place quite like ECW, either before or since. From one night to the next, from Paul's booking to the reaction of the fans, you never knew what to expect. It was always so unpredictable, and that's what made it special.

KOOL-AID DRINKERS

In between working for WWF and ECW, I started working for a promotion that has been a big part of my life the last twenty-something years. It's an independent wrestling group with a cult-like following that rivals that of ECW and even Juggalo Championship Wrestling.

When Memphis wrestling closed up in the mid-1990s, two men moved into the Louisville, Kentucky area to try and fill that void. One of those men was Danny Davis, who opened Ohio Valley Wrestling and built that company into one of the most successful wrestling schools of the last three decades. OVW is in Louisville now, but back then they ran out of a rundown warehouse on Tenth Street in Jeffersonville, Indiana.

Another guy set up shop across the river in Kentucky, eventually opening an old Kmart building on Dixie Highway. His name is Ian Rotten, and the promotion was IWA Mid-South.

A lot has been said and written about Ian Rotten and IWA Mid-South. Some good, some bad. Ian is a smart ass, but he's a guy who always tells it like it is. We've had a few falling outs over the years, but the thing I appreciate most about him is that Ian always booked me when I was about to be let go from someplace else. Matter of fact, Ian usually knew I was getting fired before I did.

"They haven't said anything to me," I would say to him.

"Well, they're going to fire you," he replied, telling me who told him and when.

I said, "Well since they're firing me, can you book me?"

"That's why I'm calling you!" he said. I was always appreciative of that, and I always enjoyed starting my long weekends on Thursdays with IWA Mid-South.

I worked for Ian on the very first IWA Mid-South show against Reckless Youth in 1996. I worked Thursdays for him when I was with ECW and WWF, and I've continued with him off and on ever since.

We had no way of knowing this at the time, but the roster at IWA Mid-South was a who's who of the future of the wrestling business. Ian has always had a remarkable eye for talent, and guys who came through IWA Mid-South included CM Punk, Chris Hero (Kassius Ohno), Colt Cabana, Dave Prazak, Ace Steel, Adam Pierce, Tyler Black (Seth Rollins), A.J. Styles, Austin Aries, Alex Shelley, Nigel McGuinness, Jon Moxley, Bryan Danielson (Daniel Bryan), Jimmy Jacobs, Claudio Castagnoli (Cesaro), Delirious, and Samoa Joe.

It was nothing to be on a show with those guys back then. We had no idea that they were all going to be who they became.

It may surprise some readers to know how many big names have worked for Ian as well. There's a well-known triple threat match on the Internet featuring CM Punk, Rey Mysterio without a mask, and Eddie Guerrero. Ian gave guys like Eddie a second chance when no one else would, and Eddie really made the most of that opportunity.

Even in recent years, Ian has continued to run shows and elevate good talent. Ian booked the Crist brothers, Dave and Jake, before they went on to Impact. He had Michael Elgin, Sami Callihan, and Mance Warner before those guys really blew up. So many guys have done the tryout show for IWA Mid-South and gone on to become not just stars for Ian but superstars for other promotions. If anyone ever tells you, "The quality of talent at IWA Mid-South is not what it used to be," don't believe it. Those guys were not names when they worked for Ian, but they are now. Many of the guys working for him now will be big names in the coming years.

I got to work with CM Punk and Chris Hero back when they were just 19 years old. The two of them, along with Ace Steel and Colt Cabana, all broke in with a guy named Danny Dominion. I knew from the first time working with each of them they had "it."

I know it's hard to believe because of where they went in the business, but back then, wrestling was a side gig for those young guys. Colt was a school teacher back then working with kids who had disabilities. Punk was a scientist and worked in a lab. He had a hell of a job making good money. I asked him once, "You've got a great job. Why in the world do you want to do this?" Punk loved the business. That's why he did it.

Punk was always a smartass. It's his thing, to be a punk. He's very intelligent, and he says what's on his mind. The dude is very smart. The best interview I ever saw on TV was his "pipebomb" on Monday Night Raw. I didn't see it live, but I watched the playback later that night. He just told it like it was, and he got a huge push out of that.

Punk and Hero had quite a rivalry in IWA Mid-South, and some of those matches are on YouTube. They went 46 minutes in a tables and ladders match and then 93 minutes. Those were some of the most incredible matches I've ever seen.

Claudio Castagnoli was one of my favorites out of that crew, and to my mind, he's the best in the world. Claudio is an absolute beast, and he should be a world champion. You knew when you were in the ring with Claudio because he brought it every night.

American Kickboxer

Tarek and I started working at IWA Mid-South the same time as Tracy. Tracy was booked to wrestle Terry Funk at a place called Shakee's Bar in Louisville. Right from the opening bell, Tracy and Terry were really snug with each other. Neither guy was giving an inch. Terry is almost twenty years older than Tracy, but he made Tracy earn his respect.

I was rooming with Tracy that night, and as soon as we got to the room, Tracy laid out on the floor. "Man, if we hang out with Funk tonight, you can't tell him I was lying in the floor just trying to get it back together!" he said.

Tracy always loved to watch Mad Man Pondo in all the deathmatches he did at IWA. He loved Pondo, and he'd never miss a chance to watch him in action. You could hear him in the locker room, reacting to all the craziness. "Aw, he's dead! He's fucking dead! It's a war! It's like Vietnam and Afghanistan out there!"

Tracy Smothers

You can't talk about IWA Mid-South without talking about the fans. IWA Mid-South had and has a rabid, almost cult-like following that actually refers to themselves as the Kool-Aid Drinkers. It's a crowd unlike any other. I always enjoyed going out to the gimmick table after my match to watch the show and the crowd. The wrestlers always gave a pay-per-view effort, and the crowd is always hot for every match.

I got to work with Bobby Eaton at IWA one night. We had built up slowly to a one on one match between the two of us, and when the big match finally happened, it nearly started a riot. The match spilled out of the ring and was planned as a double count out. Guys poured out of the locker room to try to pull us apart, and we just kept going.

The fans loved Bobby, and the more heat I got on him, the angrier the fans became. Bobby was selling for me like crazy. I hit him in the eye and he grabbed his face, screaming, "My eye!"

As if that wasn't enough, I turned my attention to Chris Hero, who was a big babyface. I went to work on him, and he was really selling hard for me. He told me to give him a punch, and when I did, he went flying back hard into the chairs. That really set the fans off.

At some point during the melee, I got bumped into a female fan wearing a halter top. I noticed right away she was also pregnant. I reached out instinctively to steady her so she didn't get knocked down, but I did not see that she was holding a baseball bat with barbed wire. I tried to do something good, to help this girl, and next thing I knew, she and her boyfriend were attacking me with that bat!

I owe a debt to big Jay Bradley, because he saw what was going on and came over to help me. Jay's a big guy who trained under CM Punk and Colt Cabana. As soon as he got me clear, he started to beat the hell out of the pregnant girl's boyfriend. It got so vicious I tried to pull him off.

"What the fuck are you doing?" Jay said. "They're trying to kill you, and I'm trying to help you!"

Nick Maniwa

The Bobby Eaton match was a sight to see live. Between Bobby and Hero selling, Tracy going berserk, and the girl with the bat, it was just unreal. Tracy was amped up at the end, head butting the support beams and screaming, "I'll fight all of you! Bring it on!"

Tracy Smothers

When I went to work for ECW in 1997, Paul Heyman used to get frustrated with me for working for Ian. He didn't like me making the trip to Louisville every week, and he and Ian had a lot of heat. He asked me once why I continued to work for Ian even after Paul hired me.

"Because he's running every week," I said. "Sometimes I'm up here and I don't work. If I go there, I know I'll get to work."

Paul said, "Well you're my talent!"

I said, "I worked for Ian, not for you!"

Paul never cut me loose, and I'm glad of that. I'm also glad for every time Ian was there to offer me a job. I didn't like getting those phone calls because I knew it meant I was getting fired, but I'm glad he always offered me that safety net.

A singles star in Smoky Mountain. Photo courtesy of Jim Cornette.

Smoky Mountain photos courtesy of Jim Cornette.

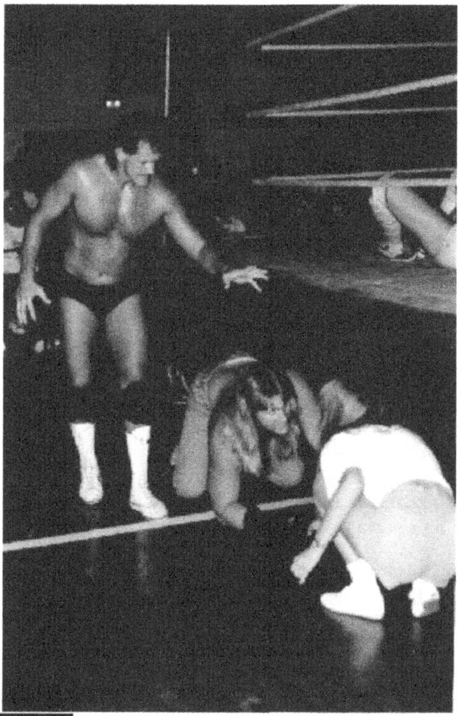

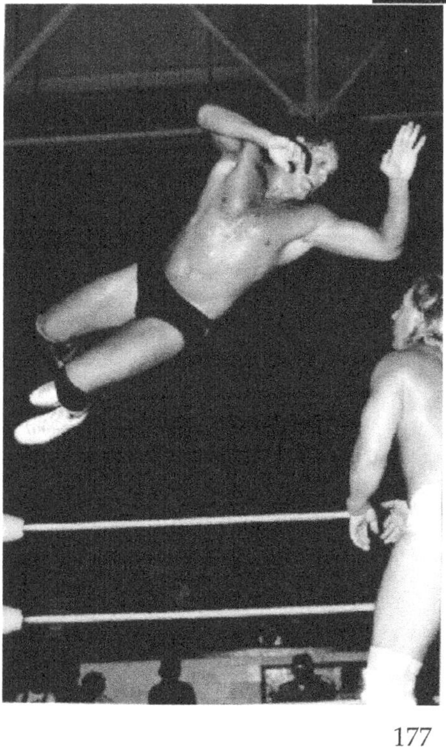

More from Smoky Mountain courtesy of Jim Cornette.

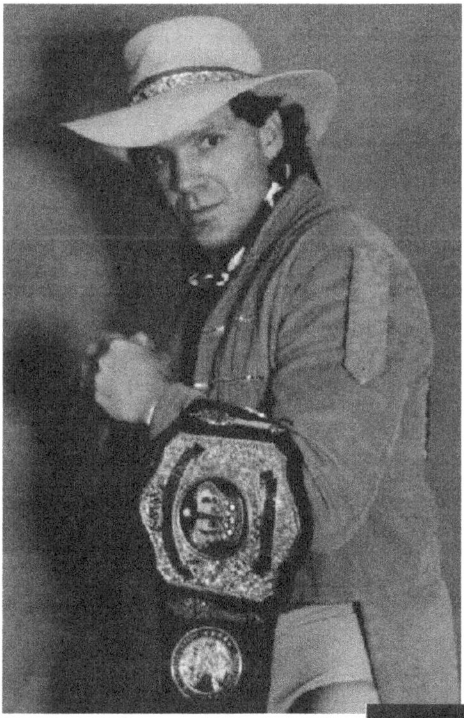

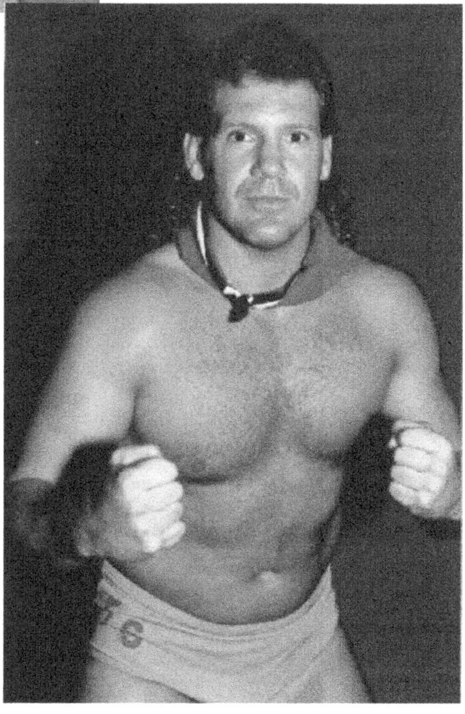

I used to have a beautiful drop kick. Top photo courtesy of Jim Cornette. Bottom photo courtesy of George Tahinos.

"From Nashville, Italy?" The FBI in ECW. Photo courtesy of George Tahinos.

ECW photos courtesy of George Tahinos.

Photo courtesy of George Tahinos.

The FBI then and now: Tommy Rich, Little Guido, and Tracy Smothers.
Above photo courtesy of George Tahinos.

THE CLOWNS

In 1997 ECW held their Hardcore Heaven pay-per-view in Fort Lauderdale, Florida. I took a flight from Nashville to Fort Lauderdale, and it just so happened the Insane Clown Posse was on the same flight. This was when they were just starting to take off as a band. They had flown from Detroit to Nashville, and they were headed south for the ECW show as well, where they we're booked in a segment with Sabu and Rob Van Dam. This was at a time when Rob Van Dam and Sabu were really in their prime, and they were killing guys in the ring. I remember seeing them against Furnas and LaFon and the Eliminators, and they loved to hurt people.

I didn't know these guys or their music, but my son Kyle, who was seven at the time, loved them. I introduced myself and asked them to sign a few things for my boy. Then I asked them, "Why are you guys messing around with wrestling? You don't have to do this. You have your music. Why would you want to do this?"

I was surprised when Violent J and Shaggy 2 Dope told me how excited they were to get involved with ECW, to take bumps, do hardcore, and literally get the hell beat out of them. "Listen," they said, "We love music, but music is our job. Wrestling is our passion. It's what we love, and we were into wrestling way before we got into music."

I found out how serious the boys were when they got to Fort Lauderdale. They promoted the ECW show as hard or harder than they ever promoted their albums, and they took a beating from Van Dam and Sabu. Van Dam kicked J so hard in a match, he developed a whistle in his ear that he still has to this day!

Shortly after that show is when their break out album, *The Great Milenko*, was released. It was a historic album release because it's the only record that was ever recalled on the day of its release. The Clowns were at an autograph signing when they learned that Hollywood Records, a subsidiary of Walt Disney, had given in to protests from the Southern Baptists to pull the album. It was released a short time later by Island Records.

I had assumed at the time they were getting into wrestling because they'd made a name in music, but I came to find out later they were wrestlers before they were known as musicians. As soon as they made money in music, they invested in a wrestling ring and started running shows in Detroit. They've had broken bones and broken necks. Shaggy and Violent J would take any bump. Matter of fact, I once saw Shaggy fall off a bus!

Back then no one dreamed that the Clowns would succeed not just as wrestlers but promoters, but as it turned out, they created one of the best places to work in all of professional wrestling. There have been many clowns who thought they could run a wrestling business over the years, but these Clowns, who are also rappers, have a real love and respect for the business. People often wonder why folks like me work for the Insane Clown Posse's Juggalo Championship Wrestling. It's because they treat you fair, they pay you well, and they put you in front of the craziest wrestling fans in the world.

The Clowns have had their share of frustration over the years, and there have been times they have quit the business. They always come back to it. Like so many of us, they love the business too much to ever get out for good.

JCW to me was the second coming of ECW. It's known mostly for the deathmatches and the blood and the violence, but the JCW roster, just like IWA Mid-South, has been a who's who of professional wrestling history with names like Cesaro, Kassius Ohno, Matt Hardy, Johnny Impact, Rikishi, Abdullah the Butcher, Hacksaw Jim Duggan, Greg "The Hammer" Valentine, the Headhunters, Terry Funk, Tito Santana, and Dusty Rhodes. These aren't backyard wrestling names but men who drew money and sold out arenas all over the world.

One of the greatest matches I ever saw took place at a JCW show. Bob Armstrong defeated Bob Orton, Jr., on a show called Wrestling Legends & Loonies 2010. Bob Armstrong came out of retirement for that match because, in his words, he could not call it a career without wrestling once for JCW.

JCW was also the only promotion to ever put on a true NWO vs. Degeneration-X match. They brought in Billy Gunn and Road Dogg Brian James to face Kevin Nash and Sean Waltman with Scott Hall in their corner. WWE never put that one together, but JCW did! I worked Tommy Rich on that same show, and I got to see those boys put on a hell of a match.

I said earlier that Haku was the toughest man in wrestling. I'll tell you who the second is. It's a guy I first met in WCW and later worked with at JCW. We used to go down to Houston, Texas, and this local kid who had been in and out of trouble with the law always came around, asking for a chance. I knew once I met him he was really a good person, but I also knew from that first handshake he was for real. I could feel it the same way I did with Haku. He ended up becoming a champion in WCW and later for WWE.

Neither promotion really gave him his due, but I'm here to tell you: Booker T is the man. Booker and I worked a match for JCW with Kevin Gill as the special guest referee. We had a great match, but I'll tell you what, I wouldn't want to get in a real fight with Book. If I'm ever in a real fight and can't have Haku with me, I'll take Booker T any day.

If I had to pick someone for the third spot on my toughest man alive list, it would be another JCW alum: Necro Butcher. That dude will mess you up. He's not a trained professional wrestler, but he is a tough mother fucker. I saw him step in the ring at JCW against Samoa Joe, who is no slouch himself, and send Samoa Joe running.

The Juggalos, as the ICP fans are known, are a crazy crowd. They aren't afraid of anybody, and they love to throw shit at the wrestlers. They've hit me with quarters, eggs, trash cans, a pitcher of beer, and a pair of jeans. One time they were selling eggs for two dollars a piece to throw at me. If you've never been hit with an egg, I'll save you the trouble and tell you - it hurts!!

The best thing you can do is to take the beating and ignore them, because the last thing you want to do is get into a fight with them. You fight one Juggalo, you have to fight them all. They are family, and they stick together.

A lot of bad things have been said in the press about the Juggalos. The Juggalos were even classified as a gang by the U.S. government. I'm here to tell you, that's flat out wrong. They are a cult in the same way ECW was, but they are not a gang. If you fight with one, you fight them all because they are family. Believe me, I experienced it myself.

I get an awful lot of heat in the ring at JCW because the Juggalos don't care for my rebel flag gimmick. Thankfully, they do have the ability to shut it off when the show is over. Unlike a lot of people, they can separate the man from the gimmick. They know it's just a character.

One night I was at a JCW event, and about twenty of them approached me at the bar with that look in their eye they get during the matches. I thought some of them were going to jump on me, so I turn to them and said, "Hey guys, I'm off. I don't want any trouble." I was relieved when they calmed down. Matter of fact, they all ended up buying me a drink, which was cool.

The independent circuit in the post-territory era was a whole different world this time around. I was now one of the more experienced guys on the shows I worked, and I was known among the boys for my work with WCW, Smoky Mountain, and ECW as well as my three encounters with the bears.

What that meant in those days was I had a target on my back. For the first time in my life I was getting called an Old Man and a Has Been. I was getting in the ring with younger guys who wanted to make a name for themselves, guys who would take cheap shots and try to take advantage of me.

The kids that wanted to work, I worked with, but whenever they took a shot at me, I fought back. These were Toughman competitors, boxers, cops, all kinds of guys, names you never heard of. I beat the fuck out of every one of them, and I enjoyed it. It was actually kind of a release for me.

A lot of these kids who tried to get cute with me were local boys who lived five or ten miles from the building. I was driving a couple of hours to the show, and they thought it was cool getting in the ring with a guy they had watched on TV. They also seemed to get a kick out of trying me, which is why I was taking so many cheap shots.

The truth about most wrestlers is that they will do anything if they think it will get them a break. They would dig up their own grandmothers if they thought it would get them ahead in the business. I've always been of the mind that I should help people the way others helped me coming up. Some I came to regret helping, but I've never stopped helping nevertheless.

I got why they thought they had to try me. I was their opportunity to try to make a name for themselves. It just got old real fast because it was every night. I tried not to take too much advantage of these kids, but when you lock up with someone who sucker punches you or tried to kick you in the nuts, you do what you have to do to set them straight.

One incident I remember took place near Jackson, Mississippi not long after I left ECW. I was really busy at the time, working part time for WWF again as well as all the independents I could book. Prior to the show, I had driven all the way from Huntington, West Virginia, to Memphis where I did two wild matches on Channel 5 TV. I went to a buffet and loaded up with food after the TV taping, which made me sleepy, and then I drove about 500 miles to the show. I was worn out by the time I arrived.

I arrived at the show and started talking to the promoter John, telling him where I had been. John told me I was in a three way with two big guys. One was about 6'5" and a former football player for Mississippi State who had recently tried to get in to ECW. The other was a cop and a bodybuilder who had worked a lot of Strongman competitions.

I sat down with the two of them to ask what they wanted to do, and they kind of blew me off. "Aww, we'll go off on you in the ring. You just sell."

For some reason, the football player took an attitude with me, blaming me for him not getting into ECW. I tried to explain to him that not only was I no longer employed by ECW, I had been fired by them. He wouldn't even listen. Both of them seemed to take exception to my old gimmick with the Confederate flag, not understanding it was a just gimmick.

I was tired, worn out, and sore all over. I had come in planning to work with these guys, maybe even help them out, and they just blew me off. "Okay, you guys caught me on the right day. Fuck both of you. I'm here to help both of you, and you're just punks. I'll see you in the ring, and I'll beat the fuck out of you."

I went and found a quiet place where I could take a nap. I let John know where I was going to be, and I lay down for about two hours, resting up for the match.

I was rested and ready when I went out that night. I let them take all the swings at me they wanted, and I dodged every one of them. Then I took them down and beat the fuck out of them.

It was the same way in a lot of places. I could have worked with these guys, but they didn't want to work. The way I saw it, I did what I had to do, not to set them straight, but just to survive.

Even though I was no longer full-time with ECW, Tommy Dreamer would book me on their house shows whenever he could. I did a TV match with Rob Van Dam as well as down in Atlanta. I was also doing shots with WWF thanks to Cornette, doing house shows and TV tapings and whatever they would offer. I booked a tour with FMW through ECW and got to work with Hayabusa. I also partnered with Masato Tanaka, who was a great guy and just incredibly tough.

I was making $500 a night whenever I got to work with WWF. Last I heard that number was down to only $200 a night. Not bad, but not near as good as the days when you could make a couple of thousand dollars a week. I made sure I was available any time WWF needed me.

I was offered a job as a trainer with WWF in 1999. I was very interested when the offer came through, but before I could start, they told me they had given the position to Jim Neidhart. This was right after Owen Hart had passed away tragically doing a stunt on a pay-per-view. It was a political thing, so I understood why, but I had turned down a lot of tours and bookings in anticipation of the new job.

I got a shoot job instead, framing houses for a friend named Jesse Gray. I framed houses a few days a week and then went back on the road every weekend. That lasted until the day I fell off a house and landed on my ear. I had to go to the hospital and get forty stitches.

As soon as I had been sewn up, Jesse's boss asked me, "You gonna come back to work tomorrow?"

I looked at him and said, "I don't think I'm coming back ever."

I was booked to wrestle that weekend, so with forty stitches in my head, I went out on the road in Tennessee and Kentucky, visiting Tullahoma, Shelbyville, Lewisburg, and Georgetown. At one of those shows I talked to Ashley Hudson and Korey Williams that weekend. They were on their way to a WCW TV show in Arkansas, about a four hour trip from Nashville, to work WCW Saturday Night. I agreed to split transportation with them and rode along.

WCW had just lost Dean Malenko, Eddie Guerrero, Chris Benoit, and Perry Saturn just a few weeks before to the WWF. They were hurting, and there were a lot of bad vibes going back stage. When Arn Anderson and Jimmy Hart found out I was there, they asked if I would work Booker T. I said yes.

Booker T ended up no showing for some reason I can't remember. Arn and Jimmy came to me and asked if I would mind working with the Barbarian. I was more than happy to do the match.

I didn't tell anyone about the stitches, not even Barb or Nick Patrick, who was our referee. I did my best to protect it myself, but at the end of the match, Barb hit me with the big boot, right where I had been busted open. I turned to Nick Patrick and asked, "Nick, are my brains falling out?"

"No," he said, "You're okay."

They paid me $500 and asked if I'd be willing to do some more house shows. I told them I had a month long tour of Japan with FMW coming up, but I would be glad to do it when I returned. By the time I returned from Japan, things had changed. Vince Russo had the book, and he didn't want to use me.

I was going through an ugly divorce at that time. My ex-wife Rose and I had been married nine years, and we were both to blame for what happened. Rose cut up all my clothes and threw them away. Then she took all my trophies and all my old photos and threw them in the river. I understood she was mad, and she had every right to be, but it wasn't just me messing around. She was seeing other men on the side too.

American Kickboxer

Tracy and I were booked on a show one time with Harley Race. Tracy has a lot of respect for Harley, but on the night of the show, as we sat in my car outside the building, Tracy kept saying "Man, Harley Race is inside. He's gonna pick me off like a fucking goof. Lightning shoots from Harley Race's elbows, man. He'll knock you out before God gets word of it!"

"Listen, Tracy," I said. "This is a big building. You can avoid Harley all night if you want to."

Tracy got out of the car. He walked up to the building, opened the door, and sure as shit, on the other side of the door was Harley Race! Tracy looked over the door and shook his head in disbelief. It's like he willed Harley to be there.

Another time we were driving down the road, and we passed a factory. "See that over there, Kickboxer? That's a penitentiary."

"Tell me about it, Tracy," I said.

"Those people in there," he said, "They have to tell somebody when they're going to take a piss. People get half an hour for their lunch. They eat their cheese sandwich and their Coca-Cola. And then later on, they'll have to tell someone when they go take another piss.

"You and me will be on this road all day. We may have to fight this promoter tonight for our money, but we ain't gonna be in the penitentiary!"

Tracy Smothers

Terry Golden called me from Memphis and asked if I was still interested in training for the WWF. Jim Neidhart had been let go, and the position was open again. I took the job, and as soon as I finished my dates on the outlaws, I headed to Memphis.

Terry Golden was the owner of Memphis Championship Wrestling. They had their own TV show at that time, and did spot shows around the area. The WWF was sending all of their developmental guys to train there.

Steven Regal was the head trainer sent by Bruce Prichard from WWF. Regal had been through some drug problems and was trying to work his way back into the company's good graces. He told me that this was his last chance, and luckily for him, things worked out. He's still with the company today.

A lot of the developmental guys in Memphis were students of Shawn Michaels, who had started his own school down in Texas. Brian Kendrick was there, along with a nineteen year old Bryan Danielson, later known as Daniel Brian. Steve Bradley was there, Joey Abs, Lance Cade, Kevin Thorn, and Molly Holly came through as well. There was also a kid named K-Kwik, who later went by Ron Killings in TNA and R-Truth in WWE. Viscera was there for a time trying to rehab some injuries so he could get back to the main WWF roster. They ended up letting him go before he could ever get a second chance.

Robby Brookside did his first stint with the WWF while I was training in Memphis. The company liked Robby a lot, and when they decided to pull Steven up to the main roster and make him William Regal, they wanted to have Robby replace him as head trainer with me as his number two. Robby was making such good money in Japan, he didn't want to commit full-time, but he got another opportunity years later after WWE opened the Performance Center. He's one of the greatest wrestling teachers around and a good guy.

Many people don't know that Reckless Youth trained for the WWE back in those early days. I knew him from the independents and from IWA Mid-South, and Reckless could do it all. He could wrestle, he could do commentary, he could do anything. WWE wanted to give him a shot, but he didn't like the character they presented him, and it fell through.

One night I had a chance to step into the ring with Kurt Angle. Kurt had won a gold medal at the 1996 Olympics in Atlanta with a broken neck, and that's no work. Kurt was learning the ropes as a pro wrestler, and he was an absolute stud. I was in the best shape of my life that night. I laid it all out, with him as a heel and me as a babyface, and Kurt loved how it turned out.

Kurt had never done a kick in the ring before that match. He didn't know how to do a working kick, so when I was lying on the mat and told him to stomp me he almost caved in my chest.

Kurt was an absolute stud. I wasn't there, but I heard from some of the guys who witnessed the Kurt Angle - Brock Lesnar shoot that took place in a WWE ring when the cameras weren't on. The Olympic champion and the NCAA champion agreed to see who was the best under collegiate rules, and Kurt just kicked Brock's ass.

Whenever I see Kurt, I rib him about kicking in my chest. He's always nice, though, and he's always grateful for helping him out.

One guy I saw a lot while I was training in Memphis was Jerry Lawler's son Brian Christopher, who wrestled as Grandmaster Sexay. Brian was a great kid and so dedicated to being a great wrestler. Despite his in-ring character, Brian was not a drinker or a party animal in those early days. He didn't do any drugs, other than the physical enhancement stuff. He loved his Pittsburgh Steelers, which was always my favorite too. He was a hell of a worker, and I loved getting in the ring with him.

Brian lost his job with the WWE in 2001 when he was busted for having performance enhancing drugs during a trip to Vancouver. The drugs were illegal in Canada but not in the United States. The WWE still took a hard line with him, and he was fired immediately.

After the Vancouver incident, Brian was a different person. He started partying and drinking, which he never did before. Brian had a mouth on him too, and if you didn't know him well, he could rub you the wrong way. He had some skirmishes with police in West Tennessee, and he got locked up several times for DUIs and disorderly conduct.

One of Brian's friends put it best when he said that Brian wasn't used to natural laws and natural consequences. Growing up, he always got out of trouble because his dad would bail him out. It was hard to live a normal life when you never had to abide by the rules until you were in your 40s. Add to all the above the pressure of being Jerry Lawler's son, Brian had a lot of struggles in his later years.

One thing I was told second hand, Brian used to laugh at the cops and the guards when he got arrested and act like he was better than them. I don't know if that's true or not because again, this is hearsay, but Brian did have a wise cracker attitude. You can't do that with the cops.

There was a lot of speculation as to what actually happened to Brian when he passed away. It's true that a lot of people do kill themselves in jail, but as Bill Dundee said, Brian would hurt a lot of people, but he wouldn't hurt himself. Brian loved himself, and he loved life. Something isn't right with the suicide story.

Bollivar, Tennessee, the town where Brian died, had a reputation even back in the day when we wrestled there. When you worked in Bollivar, you didn't hang around. You got out as quickly as possible. Brian wasn't the type to kill himself, and no one's given a good explanation why all the security cameras were turned off in the jail. Something happened to Brian that night, and I hope one day he gets justice.

I had just gotten home around 5 or 6 am the day Brian passed away. When I got the word, I was told he had no brain activity, and they were keeping him alive long enough to let Jerry get to the hospital and kiss him goodbye. No father should have to go through that, to bury his own son. I had a booking during the funeral, but even if I hadn't, I can't do funerals. It was hard enough following it all on social media.

Getting back to Memphis, I was starting to have some problems with management and the way they treated the kids. I did my best to take up for the kids and help them out. That was my job, to build them up and get them ready to move on to the next level. The kids were slowly getting frustrated by the way they were being pushed around.

The WWE would call up a few of our students each week to

work dark matches. One weekend they were in the Carolinas, which is where K-Kwik was from. He had done the last few weeks of house matches and was excited to do a show back home. Just to mess with him, they left him off the list and made him stay in Memphis. He was pretty upset after that and didn't even want to get in the ring for a while after that.

Morale was sinking lower and lower because of the way the students were being mistreated. I got called into a meeting with Kevin Kelly and Bruce Prichard to talk about how unmotivated the kids were.

"What do you want from me?" I asked.

"We want you to train them," they said.

"I'm trying to train them," I said. "But what do you expect? They came here to train, and all you do is fuck with them all the time!"

I got pretty fired up, and I knew I was in trouble. I didn't care though. It was the truth.

A few days later I showed up for the TV taping in Memphis. I was working with Joey Abs. This was right when the Rock and Stone Cold were at their peak, and the WWF was doing four to five hundred thousand dollars a night just on the house shows.

Joey had been sent down to Memphis and was working hard to try to get back on the main roster for another run. I was working babyface with Joey as a heel, and they wanted me to put him over. I was cool with that. I was a trainer, and my job was to get the kids over. I told Joey we would end the match with him using his finisher.

Kevin Kelly said, "No. We're not doing that. Joey will hit you with the finish, and when Tracy comes up, hit him in the head with a chair."

It was known in the business that since 1992, I would not take shots to the head. I had already had several concussions and head injuries to the point where I had no business taking shots to the head.

Kevin knew this the same as every other man I had shared a locker room with in the eight years since 1992. He knew my history with concussions. There was only one reason to tell Joey to hit me with the chair, and it wasn't a good one.

To his credit Joey didn't want to do it. He told me flat out he wasn't going to do it, but I told him he had to. Joey already had heat with the office and some of boys on the main roster. I knew Joey was training hard, and I wasn't going to stand in the way of him getting a second chance. I also knew Joey was benching 400-500 pounds. I couldn't believe they would even ask me to take a chair shot from him.

When the moment came I took that chair shot head on. No hands up, no ducking, nothing. I went down hard, and I didn't feel a thing when I hit that mat. I got another concussion, and I was throwing up for days afterwards.

I haven't been right ever since that night. I've had doctors look at scans of my body and shake their heads, saying they've never seen anyone alive with as much trauma as I've had on my body.

SHAWN'S BOYS

I was hired to train a new generation of wrestlers by the WWF, and despite all the bullshit they put me through, I did my very best to prepare that younger generation for the future. Three guys in particular I really enjoyed working with were Lance Cade, the American Dragon Brian Danielson, and Spanky. You know those last two better as Daniel Bryan and Brian Kendrick.

Both Brians and Lance were first trained by Shawn Michaels down in Texas. Shawn, at that time, was no longer wrestling, but he was still on the payroll. Vince had lost Kevin Nash, Scott Hall, and a whole slew of guys to WCW, and he was not going to let Shawn follow them. For four years, the hardest thing Shawn had to do was walk to the mailbox and pick up his check for $18,000 a week, just for staying loyal to the WWE. That's a shoot.

While I had no love for Shawn, I never let that affect the way I treated them. His students were all very talented, and I have some good memories working with them.

A lot of the young guys were from other places, and they had no idea about the history of Memphis Wrestling, Memphis TV, or any of that. Brian Danielson and Spanky were exceptions to that, but Spanky had a little bit of an attitude that almost cost him his job early on.

We were in Brownsville one night watching a replay of the Mike Tyson vs. Andrew Golota boxing match on a portable television I had. It was a controversial match in which Golota had withdrawn after only two rounds. Fans were pretty upset with his decision initially, but it was later revealed he had suffered several serious injuries that led to his early exit.

There was an older gentleman named Mr. Coffey who used to work for Jerry Lawler in Memphis along with his wife. He was a wonderful man and as much a part of the rich history of Memphis as any man who worked for Lawler and Jerry Jarrett. Mr. Coffey came by when we were watching the fight, and when he saw what we were watching, he simply said, "Yeah, too bad that guy quit."

Some of the guys watching with us didn't know the outcome of the fight already. Spanky got pissed and blurted out, "Oh, okay, Mr. Coffey, thanks for giving the finish. Why don't you go take care of the concessions?"

Mr. Coffey walked off embarrassed, and I thought, "Oh shit, he shouldn't have said that." Spanky was Shawn's boy, but Mr. Coffey was Lawler's man. This is a man who had Lawler's full confidence and trust, one of the few Lawler trusted to handle money. I knew Spanky didn't mean anything by it, I'm sure, but he also had no idea just how highly Lawler regarded Mr. Coffey. Being Shawn's boy would do him no favors either as Shawn and King did not get along to begin with.

The following night we did a house show that didn't draw well. I spotted Kevin Thorn and Glen Ruth, who worked as Headbanger Thrasher, telling Lawler about Spanky and Mr. Coffey. Glen was a good guy and I liked him, but he was going into business for himself, trying to get back up to the main roster. He didn't like Spanky, and both Glen and Kevin saw a chance to improve their own standing by tearing Spanky down. Lawler was already pissed because the house was down, and he didn't like what Glen told him at all. "We'll see about that at TV tomorrow!"

I pulled Spanky aside to have a little chat. "Your man Shawn is home in San Antonio. You have major heat because of what you said to Mr. Coffey." I told him I had seen Glen and Kevin stooging to Lawler and I told him, "If you want to get in and work for WWF, you better go and apologize to Mr. Coffey first thing at TV. Get there early and apologize to him and to Lawler first thing."

"Okay," he said, "But why?"

"Kevin and Glen just tried to earn themselves brownie points by stooging on you and getting King stirred up," I said. "If you don't apologize to both of them and mean it, they will kick you out of here."

I reminded Spanky he was not in WWF and he was not in Texas. this was Memphis, and for all intents and purpose, Jerry Lawler was Memphis. "If you don't do this, it won't matter if Hulk Hogan broke you in. Jerry Lawler will kick you out of here, and you will never work for WWF."

I told him I would probably get heat for telling him all this, but I didn't care. I liked Spanky, and I wanted him to make it. Spanky understood, and he did exactly as I told him. The next morning he apologized to both Mr. Coffey and Lawler. He owned up to having a big mouth and being brash and cocky and foolish with his words.

Mr. Coffey brushed it off like it was nothing, but Jerry Lawler really respected Spanky for taking ownership of what he had said. Lawler gave Spanky a huge push after that on Memphis TV, which didn't sit well with Kevin and Glen. I like those boys, I really do, but I know they were trying to get ahead by cutting Spanky's throat.

Lance Cade reminded me a lot of Barry Windham in his body and how he worked in the ring. Lance and I were paired up as a tag team, and we started traveling together.

We were down south one time with Brian Danielson in the backseat driving home from Jackson, Mississipi. A state trooper flashed his lights, and I pulled over.

Lance leaned into me and said, "Tracy, if he asks if you have drugs in the car, you have to be honest," said Lance. "If you lie to him and he finds stuff, then we're screwed."

I looked down at the ash tray and spotted a tiny joint sitting inside. I don't recall whose it was or who had left it there, but I got a huge knot in my stomach knowing that yes, I did have drugs in the car. It wasn't even my stuff, but it was in my car.

When the trooper approached my window, the first thing he asked was if we had drugs in the car.

"Yes, sir," I said. "There's a tiny roach in the ash tray."

I braced myself for his reaction, but the cop surprised me when he said, "I'm not worried about a little dope. When I see three big guys like you in the car, I'm thinking there might be harder drugs. Or steroids."

"No sir," I said. "Nothing like that."

"You mind if I check the trunk?" he asked.

I told him no, and I got out of the car to open the trunk. The first bag he grabbed was mine, which he searched and found nothing. Then he searched Lance's bag. Once again came up empty handed. Finally he got to Brian Danielson's bag. Brian was the Junior Heavyweight Champion in Memphis at that time, and when he opened Brian's bag, he pulled out the title belt.

This cop was being a hard ass up until that point, but when he took the belt out, his attitude changed. "What the hell is this? Whose belt is this?" We told him it was Brian's, and he did a double take. "Are you kidding me? You two big mother fuckers don't have a belt, but this little guy's got one?"

The tension broke, and we all just died laughing at that.

The cop looked at Brian. "You don't do drugs, do you?"

"No sir," said Brian.

"The worst thing he does is drink milk," I added.

"Is he that good?" the man asked.

"Yeah, he's great!" I said.

"He ain't that big at all!" said the cop.

"It ain't the size," I said. "It's the fight in the dog."

I've often wondered if that cop would be laughing if he knew that kid went on to win the WWE World Heavyweight Championship. We spent some more time with him talking on the side of the road, and he started telling us some wild stories about Ted DiBiase from his wilder days in Mid-South.

Tony Myers

I was in Memphis when Tracy was training for WWF. They sent a few guys down from the main roster while we were there, and one of them was Nelson Frazier, who had been in Men on a Mission as Mabel and later went back as Viscera. Tracy told us the story of the first time he ever saw Nelson at a show. Nelson was 6'9" and weighed almost 500 pounds, so he was hard to miss. Tracy asked the promoter, "Who's that big ol' guy out there?"

"Some guy showed up looking for work," said the promoter.

"And he's not booked??" said Tracy.

"Naw," said the promoter.

"Well why in the hell NOT?????" shouted Tracy.

Nelson was a very sweet man. I miss him a lot. Nelson thought the world of Tracy, and he never forgot the kindness Tracy showed him when he was breaking in. "Man, I owe Tracy Smothers everything." I think a lot of us feel the same way.

Tracy Smothers

Things continued to sour for me with Kevin Kelly. There was a friend of Owen Hart's named Jason Sensation in the territory. Jason was a tremendous talent who could imitate anybody, but for some reason, Kevin didn't like him. They would let him ring announce, but he couldn't wrestle or even manage anyone.

I got Jason hooked up with Brian Kendrick as a tag team, and the boys clicked. They were a hilarious duo as a heel team, and Jerry Lawler loved it. Jerry started pushing them on TV, which only pissed Kevin off more. They couldn't get rid of Lawler, but they could get rid of me.

After working a few matches with Lance Cade as a tag team, I turned heel on him, and we went into a feud of our own. We built up to a big pay off match in Jonesboro, Arkansas, and to raise the stakes and sell a few more tickets, wouldn't you know it, they brought in Shawn Michaels. Shawn was going to be in Lance's corner, and Terry Rocker, who was one of Terry Golden's boys, would be in mine. I really liked Rocker a lot, and we worked well together.

The day of the show things were tense, especially between Shawn and me. I kept professional, but we were not being really friendly to each other. He asked me a question I couldn't answer, and he said, "Why don't you know, Smothers? You're supposed to be the man around here."

I said, "Shawn, if I'm the man anywhere, we're in real trouble." I got a laugh out of Shawn, and that finally broke the tension between us. "Come on, man," I said. "Relax."

Terry Golden had given us the finish at TV. He wanted Shawn to superkick me and then have Lance do his finish off the top rope and hit me with his finish. Lance didn't want to do that. He wanted to beat me outright with his finish.

I didn't care how we did it. I was getting paid anyway. That said, I didn't want to get kicked by Shawn because I knew he would try to kick me to the next planet.

We went into a meeting with Kevin and Terry, and Lance told them he wanted to beat me with his finish without interference from Shawn. To his credit, Shawn took Lance's side, saying, "I shouldn't have to kick Tracy for Lance to beat him."

I was thinking to myself I didn't want get kicked either because I was pretty sure I'd get up and beat the fuck out of Shawn anyway.

Terry actually had a good reason for wanting me to take the superkick. He was trying to run a territory, and he didn't want me, one of his big heels, to lose my heat. We worked out a compromise, where Terry Rocker took the super kick from Shawn while Lance hit me with his finisher. In the end it all worked out well. Shawn and I had fun working together, and afterwards, we were cool.

"Smothers, you're alright," he said. "You're funny. I laughed my ass off out there."

"It's all good," I said. "I never meant anything. I hope you get better and can get back into the ring one day."

As good as things went with Shawn, Kevin Kelly was even angrier with me. He wanted me to take their side and overrule Shawn, as if I had the power to do that. They could have overruled us on their own, and I would have done whatever they wanted, but they gave into Lance and Shawn and blamed it all on me. They started dumping even more heat on me, blaming me for not working well enough with the ladies and all sorts of shit.

We were running bar shows in Oxford, Mississippi every Wednesday. It was never a very good crowd, and Lawler finally complained about how they were running the show. Lawler invited Bruce Prichard, who was head of talent relations, to come down one week to the Wednesday show. This was supposed to be a surprise visit, and they were going to crack the whip. Kevin Kelly got wind of it, however, and he reached out to Bruce before he came down.

When we arrived at the bar, you would have thought it was Monday Night Raw by the way they were doing things. Lawler had intended to surprise Kevin, but it ended up the other way around. This was shortly before the WWF fired Lawler's then wife, leading him to walk out. I'm pretty sure that night in Jonesboro only added to King's list of reasons for quitting.

I worked with Rodney from the Mean Street Posse that night. He was kind of a prick and we didn't get along well, but the match still went great. Of course when we got to the back, they all told us it was the shits because they were looking to get rid of me. Rodney didn't help matters, and he piled on telling Bruce all sorts of shit about me.

Bruce Prichard came into a meeting with all the developmental guys and announced that everyone had to take a drug test. They never did this with the developmental guys back then, so it was obvious something was up. I knew I would probably fail because they would no doubt find some pot in my system. As it turned out only three guys passed the test: Rodney from Mean Street Posse, Brian Danielson, and Pete Gas. As much as I didn't like Rodney, I loved Pete. He was a great guy, and I've always loved him.

In the days following the drug test, I changed our training routine up with the guys and started doing fewer in-ring workouts and more out of ring drills and exercises. It was an old school way of training, and the guys bought into it. Even Rodney, who hated my guts, took to the new plan and got a lot out of it. Things looked to be getting better.

One day during a training session, Terry Golden came to see me. "Bruce Prichard wants to talk to you."

"Okay," I said.

"Go out in the parking lot and call him," he said.

I went outside and called Bruce. "Tracy, just so you know, you failed the drug test. We're going to have to let you go."

"Really?" I said. "Okay, so I'm the only one that failed the drug test, right? I know this crew. I know who does what. I also know that only three people passed it, so you could fire the whole crew. But I'm done, right?"

"Yeah," he said, "I'd like to be there in person to tell you because I respect you."

"I'm sure you would, Bruce," I said, mad as hell. I knew it was all bullshit. Things hadn't been going well, someone had to take the fall, and Kevin wanted me gone.

Bruce went on. "Well, we don't really want a Memphis type guy doing the training. We don't even want someone who watched Memphis wrestling training our guys."

"Yeah, yeah, why would you want that?" I said. "A lot of top guys came out of Memphis." It's the truth, too. Hulk Hogan, Randy Savage, Undertaker, Steve Austin, Scott Hall, Kurt Angle, the Rock, Kane. All those guys and many, many more came through Memphis at one time or another.

"A lot of big time guys came through here and made it," I told

Bruce. "Why would you want any Memphis style wrestlers working for you?"

I hung up and went back inside, where my training class was still waiting for me to finish. "Well guys, we can wrap up for today. I just got fired."

A lot of the boys were mad. Even Rodney was mad! But the WWF needed a scapegoat, and I took the fall. I wasn't the only one to lose my job, either. They fired Glen Ruth, who was tight with Lawler, and Cindy Snow, Al's ex-wife. To this day, I still joke with Cindy when I see her, "Remember that time we both got fired on the same day?"

It's funny to me that the WWE, of all places, created the "Be A Star" Anti-Bullying campaign because bullying was just part of the job. Everything was a rib to those guys, especially the agents and management, and it all started right at the top. If you weren't in one of the main cliques - Shawn's group, Hunter's group, Taker's group, or Bret's group - you were pretty much fair game.

A lot of things went on behind closed doors. There were rumors even then of people having to trade certain favors to get a push, and those stories weren't just about the ladies. I knew it was happening the first time I was there, but it seemed to be a lot more out in the open the second time around. Some of the things that were said between the boys were just unbelievable.

The bottom line is if you played ball, if you said and did the right things for the right people, you got ahead. If you didn't, you got jobbed out quick. The WWF was just a miserable place to work. That's why I always say, "No," any time someone asks if I'd ever go work there again. Lord knows I could use the money, but I'd rather keep my soul than take what they have to offer.

I've seen Kevin Kelly and Bruce Prichard a few times over the years. They smile and offer to shake hands and want to let bygones be bygones. I'm sorry, I can't. I never should have been in that position, and I still hold them responsible. One of these days, I'll have my say.

Several years ago, Billy Jack Haynes filed a class action lawsuit against the WWE for injuries sustained within the ring. Billy Jack, like many wrestlers, had suffered a number of head injuries and concussions, and with his attorney Konstantine Kyros, he opened the door for other wrestlers and workers to join in the lawsuit. Over time more than 60 people joined in the suit including Road Warrior Animal,

Jimmy Snuka, Paul Orndorff, Sabu, Shane Douglas, and Bobby Fulton.

It was Bobby Fulton who contacted me about the lawsuit and gave me the number for the law firm representing the wrestlers. I wasn't too keen on getting involved, but Bobby urged me to at least call up the attorney and talk to him.

When I called the lawyer, he asked me if I had ever had an incident in WWE involving a concussion. It didn't click with me at first, but after I hung up, I remembered that night in 2000 with Joey Abs. I called the attorney back while I was driving home from a School of Smothers program, and he recorded my entire story. I've had concussions since that time, but that one, at age 38, was the one that really got me. That kind of shit shouldn't happen to anybody. When you have any sort of concussion problems, nobody should make you take any blows to the head, ever. I've had a lot of problems coming from that injury including several mini-strokes. It's only by the grace of God I'm still alive.

I've taken a lot of flack for joining in the lawsuit. I've been reminded I was just a jobber who had "a cup of coffee" in the WWE. That's all true, but it's also true that the WWE management decided I should take a shot to a chair from a big, strong kid like Joey Abs when they knew damn well I had a history of concussions.

Here's the reality. A lot of guys are gone because of injuries they sustained in the ring. They did it to provide for their families, and now their wives are widows and their kids don't have their dads. You wish there was something you could do to help, but at the end of the day, there's nothing you can do to bring those people back.

As many of you probably know, pro wrestlers are independent contractors, at least as far as WWE is concerned. They do not get any medical insurance from the company. All their medical expenses are out of pocket. There's no protection if you say no to the company or tell them you don't want to do something. If you say no, they'll just get rid of you and find someone to say yes.

There was talk as early as WrestleMania II of wrestlers forming a union to help protect themselves from the company. Jesse Ventura wanted to start one, but guys like Hulk were making so much money, they didn't want any part of it.

In September of 2018 the lawsuit was thrown out of court. Of course this happened in Vince McMahon's home court of Connecticut, and Vince has some of the best attorneys in the world. The judge not only tossed the suit, she ordered our attorney to pay the WWE's legal fees.

Last I heard, the suit is being appealed, and this time, it won't be in Vince's backyard. The judges in the appeals court are much more likely to give us our say, and I cannot wait to take the stand and tell my story. Time will tell if anything comes from it, but I hope and pray the day will come that I can get on the stand, testify about what Kevin Kelly put me through, and bury him.

THE SUNDANCE KID

I was renting a room in a trailer with a lady named Anita at the time I was fired from WWF. As soon as I left work that day, I went home, picked up the phone and got myself booked. I started booking as many dates as possible and was back on the road, working 15-20 days a month.

What was really great was for the next three months and two weeks, I still received a check from the WWF. They gave me three months pay as a severance package, and then at the end of that time, they forgot about me and paid me for one more two week cycle. That money on top of the money I was making in the indies made for a good living.

I was still pretty pissed off. I was hired to train guys, which I did. I was hired to help guys, which I did. It was all political, and it just made me angry the more I thought about it.

I ended up taking a really cool gig in 2001 working as an extra on a movie for Dreamworks. I think it was Candy Devine who told me about the job. It paid $100 a day for five days a week, plus you got two free meals each day and could work out on the set. And you get to be in a major motion picture. I didn't have much going on, so I figured what the hell.

The movie was called *The Last Castle*, and it was filmed at the Tennessee State Prison in Nashville, where they also filmed *The Shawshank Redemption*. The movie starred Mark Ruffalo, James Gandolfini, and the Sundance Kid himself, Robert Redford.

I had never been on a movie set before, and I learned so much about how movies are made. I never dreamed so much work went into making a movie. We went from 6 am to 6 pm every day for a full six weeks, just to shoot a two hour movie. It amazed me how many times they would reshoot some of the simplest scenes, trying to get things just right.

There were a number of days on set when we would get "wet pay." When a scene took place in the rain, they would wet down the ground and use a rain machine to make it appear as if it were raining on us. Any time we did these rain scenes, we got an extra $20 wet pay on top of our $100 per day.

When we first started, they lined a bunch of us extras up. One of the directors came down the line, checking us all out. I'll never forget when the director got to me. He pointed and said, "You. You got a good look. You're ugly."

I started laughing, and he gave me this serious look. "Something funny, young man?"

I said, "No, sir, nothing funny at all. I'm sorry."

Some of us, we were told, might get a line or two in the movie. If we got a line, we'd also get a Screen Actor's Guild (SAG) card, which means we'd be part of the actor's union and be able to get in more movies. I was there just to make the $100 a day, but a lot of guys were hoping to get that SAG card.

The sad thing is I came very close to getting that SAG card. The production crew really liked me, and they were going to give me a line in the movie. I didn't know this because no one told me, and the day before that was to happen, I left early to get on the road and go work a wrestling show I had previously booked.

I didn't think it was any big deal, but the production got mad at me for leaving early. They cut me out of a lot of scenes after that as punishment. "You should have told me!" I said. "I could have canceled out of my booking and found someone to take my place!"

Despite all that, I got to work in a lot of scenes with a lot of great people and eat all day. One of the other extras was a boxer named Nick Rupa. He used to spar for Sweet Pea Whitaker and a few other big names, and one of Nick's last fights was against Terry Norris, the man who knocked Sugar Ray Leonard off his throne.

There was a whole workout area set up in the prison yard because, well, it was a story about prison. There were weights and punching bags, and all sorts of things. Nick and I worked out every day. He taught me about boxing, and I showed him a few things about wrestling. Nick had a lot of respect for wrestlers, and he was fascinated by the sport.

One day I was working out when I heard someone hitting the bag pretty hard. I looked over and saw Nick standing by while James Gandolfini was throwing punches.

James Gandolfini had just finished shooting season three of *The*

Sopranos. The HBO series was the biggest show on TV at that time, and James was a huge star. He got paid $5 million himself to play the heel to Redford's babyface in *The Last Castle*.

I walked over and held the bag for James. He didn't have a lot of skill, but he was a big old rawboned guy who could hit the bag pretty hard. He weight 280 pounds and stood 6'1" but he looked more like 6'6". He had worked up a good sweat hitting that bag while Nick was giving him pointers like he was a real fighter.

James finally dropped his arms. "Look, I'm winded, and I need to go. Thank you for the workout." He reached into his pocket, pulled out twenty bucks, and said, "Here. You guys get some dinner on me. Thank you so much. I learned a lot."

James was pure humble pie with Nick. As a matter of fact, James knew who Nick was because James was a big boxing fan. Nick was still coaching him as he walked away and headed to his trailer. "You're a big guy, but he'll eat you alive with body punches! Quicken up that left!"

When James left, I asked Nick, "You do know who that is, don't you?"

Nick said, "He said his name's James."

"Nick, that is James Gandolfini," I said. "He's the star of *The Sopranos*. He's Tony Soprano. He's the second lead star in this movie!"

Nick just said, "Well, heck, I didn't know! I just thought he was a regular extra."

James Gandolfini was just a really cool guy to be around. He loved to eat pizza and Italian foods. He was really funny and very down to Earth.

We were told that we were absolutely not to talk to Robert Redford, but one day when I found myself standing behind him on set, I couldn't resist. "Mr. Redford?"

He turned and looked at me. I pointed my finger at him like a gun and said, "*Butch Cassidy and the Sundance Kid* is one of my favorite movies." It is, too. I remember seeing him step off the bus in that one scene like he was the man. He was so fucking cool.

Robert Redford had an extra on set, and the man looked exactly like Robert. The two of them had worked together for decades, and when they were younger, they really looked alike. He received

$10,000 a week on every movie Robert Redford made, just to stand in for Robert Redford when he wasn't on camera. Robert Redford got a whole lot more than that, but that $10,000 was pretty good money too.

It was a real experience watching Robert Redford and James Gandolfini work every day. I learned a lot from them just watching the way they carried themselves on set.

There were a number of scenes in the movie that called for stunts, including some sequences that took place involving a helicopter suspended from a crane. They had a great team of stuntmen on set for the movie, and they were a really tight knit group. Unlike the cast, they wouldn't hang with the extras or even let us sit with them. I know because one day, I tried to sit at their table. They all just stared at me like we were really in prison and I had just tried to sit with the wrong clique. The lead stuntman actually came down and said, "You can't sit here. You need to eat over there."

I didn't do it on purpose or anything. No one clued me in that their table was off limits. "Okay, I gotcha," I said. "I didn't mean to do that." He just looked at me with a mean expression until I left.

I wasn't the only wrestler on the set. I got Jamie Dundee in as an extra as well. Jamie made sure everyone knew he was Bill Dundee's son, and he quickly became the life of the party. There were a lot of guys on set who remembered the old USWA, and they loved having both of us around.

One day Jamie and I started messing around in the yard with some of the extras. One of them, confused why two former rivals were getting along so well, asked us, "How come y'all aren't fighting each other like y'all did on TV?"

I said, "Well you know what? It's business out here, but fuck Jamie Dundee!" I started cutting a promo on him, acting like I hated him, and Jamie joined right in. "Oh yeah? Well fuck you too, Smothers!"

Our exchange of words led into us actually locking up and putting some submission holds on one another. We were just messing around and having fun, but the stuntmen got really pissed off at us! The same guy who told me I was at the wrong table came over to us. "What do you think you're doing? If you're going to do all that, you're out of here! That doesn't look good, and it's not needed."

Jamie stayed quiet, not wanting to get into it, but I had to say something. "We're not doing anything on camera! What does it matter?"

"It does matter," he said. "Do it again, you're out of here!"

"Okay," I said. "That's cool."

The stuntman walked away. I could see all the other stuntmen were sizing me up and talking about me. One of them, who stood about 6'7", came walking right up to me after that, just staring me down. I stepped aside and said, "I hope you had room to get by."

He just glared at me and said, "Yeah. Yeah I did!"

After he passed, another one of their clique came up to me. "Man, those guys are hot at you."

"Really?" I said, "Why the fuck are they worried about a guy who's playing fake wrestling as they call it?"

The guy sad, "You understand what I just said to you, right?"

"I understand," I said. "I also understand we weren't on camera, and you're not my boss. You don't sign my check, and I didn't do anything to disrespect you. But I get the point. I'm just here to make my hundred a day and go home."

The guy said to me, "Well, don't be doing it again."

"Don't worry about what I'm doing," I said. "I got something for you all."

I'm sure many of you know the big, wooden stick that I carry to the ring with me sometimes. I was already carrying that around back then because I used it as part of my daily workout. I had it stashed away in my locker on set. I went and got my stick and brought it back to the set with me. I set it down and started punching the big bag, letting everyone get a good look at it.

We had a lunch break shortly after and then got back to work. They had me way in the back in a scene, where I was standing with a small clique of guys I usually hung out with on set, all of them Vietnam veterans who knew what was going on.

I still had my stick on me, and I had to walk past a gang of stuntmen to get to my mark. I carried that stick with me and greeted everyone of them as I walked through. "What's up, guys? What's up? Everyone have a good lunch? Okay, cool. Have a good day." They didn't bother me, and I walked right on through.

Honestly, I was a little scared. I knew if the stuntmen turned on me, nobody except for my handful of Vietnam vets would stick up for me. I made sure the stuntmen heard me when I repeated what I had said earlier. "I don't want any trouble. I just want to make my hundred and go home."

Even though I didn't appreciate the way they treated us, I had nothing but respect for the stuntmen. They are a small but proud crew who beat up their bodies week in and week out doing incredible things on camera.

I saw some of those guys do some incredible stunts on the set of *The Last Castle*. One guy got $10,000 to get set on fire. Another one got $5,000 to do a pretty big fall. He landed in a big air bag, but he had to fall a long way before he hit that bag.

I would have fought one of them if I had do, but I'm glad it didn't come to that. I knew they were tough, and I wanted nothing to do with them in a real fight!

I still regret that I took off to work that show and missed my chance to get a line. I had heat with the production crew from then on, and it only got worse when the stuntmen got mad at me. I could have had a line in a Robert Redford movie and received a SAG card. But no one told me to stay on set or I would have canceled my other bookings. How was I supposed to know if they didn't tell me?

I was there because it was a cool thing to do. It wasn't my job, and it wasn't my dream. They thought that everyone on set wanted to be an actor, and I'm sure the guys who got the lines and the SAG cards were there for that reason. They got really pissed off at me, but I still got to be in a movie, and I had an incredible time.

Working on *The Last Castle* was an awesome experience. Working on a major motion picture is an experience that everyone should try at least once if they get the chance. After you finish my book, go find the movie and see if you can spot me in the background.

MAIN EVENT CHAMPIONSHIP WRESTLING

In 2001 I got a call from John Collins who was trying to start up a new wrestling company in Evansville, Indiana. The name of the new promotion was Main Event Championship Wrestling, and Collins invited me to meet him and a bunch of other guys at a Buffalo Wild Wings to learn about his plans.

Main Event came along right at that moment in time when there was only one national wrestling company left in the business. ECW had folded in 2000, and it was in early 2001 that Vince McMahon bought WCW. The WWF roster was bloated with WWF stars as well as former WCW and ECW wrestlers, and a lot of guys found themselves on the outside looking in. John was able to draw a lot of interest because everybody not under contract to Vince was out of a job!

When I arrived at Buffalo Wild Wings, I saw a lot of familiar faces in the restaurant that night including Public Enemy (Johnny Grunge and Ted Petty), Steve Dunn, Chris Champion, and Wolfie D. John told us he had big plans for MECW, including taking us national with a cable TV program. He wanted us all to be a part of it.

John seemed like a good guy. Not only did he pay for the meal and our drinks, he paid us all to drive up there and even paid for our hotels. He held a second gathering closer to where he lived in Lawrenceville, Illinois. Same deal, he paid for dinner and drinks and hotel to invite a bunch of guys to join his company. Guys were glad to accept the invitation not only because it was all expenses paid, but because we had nowhere else to go!

John asked me to help out with the booking at Main Event. It was a non-exclusive deal, which allowed me to work independents, and he put me on salary so I wouldn't have to work another job. I spent a few days a week working with him at the office while we tried to put something together.

John was interested in signing younger guys who had potential as well as veterans with name value. He and I drove out to Chase Stevens' place in Indiana one time. It was raining that day, and Chase had his students working in the rain.

He had a kid who wrestled under the name Glacious. I knew

him from a few bookings I had taken, and I liked him really well. He was young, though, and still hadn't fully gotten his head in the game. One time he missed a booking because he had bought a new boom box. I had to lay into him over that one.

John ran the first big Main Event show at Viking Hall, the former ECW Arena in Philadelphia. MECW was the first promotion to run the building after ECW folded, and he booked a lot of big name guys for the show. He printed some fliers that he passed out at a WWF show when they were in town, and he did some internet interviews as well.

When ticket sales got off to a slow start, John decided to make the show in Philadelphia free. That raised some red flags, and a lot of us wondered how he could afford to pay all the wrestlers and run a free show. He assured us "the man above," his big investor, had plenty of money to cover. Public Enemy wrestled the FBI, Curt Hennig wrestled Chris Harris, Simon Diamond worked the Blue Meanie, Sabu wrestled Sandman in a ladder match, and Buff Bagwell defeat Jack Victory. Barry Windham made an appearance as well.

Everything seemed to go well, but after the Philly show, John decided to run some shows closer to home before our next big venture. The next MECW show took place at the university in Vincennes, Indiana, and we drew a really strong crowd. I wrestled Mike (IRS) Rotunda. He also brought in Tommy Rich, Curt Hennig, and Terry Gordy.

This was after Terry had had a major overdose on a plane ride to Japan. As a matter of fact, I was on that trip when it happened, headed over for one of my runs with All Japan just a few years before. It was scary as hell. Terry wasn't all there mentally anymore, and he'd had a lot of health problems. He was in good spirits that night in Vincennes. Terry talked to me a lot that night, telling me about how his son was preparing to go to train in the dojo in Japan. He was so proud of his son not only for going into wrestling, but staying clean with no drugs.

Terry had ridden up to the show with Tommy and his wife, who drove. They dropped Terry off first at his place before going on home.

The next day, Terry was found dead in his recliner at home. We were all stunned. You never think when you see someone its going to be the last time you ever see someone, but you just don't know, especially in this business.

We were starting to realize that John Collins was a con man even before that night in Vincennes, but that night, it became clear the man who brought us together was our greatest liability. John Collins was married, but he was messing around with another woman. Something happened between him and his mistress, and before the Vincennes show, the other woman got him thrown in jail. John managed to get out of jail and barely made it to the show before it was over so he could pay everyone.

We ran shows every Wednesday at the Coliseum in Evansville, and John brought in some top guys who needed work including Mike Rotunda, Curt Hennig, Barry Windham, Sandman, Sabu, Terry Taylor, Tommy Rich, and Public Enemy. He also booked some younger kids I was training like J.C. Bailey and Johnny Richards.

The guys were glad for the work, but only a few weeks in, John was shorting them on pay and making excuses. After one show, a lot of guys got left stranded at the airport when their travel reservations ended up being no good. John blamed it on Paul Heyman, saying Paul was trying to sabotage us, but in the end, the guys had to pay for their own flights home.

John was definitely a con, but he was getting screwed by a lot of people himself. I remember there being a lot of conflict between John and Mr. Acker, who ran the Coliseum. Mr. Acker was charging him a ton of money every week to use the building, and he never got a dime of the confessions money. John also bought a ring from Doug Gilbert, who screwed him over on the price. Doug claimed it was the old Memphis ring, but who knows where it really came from. I remember setting that ring up, and it was a total piece of shit. Reno Riggins sold him a ring that wasn't too bad, but he overcharged John as well.

You had a promoter who was not very smart with money, and a lot of guys saw an opportunity to make a buck. Everybody who thought they could get him would get him. I tried to help John when I knew guys were ripping him off. The problem was it was happening all the time. We were overcharged to use the Evansville Fairgrounds and different buildings, and I'd call guys out on it. John would pay it, as he paid for a lot of things.

John enjoyed being a promoter and hanging out with wrestlers.

He wanted to be big time, and he was talking to everyone from Brian Christopher to Bret Hart to Randy Savage about coming in. You would not believe the money they were asking for. They didn't have anywhere else to go, but they were still asking for the moon. I tried to explain that to John, to tell him these guys didn't have any leverage to ask for all that money, but he paid it anyway.

One night in the airport while we were waiting for everyone to fly in, John opened up a tab for all of us at the bar. We drank for a good two hours before the show, which we shouldn't have done. Then after the show John took us all to Buffalo Wild Wings to drink some more. I can't imagine what the bar tab was. It was like the old WCW days, with Eric Bischoff spending all of Ted Turner's money. You offer wrestlers something free, and they will take advantage of you all they can.

In defense of the guys, they were taking what they could because their livelihood had been wiped out by WWF. If you weren't working for WWF, there was nowhere else for a wrestler to make a full-time living anymore. A lot of guys started to overdose and die at that time because they had no place else to go. It was really a sad time.

MECW was a last hope for a lot of guys. We were only running once a week, but it was something. Guys like Buff Bagwell, who had burned his bridge with WWF, were desperate for something to pick up and fill the void left by WCW. Everyone was taking what they could get, and deep down, we knew it wasn't going to last.

John always talked about "the man above," a mysterious money man in Canada who was funding MECW. We came to find out his backer was a man named Garry W. Stroud, who was under investigation in both Canada and the United States. Stroud had allegedly been running a number of pyramid schemes, and the government was just then closing in on him. John was warned about the investigation prior to receiving any investments from Stroud, but he still took the money.

Garry had a number of scams. One that I believe John was involved in was they would look up people in the obituaries who had died and send someone to visit their relatives while they are in mourning. They posed as Bible salesmen and showed up with Bibles engraved with the deceased person's name and say they had ordered but not paid for the Bibles. Pretty shameless.

John was no angel himself, of course, and he was pocketing

plenty of money from Garry. John would negotiate an appearance fee for someone for $5,000 and tell Garry he needed $10,000. He would pay the wrestler $5,000 and pocket the other $5,000. John was also booking *Playboy* models and other beautiful women to work as valets, all because he was trying to sleep with them.

I don't remember exactly how it happened, but John got in trouble with the Mafia in Canada. John owed them money or something, and he blamed it all on Garry. One day the Mafia showed up at Garry's house demanding money. Garry would have been killed, but he had enough cash in the house and was able to pay off the mob.

Guys were getting stiffed on money more frequently, and Garry was getting tired of John's shenanigans. John even faked a heart attack at one point to try to get out of paying guys. Chris Hays ran one more show in Evansville and took care of the local guys who worked MECW. He didn't bring in all the big names, but those of us who were local got paid.

Then September 11 happened. That morning I got a call from John Collins, who simply said, "We're done, brother."

"What do you mean?" I said.

He said, "Turn on the TV." I turned it on and saw the two towers of the World Trade Center on fire.

9/11 changed everything in America. The economy took a dive, and people with money started pulling back on investments. A lot of businesses went under during that time, and every industry was hurting. My parents took a trip to Vegas shortly after September 11, and they couldn't believe how dead it was. Not just the casinos and the hotels, but the airport and everywhere.

9/11 was the end of MECW, but we were already on the way out. John was involved with so many schemes, all 9/11 did was shorten the timeline. John was arrested and convicted, but he only served 71 months of his sentence. How he got out, and what he did next is a whole other story to be told in a later chapter.

TROUBLESHOOTER

With the wrestling business becoming a monopoly and my being on the outside looking in, I had to look for work outside the ring to pay the bills. I went through another ugly divorce in the early 2000s, and I was semi-retired from the ring.

I had met a couple called the Westcotts, who lived in Rockford, Illinois, when I was working for John Collins. They took a liking to me, and Jean Westcott, the wife, took my number. Mr. Westcott was from Baltimore, and he used to work security for the wrestling shows when he was still in Maryland. He got out of that and got into the wood business until he retired. Mr. Westcott had a nest egg that he kept in the house somewhere in the neighborhood of $65,000 in cash that he called his babies.

He and his wife Jean were wonderful people, and they hired me to work for them. I was their security guard, handy man, gardener, driver, errand runner, and whatever else they needed. They paid me $1500 a week and let me live in the house, which I did for about six months. I got some extra work at a restaurant called The Hiding Place, which took care of battered women and their children. I also made some extra cash working as a troubleshooter for a man named Bobby Bell.

Bobby Bell wasn't his real name. He was a bounty hunter, a half-white/half-Native American from New Mexico who wore a cowboy hat and carried a .38, which earned him the nickname Dirty Harry. Bobby was a really slick operator, and most of the time he didn't need me. He knew exactly when to go in and grab somebody, whether it was in the middle of the day at their work or 3 am in the morning. He loved wearing disguises, and he could be anything: a roofer, a house painter, a mailman. He was good at it, and he could blend in anywhere.

Bobby was so good, I saw him talk many people into putting on the handcuffs without a fight. He was really good at reading and working people. "You can run," he'd tell them, "But then you'll have this charge and that charge added to you as well as the charges you already have. Just come back with me, and it'll be easier."

Not everyone went so peacefully, and that's where I came in. I was the guy they never saw coming, always within earshot but out of sight unless I was needed. I never carried a gun, but if there was any trouble, I handled it. I beat the fuck out of some people in real life, which was great because I really needed that outlet.

One night in Springfield, Missouri, we tracked a target to a bar. We had contacted the cops and were supposed to wait for them before moving in, but when the cops didn't show up, Bobby told me to go in and grab him by myself. "If you want to make it in this business, prove it. Go in there and arrest him yourself."

The guy we were after was sitting at a table surrounded by women and drinks. I swear, it was just like a scene out of a movie. I walked up with my cuffs in hand and said, "What's happening?" Without waiting for a reply, I knocked the table out of the way. I didn't even give him a chance to resist. I took him straight down into a Full Nelson and put the cuffs on him. "You're under arrest!"

The bouncers saw me coming, dragging this guy along in handcuffs. "This guy is going to jail," I said. "Get out of my way, or you're going to jail, too." I didn't have the authority to arrest anyone, but the bouncers let us go anyway.

The guy was jawing at me the whole way out to Bobby's truck, saying, "I'm gonna kill you if you don't let me go. You fake wrestler, I could kick your ass!" Like a dumbass, I let him get to me.

"You think you can kick my ass?" I said once we got him to the police holding area. "Only one way to find out!"

I took the cuffs off him, and when he came at me, I took him down. I didn't hit him, and he didn't know how to box or wrestle, but I hooked him and took him down with my elbow in his throat until he gave up. Looking back, it was a foolish thing to do. He was high on drugs and crazy, and he didn't know what was going on. I was already tired and worn out as it was, and things could have gone really wrong. I put the cuffs back on him, and we turned him in.

There was a dance bar in Springfield where we used to pick up a lot of guys we were after. Bobby would go in ahead of me and pay a few of the girls to spend some time with our target. The girls would make the guy drop his guard, and they sometimes made it a competition to see who could get the most money of out him. Bobby would often up the ante, paying the girls with money they had already taken from the bad guy, just to make the guy spend more in the hopes one of the girls would go home with him.

I would slip in an hour after Bobby. I got a table within earshot of Bobby and the girls and our target, waiting and listening. I don't know how many times we ran this game, but it was something to watch, seeing these drug dealers shell out big money to try to outspend Bobby.

At the end of the night our target would leave the club with one or both of the girls and head to his car. That's when we grabbed him. The girls knew to play innocent, as if they didn't know what was going on, while we put the cuffs on the poor guy who thought he was going to get some. They did some good acting too, saying things like, "Don't hurt us! We don't want a fight!" The ladies did their job well and went home with a lot of extra cash while our target went to jail, never realizing how we nailed him.

It took a real man to do that kind of work, and I wasn't the only wrestler who did it. As a matter of fact, even where we were in the Midwest, everyone knew the name "Dr. D" David Schultz. David did his bounty hunting based out of Connecticut, but he traveled the world bringing people back who had fled from justice. David had a different approach than Bobby. Where a guy like Bobby would use disguises to blend in, David couldn't exactly blend in anywhere, being 6'5" and white with that big head of blonde hair. People don't mess with him, though. They knew David was a crazy mother fucker, and if David was coming after them, they might as well just give up. He always got his man.

Bobby spent a lot of time hunting people down in Branson. When most people think of Branson, Missouri, they think about vacations and tourists and big name music stars, but there was a hell of a lot of crime in Branson. A lot of the folks who worked in Branson actually lived 30 minutes to an hour out of town, but they'd also rent a room in Branson with some other folks for the days when they were working. There was a lot of drug dealing going on, and meth was just starting to become a big problem. Some of the elderly tourists used to make extra money selling their prescription pills to the locals as well.

The son of one of Jean Westscott's friends had screwed over some drug dealers in a nearby town called Hollister. Jean asked me to go with her friend to get her son's car, which was now in the possession of the drug dealers. We went over to a house that had about thirty guys who looked like they were part of a gang. They were partying hard with alcohol, pot, meth, you name it. This was in broad daylight in the middle of the week!

I told the lady this was dangerous, trying to get her son's car back, but she was really brave about it. She was a born-again Christian, and she told me, "I'm not afraid. I've got Jesus."

I told her, "The only thing godly you're going to hear in there is hearing God's name in vain. These guys are no joke, and probably every one of them has a gun."

We walked up to the house and knocked on the door. When someone answered, Jean's friend asked for the guy who had the car.

"I came to get my son's car," she said.

"Well, your son owes me some money," the guy said. He was very cool and very respectful of her.

The guy took us around back and showed us the car, which was parked in a puddle of water. The lady and the guy went off to talk a moment by themselves, and he told her how much money he was owed. He wouldn't let her take the car without the money, and she started to get irate with him.

The lady was causing such a ruckus, some of the other folks in the house came out and gathered around. A few of them started looking at me, and I put my hands up. "Hey, calm down guys. We don't want any trouble."

They knew the lady just wanted to help her son, and they weren't going to hurt her. It was her son they were mad at, and they just wanted to get her out of there. They kept telling me, "He fucked us over!" The lady demanded he give her the car, and the guy kept telling her no.

It was a funny scene in a way because the lady kept telling these guys not to cuss. You just can't tell people like that they can't cuss, and I had a hard time keeping a straight face while she was doing that. Some of the gang members saw me trying not to laugh, and that made them smile, too.

"I'm just trying to get out of here so you guys can get back to your party," I told them.

We finally walked away without the car. The lady was pretty upset, but I was just glad to get out of there alive.

One night I got a call from a couple of buddies of mine, one who was a DJ and one who was a bartender. They were in another bar one night that was popular with the tourists, and things were starting to get ugly between some friends of theirs and another group of guys over a woman. "There's gonna be a fight in a minute. We need you."

"Are you crazy?" I said. "I'm not coming down there to get shot!"

"Well, is there anything you can do?" they asked.

"No," I said. "Not unless you can run them through the computer and see if they have warrants."

"Can you do that for us?" they asked.

"No," I said, before telling them to stay the hell out of the fight. My friends were smart enough to take my advice, and they didn't get involved when a fight broke out in the parking lot. My friends' friends got beat up pretty bad, and the cops got involved.

You'd be shocked how many times fights broke out at the bars down there. There was a lady who owned one bar who loved the fights. Seriously, she loved when a fight broke out, and she loved seeing the bouncers get involved.

Another way Bobby made money was repossessing cars, which is how I got into that line of work. That was even more dangerous than bounty hunting. People will shoot you over a car.

There was one grab I will never forget. Bobby was hired to repossess a really nice BMW. The guy who had the car was a friend of Bobby's, and Bobby knew the guy had a warrant out for his arrest. Bobby and I rode over in his big truck to make the grab. He sent me in first, and I slipped in the side door of the garage. The guy must have heard me coming because as soon as I got into the garage, he sent two big pit bulls after me!

I always carried my big stick in case there was trouble, but I only ever used it on people. I love dogs, and I would never, ever do anything to hurt a dog. When those pit bulls came after me, I took off running! I raced back and jumped in the cab. Those dogs were all over the door, barking and snarling at me.

The guy came out of his house, I yelled at him, "That's fucked up, man, sicking the dogs on me!"

He yelled back, "You ain't gonna take my car, mother fucker!"

Bobby got out of the truck and went over to talk to him. Bobby pulled out his .38 and fired it up in the air, saying, "It's whatever you wanna do, man." He was ready to do whatever it took to get the car, and the guy knew it. He wasn't up for a gun fight.

"Man, what do you want with me?" he said.

Bobby said, "You're three months behind on payments."

This guy actually lived in a nice place, and he had the money for the car. For whatever reason, though, he didn't want to pay it. Bobby told the guy, "Look, there's a warrant for your arrest. I could take you in on that. All I want is the car."

The guy calmed down, and they talked it out among them. Everything was cool between them, but I was still in a bad spot. I cracked the window and yelled out, "Hey, I'm glad y'all are cool, but somebody come get these damn dogs away from me!"

Meth was just starting to become a serious problem at that time. We saw some really messed up things, all as a result of meth. I remember one time being in Wal-Mart with the Westcotts. Mr. Westcott was in a wheelchair, and this meth head almost knocked him out, running through the aisles trying to get the stuff he needed to cook more meth.

We picked up a lot of guys strung out on meth. I remember seeing a lot of people who shot their dogs under the influence. I always hated that. Animal cruelty was pretty common, too, because of some occult things that were going on, especially out in the woods. Devil worship went hand in hand with drug use, and you'd find animal sacrifices that just made you sick.

I got to know the smell of a meth lab. I smelled it in houses, out in the woods, and even in caves. I smelled it from time to time in the woods where the Westcotts lived. They would tell me it was just the sewer, but I knew that smell.

Jean Westcott had a husky named Moby that I used to walk through the woods. One night I caught that unmistakable smell, and we came upon a place where people had obviously had a big party the night before. The two of us got out of there and left everything behind.

The next night I took the dog for another walk. When we got to that spot, someone had left a handwritten note. I remember when I found it, the husky gave it a sniff and then the hair stood up on its back as if it were suddenly scared of something, which really gave me a bad feeling.

I opened up the note to see what it said. It was poorly written, but what I read gave me chills. "I see you. You boy or girl?..." It went on and on, getting worse from there. The words got pretty perverse and then downright threatening. It was obvious whoever wrote it was really strung out. I'll never forget it.

About the time I finished reading the note, I heard a boat down in the ravine nearby. I saw Moby looking down into the ravine, and I shouted, "Moby, what do you want to do?" The dog took off down the trail, and I followed behind him. We heard these crazy sounds in the woods as we ran. They were human voices, people strung out on drugs, but they sounded monstrous.

We got down to the bottom of the ravine and could see some people going in and out of a cave. They had run electricity into the cave, where they were cooking meth. We watched them for a little while, and I'm pretty sure they knew we were coming.

After a time, Moby and I turned and walked back up the trail. A short ways away from the cave, we spotted a lawn chair. I knew that chair had not been there the first time we walked past that point not twenty minutes earlier. When I saw the tree, I started jogging. I tried to play it cool and act like I was just working out, but I was scared. Moby picked up the pace and came running beside me.

I was blown up tired when I got back to the Westcott's house. I told Mr. Westcott all that had happened, and when he heard the story, he laughed. "You think you're some big, badass bounty hunter! They could have shot you, buried you, burned you, and no one would have found you. The old man is fucking with you, and whoever wrote that note was probably zooming."

Mr. Westcott knew exactly who he was talking about. The "old man" was the leader of a group of ridge runners who lived in the woods. They were cooking meth and into all sorts of weird shit. Not only that, they were in with the cops. If they had wanted to be rid of me, no one would have ever found me again.

"You leave them alone," Mr. Westcott said. "They're going to do what they're going to do, and there's not a damn thing you can do about it."

One time Mr. Westcott had a medical emergency. We didn't

have time to wait for an ambulance, so we loaded him into the car and I took off. I had an emergency light that I put on the top of the car, but the cops pulled alongside us anyway. Without stopping, I pointed to the backseat. Mr. Westcott's eyes and mouth were wide open, and he didn't look good. The cops recognized him, and while they didn't like the way I was driving, the took the lead and gave us an escort to the hospital.

By 2003 wrestling was starting to come back, but there wasn't much going on. I'd do some shows for Ed Hillyard in Minnesota and J.T. Lightning in Cleveland, but it was hardly enough to support me full time.

A guy in Branson named Brian Gorey, who sold time shares, decided he wanted to run a show. He found a nice building and got some backers to finance the show. He asked me to help run the shows, and we brought in Wildcat Chris Harris, the Naturals, Cassidy Riley, Christy Richie, Dusty Wolf, and a few others.

Brian hoped to incorporate wrestling in with some of the vacation packages he was selling. He wanted to run shows twice a day, and people would have the option of adding wrestling tickets to their package. We had a good response from it, but the economy was still pretty rough, and it just didn't work out.

Meanwhile, Jean Westcott was having trouble with another couple, a preacher who was kind of a carnie/con man and his wife, who were trying to get into Mr. Westcott's good graces. They pretended like they had good intentions, but they were trying to get Mr. Westcott to sign over power of attorney to them. At one point they had the papers drawn up and were very close to getting Mr. Westcott to sign!

I was living in Rockford, working for the Westcotts and wrestling wherever I could, when all this was going on. I tried to stay out of the situation as best as I could. One day I was in Indianapolis with Ian Rotten when I got a call from Jean.

"What are you doing?" she asked. I told her, and she said, "Can you get up here right away?" Jean had gotten wind that someone found out about Mr. Westcott's cash and was trying to steal it. I headed up to Rockford and hung out, keeping an eye on things until the situation blew over.

Mr. Westcott never trusted Bobby Bell either. Bobby knew about the 65 grand that Mr. Westcott kept in the house. He was very leery of Bobby robbing them. Bobby played dumb about it, but I slept by the front door with one eye open for six months.

I had my suspicions Bobby was involved in some illegal stuff himself. There were some storage units that got robbed, and the authorities were convinced it was an inside job. I was pretty sure Bobby was in on all that, among other things.

Bobby worked with me at The Hiding Place. One day Bobby asked me to deliver food to someone, but after driving around for a while, I couldn't find the address and gave up. As I was pulling back in at The Hiding Place, I saw a freight truck, either Yellow or Rodeway, pulling away. I was suspicious something was going on because this was on a street that 18-wheelers could not access. I couldn't imagine how the truck even got down that street, but when I got there, the driver was booking out of there pretty quickly.

I couldn't tell if the truck was picking something up or dropping something off, and I never found out. Bobby didn't say a word about it. Nothing at all.

I saw a lot of bad things during this time of my life, but not everything turned out for the worst. One time at the hiding place we had a lady arrive from Las Vegas. Her husband was a big shot who worked at a big casino in Las Vegas. He found out where his wife had gone, and one day, he showed up at The Hiding Place.

The man had a long talk with Bobby and the guy who had founded The Hiding Place. He said he and his wife had been childhood sweethearts, and after his wife left, he became a born-again Christian. He left Vegas to move to Missouri so he could be close to his wife. He turned his life around, and they ended up being really happy together.

There was a girl who used to mess around with some retired Hell's Angels. There were 40-50 of those guys all living outside Branson, and even though they were retired, they were still some bad dudes. Bobby always looked out for her, maybe because he was screwing around with her too. Something happened involving Bobby and the girl, and they tried to put the heat on me with the Hell's Angels.

The bikers tried to ask me some questions about Bobby and the girl. I just told them, "Whatever's going on with them, that is their business. I know nothing about what you're talking about. I'm an old, beat up wrestler, and I work for the Westcotts." They could tell I was telling the truth, so they eased up on me.

On my way out the door, I ran into Bobby, who pulled me over to talk. I got in his face and gave him a piece of my mind. Bobby tried to play it cool and said, "See, I like that about you."

"I'm sure you do," I said. "I don't like you, and I know you're into some bad shit. It ain't none of my business. I just work for you."

Bobby was a shady character, but the big reason I got out of the business was the cops. I learned real quick that cops didn't care too much for bounty hunters, and the biggest reason the cops didn't like us (at least in the area where we were) was we were hurting their side businesses.

A lot of the cops we knew were dirty. My girlfriend at that time got to know the ex-wife of one of the cops in Branson. He would run sting operations to bust people who were working two and three jobs. He'd lock them up for a day or two, take their drugs, and then drive across the bridge and sell the drugs back on the street.

The cops in Branson really had a racket going. These little busts made the county look tough on crime. They'd bring in revenue through fines and court costs and attorney fees. Then they'd make some extra cash on the side reselling the drugs. It was like a business all unto itself. Seriously, there were some corrupt people out there in Branson!

Bounty hunting and being a repo man was dangerous enough, but when the cops decide you're a problem, that's too dangerous for me. It wasn't the last time I'd do work like that, but I was glad to get out of it at the time.

ECW REUNIONS

By 2004 I was starting to get back on the road. I was wrestling more and more, and I was getting to spend time with my boys back in Tennessee. My now ex-wife Renee had found an apartment for us in Nashville, and I finally left the Westcotts in Rockford to move back home.

I got a job doing maintenance at an apartment complex. I'd work out at the YMCA every morning, work during the day, and travel to a wrestling show in the evening. Then one day I got a phone call offering me a chance to work a tour of Germany. I had never wrestled in Europe, so I jumped at the chance to go.

Germany ended up being more than just one tour. I got so busy with bookings there and in the US, I quit my job to go back to wrestling full time.

Some terrific British wrestlers were on that first tour including Drew McDonald, Doug Williams, Dave Taylor, and Robby Brookside. The latter two guys are phenomenal trainers and work for WWE now. In Germany they wrestle rounds like in a boxing match, which I had never done before.

I did my first rounds match with Robby Brookside, and we had a really great match. Robby walked me through the match, and we called everything on the fly. Robby was a terrific athlete. His father had been a professional soccer player, and Robby was pretty good at soccer himself. He had incredible cardio, and Robby was just so good at everything he did. .

Later on I wrestled Doug Williams in a rounds match and also in a regular match. Both of those matches turned out pretty good as well.

When I arrived home from Germany, I received a phone call from Shane Douglas. Shane, Cody Michaels, and Jeremy Borash were organizing a show called Hardcore Homecoming in Philadelphia at the Alhambra Arena. The plan was to reunite as many former ECW stars as possible for one show and possibly more. A lot of guys were not working for WWE and not available, but I was happy to sign on for the event.

Shortly before Hardcore Homecoming, I worked an independent show in Spartanburg, South Carolina where I took One Man Gang's place in a match against Lex Luger. This was just a few years after Miss Elizabeth had died in their home of a drug overdose, and Luger was still trying to get his life together. Lex still looked pretty good back in 2005, but he was still messed up on drugs. I did the best I could with him, knowing that if we had a good match, it could lead to more bookings on the independents. The match came out okay, and it did in fact help me out.

Just a few days later, Tommy Dreamer called me. Tommy was working with WWE at the time, and he told me they were planning to do their own ECW reunion. It was going to be a pay-per-view called ECW: One Night Stand. Not only were they going to use the former ECW wrestlers they had under contract, they wanted to bring in as many guys as they could who were not signed. The show would take place at the Hammerstein Ballroom in New York. It was actually Rob Van Dam's idea, and it's a shame he got hurt and didn't get to actually wrestle a match on the show. It did a huge buy rate, and it led to a short term revival of the ECW brand under WWE.

One Night Stand was scheduled for June 12, just two days after Hardcore Homecoming. A lot of the guys booked on the Homecoming show were headed to the Hammerstein Ballroom in New York for One Night Stand, and I was glad to join them.

I arrived in Philly on June 10 for Hardcore Homecoming. WWE wouldn't allow any of the guys under contract to work the event, but there were plenty of guys under contract available to put on a great show, including Mikey Whipwreck, Chris Chetti, Simon Diamond, C.W. Anderson, 2 Cold Scorpio, Kid Kash, The Gangstanators, Axl and Ian Rotten, Jerry Lynn, Justin Credible, Raven, Sandman, Sabu, Shane Douglas, Francine, and the most hardcore of us all, Terry Funk. Mick Foley wasn't under contract with WWE, and he surprised the crowd by making an unannounced appearance as the special guest referee in the main event.

I worked the Blue Meanie that night with J.T. Smith in my corner. We wrestled and did a dance off in the ring. Later that night Meanie got involved in a match between Raven and Sandman and took a chair shot to the head that required stitches.

Hardcore Homecoming ended up being successful enough,

they did three more shows in the fall of 2005. I worked one of the two shows in September, defeating Blue Meanie again.

Ian Rotten was running a show the following night, June 11, at the Arena in Philadelphia, and he asked me if I'd stick around to work that show.

"Sure," I said.

Ian asked me, "You don't mind putting Claudio over, do you?"

"No, of course not," I said.

Claudio was Claudio Castagnoli, who you probably know best as Cesaro in WWE. Ian knew Claudio was going to be a big deal, and of course he was right. Claudio was a beast in the ring.

I saw CM Punk at that show, too. Punk told me he was getting ready to sign a contract with WWE. I don't have to tell you how well that worked out, at least for a time.

There was a brutal match between Necro Butcher and Samoa Joe that night. Necro had beaten up some of Joe's students or something prior to the show, and he had heat with Joe. I was at the gimmick tables during that match, and I ended up moving up to the rail to watch those guys beat the crap out of each other.

The next day I went to New York for what was easily one of the most memorable shows I have ever worked. The WWE did a great job building up the event on television. Raw and Smackdown were separate shows at the time, and a faction of heels from each brand came together under the leadership of Eric Bischoff and JBL to oppose the revival of ECW. In the weeks leading up to the show, the anti-ECW factions began to harass the former ECW stars now working for Raw and Smackdown. That essentially set up Bischoff and his cronies as the heels for the night while every ECW wrestler would be treated as a babyface. It was just what the sold out crowd of die hard fans wanted.

When I got to the Hammerstein Ballroom, there was some new heat on me and the other boys who had worked Hardcore Homecoming. A lot of WWE wrestlers and even the top brass didn't want us there.

We all heard talk that Vince was thinking about reviving the brand and offering a lot of us full-time jobs. I was just glad to be there and have a job, and the prospect of full-time wrestling for WWE sounded good to me. A lot of the WWE guys were not fans of the hardcore stuff, and like all wrestlers, they were concerned about losing their spot.

I felt some friction with JBL, too, who I had heard putting me over on his radio show just a few days earlier. During rehearsal, I went up to talk to him about his radio show when he was down by ringside. JBL was drunk, which was my first sign something was wrong, and he blew me off when I went to talk to him.

I hadn't had any issues with JBL after those first few matches we had back in 1996, but from what I heard, JBL was mad about Blue Meanie calling him a bully on a shoot interview. During rehearsals earlier in the day, I heard him talking to some of the agents and the big, younger guys on the WWE roster, including Tyson Tomko, Matt Morgan, the Bashams, and Snitski. "If any of these guys gives you a problem, don't be afraid to knock them the fuck out."

John knew I had overheard him, so I said, "Hey, man, that's cool. Just remember, that's a two way street." I was joking, but I knew he wasn't joking. As the night went on and the big ending got closer, we really didn't know what was going to happen.

Joey Styles was the voice of ECW, and the WWE brought him back to call the show. They paired him with Mick Foley, who was not only one of the real innovators of hardcore violence, but a very smart guy. I still remember one day in 1999 when I was working for Cornette in Pittsburgh, Mick showed us a handwritten manuscript for what became his first book *Have a Nice Day*. I read just a few pages of the book, and I knew Mick was going to do well with it.

The three way dance between Guido, Tajiri, and Super Crazy was a classic. Guido was a consummate wrestler and still is. All three of those guys were in ECW at the time they really innovated the three way dance, and they were unbelievable.

One of the hardest matches to go back and watch on that show is the one on one contest between Eddie Guerrero and Chris Benoit. Both men had worked for ECW prior to WWE, but they had never worked against each other in ECW. The WWE wanted the match for that nostalgia factor, but those guys were both completely worn out. They had been on the road constantly, and they were not their best selves that night.

I remember seeing Eddie lying on the floor of the locker room. I asked him if he was okay, and he didn't even speak to reply. He put his hands together in the shape of Texas, which was his way of telling me he'd rather be home. I checked on him a few times that night, just knowing how he was feeling.

I didn't know Benoit as well as I knew Eddie, but I'd known both guys a long time. Benoit came walking up to me and asked how I was. I asked him the same. Benoit, physically, looked great. His body had never been in better shape, but his eyes told another story.

"I'm tired," he said, "I need a break, man. I need a break. I need a long break." He told me he had some time coming off, but he admitted he wouldn't stay away the whole time he was given. He had to protect his spot, but more than that, he loved what he did.

It wasn't long after that night that Eddie passed away. He was followed by Benoit in that horrible tragedy. It's a shame WWE couldn't see both those guys needed a break. I can't say whether or not it might have changed things, but you never know.

Two guys who weren't road fatigued and put on a hell of a match were Mike Awesome and Masato Tanaka. Mike had been sitting around at home after being fired by WWE, so he was well-rested and ready. He and Tanaka stole the show, which was no surprise to anyone who remembered the matches they did in ECW. Mike and Tanaka didn't work; they fought. And those punches and chair shots between the two of them were as real as it gets.

The fans loved the match, and they gave the two of them a standing ovation. The WWE, however, continued to just bury Mike Awesome, and I think it really got to him. Sadly, it was just two years later that we lost Mike when he hung himself at home.

Paul Heyman cut an amazing, unscripted promo that was more shoot than it was work. He called out Edge for his affair with Lita by dropping Matt Hardy's name, and he nailed JBL when he said, "The only reason you were champion for a year was because Triple H didn't want to work Tuesday!" Ouch!

The show ended with a main event tag match between the Dudley Boys and Tommy Dreamer and Sandman. There were countless run-ins throughout the match by the BWO, by Francine and Beulah, and others before the Dudleys put Dreamer through a flaming table. There was a whole lot of blood, which was to be expected from those guys. There was even a spot with a cheese grater.

After that match ended, anti-ECW stars came down to ringside to face us. By the time we reached that moment, the atmosphere was really tense. The crowd was red hot, the WWE guys were all worked up, and the ECW guys were worked up. We were all standing in the ring, face to face with these guys who really didn't want us there. One of the boys on our side whispered to me, "Are they gonna shoot on us?"

"I don't know," I said. I was on the front line, standing nose to chest with Matt Morgan. Matt was a huge boy about seven feet tall. He was one of Jim Cornette's students from Ohio Valley Wrestling in Louisville, and even though they gave him a terrible gimmick as a stutterer on WWE TV, I knew Jimmy really liked him. Earlier that day in rehearsal, I broke the ice with him.

"So you play football and basketball?" I asked.

"Yeah," he said.

I said, "If you ever get full grown, you'll be a good help to your Mamma!" That got a chuckle.

Standing across from me in the ring, he said, "Hey man, give me a nut shot, and that'll be my way to get out of here." Matt was a good kid, and I knew then he didn't have any problem with us. I think he knew something bad was about to go down.

The battle royal started, and everybody went at it. I went low with a shot to Tyson Tomko, another huge, young guy. "Man, you all right?" I said after I connected.

"I'm okay," he said.

"Good," I said. He was another big boy like Matt I didn't want to cross.

I caught JBL out of the corner of my eye as he waffled Blue Meanie. Meanie had taken a chair shot from Raven at the Hardcore Homecoming show and had staples in the back of his head, and JBL was going right after those staples. I went over to him and said, "What the fuck is going on?"

"Fuck you!" he shouted, hitting me with a rabbit punch.

I came back up under him and caught him under the eye. "Aw, fuck, Floyd!" he said. I went on and JBL yelled at me, "Come back here!"

"I'll be back! Fuck you, man!" I said.

I looked over and Steven (then William) Regal was working with Balls Mahoney and Axl Rotten. Regal was WWE, but he was one of the guys I knew was okay with us. "Hey, Steve," I said, "Come over here with me, I'll get you to safety."

"Hold on, mate!" he shouted. Regal was a real tough guy, and he was kicking some serious ass, but even he knew when it was best to cut and run. He went out over the top to safety, which was his spot.

No sooner was Regal out and safe, Axl and Balls turned their attention to JBL. Sandman came up behind John and was holding him, so I slipped in and got in a few body shots on the guy and lit him up.

JBL got me back with a few shots before he got out of the ring and made his way to the back. He was steaming mad by the time I got back there. Meanie came over and thanked me for bailing him out.

The fallout was immediate. John Laurinitis stormed into the locker room, yelling at everyone. "We don't do that here! We don't do that here! What brought that one out there?"

I kept my mouth shut while Johnny was sorting things out, and I kept quiet for quite a while afterward. If there was a chance of me getting a job with the new ECW, I wasn't going to get any heat with the office. Social media was still a pretty new thing, and everyone back then was on a website called MySpace. (Anyone remember MySpace?) I knew better than to say anything, and I kept my mouth shut.

I went back on the road, keeping my thoughts to myself, but then I started getting messages from people asking me about things that were being said about me. I was told that everyone from the Lords of Pain website to Dave Meltzer were looking for my response to JBL calling me a bitch and saying I had sucker punched him.

I still didn't want to say anything back, but on a show in Knoxville, I was asked to give a working response to JBL, which I did. It was the best interview I ever did, and it went viral on the Internet. I shared my thoughts about JBL on MySpace as well. I can't say for sure that speaking up cost me a shot with WWE, but it made me a lot of money. I went back to Europe and Japan and got a lot of bookings thanks to that interview. I guess I owe JBL a beer.

In 2010 we got to have one last hurrah when TNA Wrestling put on its own version of an ECW pay-per-view. The show was called Hardcore Justice, and TNA brought in Rob Van Dam, Sabu, Raven, Tommy Dreamer, the Dudleys (as Team 3D), Axl Rotten, Balls

Mahoney, Rhino, Al Snow, Brother Runt, the BWO, P.J. Polaco, Kid Kash, Johnny Swinger, Simon Diamond, and the FBI - Guido, Tony Luke, and me. They even got Mick Foley to come in as a guest referee for the match between Dreamer and Raven.

Hardcore Justice took place at the Impact Zone in Orlando, Florida on August 8, 2010. It was a spin off of an annual show called Hard Justice. The original plan was to feature TNA's regular roster, but the TNA card was pushed back four days, and the promotion chose to push what became an ECW reunion as the main show.

I scheduled some shows so I could work my way down to Florida and work my way back up, scheduling a day off at the beach as well. It was great to see everybody again, and I have Tommy Dreamer to thank for booking me. It also helped me get some more bookings on the independent scene.

I stayed pretty busy in the wake of One Night Stand. My appearances at all three shows that weekend in June of 2005 helped me to get booked on the independents, especially when people heard about the blow up between JBL and me. The term "going viral" wasn't a thing yet, but that story circulated by word of mouth and over the Internet, and it got me a lot of bookings.

Sabu told me that he had heard from Dreamer that Stephanie McMahon was pretty upset about my JBL rant. She accused me of using that incident to get more bookings. Of course I did! This is a business, and that rant brought me a hell of a lot of bookings.

WWE probably could have made some money off JBL and me, but I knew that was never going to happen. Guido had told me at One Night Stand that I still had heat with them from my time as a trainer. I was never going to work for WWE again, and that was okay with me.

It was a year after One Night Stand when they finally reopened the ECW brand and started hiring some of the old ECW guys. They hired a lot of the old ECW guys to try and draw an audience, but I knew they were just bringing them in to tear them down. WWE had a bunch of young stars they wanted to get over, and that's just what they did. They put the new guys over at the expense of the ECW legends, and they killed the ECW brand once and for all.

I was doing just fine in the independents, I was fine with it. I was doing well overseas and working about twenty shows a month. I got to tour Europe again as well as the United Kingdom. All told I did eleven tours, everything from a few weeks to three months at a time. I worked singles, tags, and even eight mans.

One guy I worked with a lot over there was Drew Galloway, who became Drew McIntyre in WWE. He got stuck in a jobber gimmick for a while as part of Three Man Band, but he came back and got a huge push later on. I also worked with Sheamus before he signed with WWE and worked a lot with Tyson Kidd as well.

I also worked with guys like James Mason, Robby Dynamite, Brian Dixon, Frankie Sloan, and Robby Brookside. Those guys were an incredible crew. They could all call matches on the fly with nothing planned in advance.

In 2006 I came back to the States. Things began to slow down, both in the wrestling business and in the economy in general. I had split from my then-wife Renee and was living in Southern Indiana when the Great Recession hit in 2008 and the economy really got bad.

Fannie Mae and Freddie Mac, two government-backed mortgage companies, went bankrupt. The stock market crashed. The big Detroit auto companies were in serious trouble, laying people off and closing production plants. That fall Barack Obama was elected President, and a lot of people had high hopes he could turn things around.

The wrestling business was hurting just as much as any other business, especially the independents. It was difficult to make a full-time living outside the WWE before the Great Recession, but I was still doing it. After the economy tanked, it became impossible. Gas was $4 a gallon. Companies went out of business left and right.

As if that wasn't bad enough, I had lost most of my life savings thanks to an investment that turned out to be a bad deal. I had never made a ton of money in the business, but I made a decent living working for WCW and WWF. I'd been smart with my money, done my taxes, and saved aside what I could, and I ended up putting my savings into some sort of overseas investment fund. I was making good money off that investment at first, but then the federal government stepped in. It turns out the fund was being used to launder money for the mob, and all that money I had saved was gone.

My girlfriend Rachelle, who I'm still with, had just lost her job as an inspector for McDonald's. She had a great job with them, full benefits and everything, but when she lost that position, she had to go to work in a store for one of the managers she knew well.

I got a job making deliveries for a place called Munchie's Pizza in Evansville. It was a good job, but I wasn't being paid hourly. I was doing okay, living off the tips and gas money, but I wanted to find something with benefits. I was still driving a van that used to carry several wrestlers to and from shows, and that thing only got 12-15 miles to the gallon. Fortunately, my girlfriend let me use her car to deliver pizzas, and she took my van to work.

Money was still pretty tight, so I put in an application at McDonald's where my girlfriend worked. I got called in for an interview, but the day of my interview, I had an anxiety attack. I got physically sick, and I just couldn't do it. I had worked in restaurants previous to that, and I was okay with it, but that day, I just couldn't do it. Lucky for me, I got a second chance, and after a good interview they hired me.

It was a humbling experience, but it ended up being a very good one. I was working two jobs, doing a shift at McDonalds in the morning and early afternoon and delivering pizzas in the evenings. I wasn't making big money, but I was catching up on my bills. I've pretty much worked two jobs ever since that time.

Both my jobs were very flexible with my wrestling bookings, which worked out great. Most of the time I was working for the Clowns at JCW, and since they never gave me a lot of notice, I was grateful McDonald's and Munchie's would work with me.

The Clowns hired me to work a Halloween show up in Detroit with less than a week's notice. Detroit had been hit hard by the recession, but the Juggalos still came out in force, as they always do. Scott Hall was on that show, and I hung out with him that night. Scott's gotten his life straight in recent years, but back then, he was struggling. He got wasted as soon as his match was over.

One of the big reasons I took the job at McDonald's was to get benefits, something I'd never had in the wrestling business and something the WWE still does not offer its wrestlers. I never got those benefits because I ended up leaving the job before I became eligible. A late night pizza delivery led to a chance encounter with someone from my past I never saw coming.

There was a young lady who delivered pizza for Munchies as well. She was good at her job, and because she was attractive, she made some really great tips, especially between 10 pm and 1 am. One night we got an order from a gentleman at a local hotel. For her own safety, the policy was that if a man called and ordered a pizza that late at night from a hotel, she had to have a guy go with her. I got in the car with her and headed out to make the delivery.

I followed her to the door to make the delivery and stayed off to the side, where I could see the door but the guy on the other side wouldn't see me. She knocked on the door, and the customer opened it. The man had a beard, and he was a few years older from when I had last seen him, but when I heard his voice, I knew exactly who it was.

I leaned around the corner and said: "John Collins!"

It had been eight years since I last laid eyes on John Collins. He invited me into the room, and I stuck around for a few hours to talk. John had moved away from the area to North Carolina, and he told me he was now a preacher. Matter of fact, I believe that was the same time he was doing the scam with the Bibles that Garry Stroud used to do.

The following day I met John for lunch, and he told me why he was back in town. He had turned informant for the FBI while he was in prison, which is how he ended up getting released after serving only 71 months. John had made some connections on the inside that made him more valuable to the FBI on the outside. He was still working undercover for them, helping to bring down some of the biggest gangs in the country.

I've told a lot of stories in this book and named a lot of names. I'm too old to care about wrestlers or promoters getting their feelings hurt from me saying what I really think of them. That said, for the remainder of this story, you'll forgive me if I do not name names or even give the names of the two major (and I do mean MAJOR) gangs involved. I'm not afraid of the WWE, but I am afraid of these people. That alone should tell you something. If you knew who they were, you would be nervous, too.

John told me about some of the things he was doing, though he didn't tell me everything. He gave me just enough as we went along so that I knew what was involved and what he wanted me to do to help. The main thing he wanted was to use me as a troubleshooter, like I was for Bobby Bell. I would be the muscle used to bring these guys in, and in exchange, John was going to help me get jurisdiction to do bounty hunting and repo cars. That was the only reason I signed on to help.

John ran the point on these assignments. He was the guy who knew people and could draw them out into the open. I was the guy they never saw coming. When the moment was right, I would step out of the shadows and put the cuffs on them to take them in.

We worked under a U.S. Marshal who was based out of Michigan. He looked a little like Randy Orton, only he was 6'5" and weighed around 250 pounds. He was 45 years old, but he was an absolute beast. He had sent John to Evansville because of its centralized location in the Midwest. It was an ideal point from which he could send us out to pick guys up.

There was a bar in Evansville that was also of interest. It was a popular strip bar that was a front for drugs and prostitution. As a matter of fact I soon learned that the big gangs in the U.S. own a lot of restaurants and businesses. You'd be shocked to know how many are really fronts that gangs use to launder money.

John and the U.S. Marshal wanted me to go undercover into the club wearing a ring and necklace that concealed a camera and a microphone. Before I could do that, I had to sign some paperwork stating that I was working for them as a precaution. If the police were to raid the club while I was inside, I would be arrested, too. The paperwork would give them a means to quietly get me released from jail without anyone knowing.

I didn't like strip bars, I didn't like the paperwork, and I really didn't like the things they were asking me to do. Not only would I be subject to arrest if the club was raided, they wanted me to do whatever the bad guys inside asked me to do: pot, crack, LSD, you name it!

John had no problems doing these things. As a matter of fact he sold a lot of cocaine to guys from one of the major gangs. John had had to move several times, all on the FBI's dime, to protect himself and his family. One of the gangs had tracked him down to a house he had outside of Evansville, which is why he had moved to the country outside Asheville, North Carolina.

One time I ran into Pat Tanaka on a show. I told Pat I was working with John, and Pat ended up tagging along with me to go and see John. John didn't go out much because he was afraid of being spotted by someone from one of the gangs who knew he was working for the Feds. Somehow Pat and I were able to convince John and his wife to go out to a bar just to have a drink.

The bar was a regular spot for a biker gang that was connected to one of the two big gangs John was working against for the FBI. Things were cool at first. John got on YouTube and started to show these guys videos of Pat and me from our younger days. But then John's old vices put us all in a bad spot.

John was still a big womanizer at the time, which was no surprise, and while we were in the bar, he got a lady drunk and took her out to his Hummer to have sex. The problem was the girl's boyfriend was one of the leaders in the gang at the bar.

I found out what John had done because John's wife asked me

to dance. I wasn't comfortable with that and told her no, and that's when she told me about John and the girl. Pat and I started to realize the mood in the bar was turning. We had done nothing wrong, but these guys were definitely not cool with us anymore.

The gang members played it off at first. When John and the girl came back into the bar, she started apologizing to all the guys in the gang. They acted like it was cool, but then somehow, word got around that John was a narc.

The next day when we woke up, John told us we had to leave. "I might have fucked up last night," he said. Pat and I packed our stuff and hit the road.

About an hour after we left, John heard a noise in his garage. John went out on his deck and saw a few men holding weapons, looking for a fight. They called John a rat and wanted to beat him up. They weren't going to kill him, but they were prepared to fuck him up. John's wife got on the phone and called the cops, and the guys took off. Needless to say, I never went to Carolina to visit him again.

I continued working with John for a few months. I had lost the McDonald's job but was still delivering pizzas and wrestling when I could. John moved to a new place in Eastern Kentucky. It was a beautiful place out in the country, and I went down to visit him one time with my dog Ruthie.

A retired U.S. Marshal moved into a house out near the back of John's property. When I was down visiting, John told me he had noticed a steady stream of traffic headed toward the marshal's house. We came to find out the marshal was making and selling meth out of his house.

The FBI came in to investigate, and as soon as they were moving in, John told me I had to go. I hopped in the car and headed home with Ruthie.

John had gotten involved with a woman who owned a huge house outside of Lexington. The woman was an ex-cop who had been married three times and taken her husbands for everything. She was crooked, and she had dirt on all her exes that she used to her advantage. She owned a horse that had won quite a few races that she kept as a pet. However, she was a lovely woman and was always nice to me.

John had a good thing going with the FBI, but got back to

running a lot of the same cons he had previously done with Garry. He would rent a place from this lady in Lexington, tell the FBI he needed money for rent, and then pocketing the FBI's money without paying the lady. He owed her a lot of money, and she was getting pretty upset with him.

One night the FBI got wind that some gang members were on their way to get John, whom they knew as "Cowboy." They had been in Louisville and let it slip to another undercover agent that they knew John was living on a farm in Kentucky.

The gang had done some research on the Internet and found where he was living. They reached out to the lady John was renting from, posing as business men, and invited her out to a pub to shoot some pool and have a few drinks. The woman knew who John was and all he was up to, and she started talking. She told them everything! She did not know these guys were out to get John, but she was mad and didn't care what she said.

The next morning, I was with John when he got a call from the FBI. The conversation was heated, and I remember John saying, "I didn't tell them anything!" He got off the phone and told me we had to split. I grabbed my things and got out of there fast.

I was working another job on the side at that time for my friend Beau James who had started up a carnival. The economy was still pretty bad at that time, but according to Beau, carnivals lasted through the depression, and he believed his would weather the recession. Turned out that wasn't quite the case, but Beau sold me on going to work for him.

I went on the road with the carnival for a while, traveling from town to town and sleeping in an RV. It was pretty rough, as far as sleep goes, because the bright lights of the carnival were lit up all night long. When we arrived in town, I helped set up the rides, and when it was time to leave, I helped pack them away. In between I worked security on the grounds.

The customers were never really any trouble. The people you had to watch out for were the carnies. Brother, let me tell you, they are the worst. They used to get really mad at me, too, because I could speak carny. They'd try speaking carny in front of me, thinking I couldn't understand, and I'd tell them what they were saying.

"I'm a wrestler!" I told them. "Wrestling came out of the

carnivals!" They couldn't wrap their heads around it.

One day they fired a guy for breaking the rules, and they refused to pay him some money they owed him. He left and came back with about a dozen guys to get his money. I was the only one standing between the thirteen of them and the people refusing to pay up. Scary stuff, man.

I was out on the road, preparing to head home from a carnival gig in Knoxville, when both John and his wife started calling me. I didn't answer right away, but I finally answered a call from his wife, who told me they were back in North Carolina. "There's a lot going on right now. We need your help!"

John was in deep. He had screwed over the lady in Lexington, the FBI, and one of the most dangerous gangs in America. John and his wife wouldn't give me any details, but they were begging me to come and help them out. I remember I was on I-40, coming up to the turn for I-75 North that would lead me home. I was back and forth several times trying to decide whether to head back to Evansville or head back to North Carolina and help John.

"Look," I said, "I don't know what all John's told you, but he's pissed off some dangerous people. I have three boys to live for, and I just can't get involved again." I know it sounds dramatic, but I took I-75 North and went home. I liked John a lot, in spite of all his faults, but knowing all he had been up to, I was too scared to get involved. They didn't even know my name, as far as I knew, and I wanted to keep it that way.

I think it goes without saying at this point I've never been one to back out of a fight. Whether it was a bear, an angry mob of fans in Mexico, or even cancer, I'll jump in and go down swinging. But there's a difference between being brave and being stupid. I said before I won't give the name of the two gangs John was working against, but if you knew the names for yourself, you'd understand. Sometimes you stand and fight. Sometimes it's just better to get the hell out of Dodge.

The carnival gig didn't last much longer than that, but I got a job delivering pizzas in Evansville for Sandy's Pizza. It was my girlfriend who spotted the "Now Hiring" sign out in front of Sandy's place, so I went in and introduced myself to Sandy, who was kind enough to interview me.

"So what's your story?" she asked right off the bat.

I told Sandy that I was a professional wrestler and had also worked as a bounty hunter and a pizza delivery person. She tried to discourage me from taking the job at first, saying it was just a few days a week during the day, but I was glad to take it.

"When can you start?" she asked.

"I can start right now," I said.

"How about we start you Saturday?" she said.

Ouch. Saturday, I had a booking for JCW working for the Clowns. It was just a run-in appearance on Terry Funk, but they were paying me $500. I couldn't break my booking, but I also couldn't say no to Sandy. I said yes.

That Saturday I came in and trained with a guy named Jordan. He was a very nice man, but sadly, he drank himself to death. Jordan took me on his rounds, showed me how to do the job, and we wrapped up just in time for me to hop in the car and drive up to do the show for the Clowns.

Sandy was a hard working lady who didn't take any crap, and she sold a lot of pizza. Sandy's was very popular with families, and they had a giant 30" pizza that they sold a lot. She was a wonderful person to work for.

I did double shifts every chance I got, and they were always willing to let me off to go work a wrestling show when I needed it. I didn't wrestle much in 2009 and 2010, but I made a lot of great money. I paid off my car, some credit cards, and caught up with my child support payments. The economy started coming back as well, and things were looking up all over.

THE SMOTHERS FAMILY

There were a few times in my life when I was done with wrestling. I was ready to give it up completely, get a regular job, and be done with it. Working at Sandy's Pizza was one of those times when I nearly walked away. I was making great money delivering pizzas, working the ovens, getting all the hours I could.

Then along came Jessie Belle Smothers.

Jessie Belle was not the first of my many Smothers "daughters," but she is the only one who can say she has actual documentation that says she's my daughter. She's not, but I have a paternity test signed by a doctor that says she is.

Jessie Belle Smothers

I first met Tracy Smothers when I was working for XCW in New Albany, Indiana. I was working as a manager at that time, and Tracy asked me before the show if I would work his gimmick table for him. He ended up doing really well that night, making $400-500. Tracy was really impressed, and he told me I had the look to make it as a wrestler. "You should go on the WWE Diva Search," he said.

I was pretty excited to hear someone like Tracy say that, but my first husband shot it down. That was the end of that - for the time being.

I split from my first husband and moved into an apartment in Louisville, Kentucky. I was working out at the gym in my apartment complex, and I spotted a man who looked like Tracy. I wasn't really sure because I'd only met him a few times, but one day I took a chance.

"Are you Tracy Smothers?" I asked.

He said, "Yes."

"I'm Jessie Belle." Tracy remembered me, and while we were catching up, I told him I wanted to be a wrestler. Tracy hooked me up with a woman he was dating who could train me, and the two of us started going out to dinner to talk about wrestling.

I had a falling out with my trainer, and I ended up moving to Louisiana. I found Tracy on MySpace, and I reconnected with him. I was still trying to break in to the wrestling business, and I told Tracy if he ever needed anyone to go on the road with him to let me know.

Tracy said he would look into it and get back to me. What I didn't know at the time was that Tracy had actually walked away from wrestling. He had another job, and as far as he was concerned, he was DONE. Tracy told me later he got back into it solely so he could go on the road with me.

A few shows fell through, and Tracy started to get disheartened. He didn't tell me this at the time either, but I stayed positive. "That's okay, we'll get the next one." Finally, we booked a loop that had us going through West Virginia, and we hit the road.

It was in West Virginia we worked a show with a bunch of guys Tracy had known for years including Ricky Morton and Tommy Rich. I was just going by the name Jessie Belle at the time, but based on the way Tracy and I interacted with each other, Ricky and Tommy and the other guys all assumed I was actually Tracy's daughter. Afterwards, Tracy talked to me about it.

"When people start a fire, you have to throw gasoline on it. We're going to start telling people you're my real daughter."

"People won't believe it," I said. "I've been working as a manager for two or three years as Jessie Belle."

"Look," he said, "If I swear to it, and you swear to it, they can't disprove it. We're going to tell everybody that it's a shoot."

At that time, I was working as a house cleaner, and one of my clients was a doctor at Norton Hospital in Louisville. I went online and printed off a paternity test, and I filled out the form, editing the results to make it appear that Tracy was my real father. I gave it to the doctor, who took it to work and printed it off on hospital letterhead and signed it for me. We now had a DNA test signed by a doctor saying I was Tracy's kid!

Armed with that document, we treated our relationship as father and daughter like a shoot. I called him Pops, and he told everyone I was his real daughter. We even told Tracy's real kids that I was their half-sister. That's how far we went.

Tracy Smothers

Jessie Belle was one of several STDs: "Smothers Twisted

Daughters." Mickie Knuckles was the first of my girls, Isabelle Smothers, back in JCW. I was working against 2 Tuff Tony on a show in Cleveland, and a girl had come up and hit me hard in the head. Mickie jumped on the girl and beat the crap out of her. The next night, they put Mickie and I together as father and daughter. The Juggalos hate rednecks, so that got us a lot of heat.

I connected Mickie and Jessie Belle, and Mickie started to train Jessie Belle. They worked tag matches and singles matches against each other, and they also worked as valets at ringside with me.

In addition to Jessie Belle and Isabelle, there was also Mae Belle Smothers (aka Delilah and later Lovely Lylah), Anna Belle Smothers, Mary Belle Smothers, and Khloe Belle Smothers.

The Smothers Sisters were the very first wrestlers brought into Ohio Valley Wrestling in Louisville who were not either WWE or Impact signees or students at OVW. Al Snow brought them in back in 2010, and Jessie Belle has been there off and on ever since.

Jessie Belle

We worked in West Virginia for a promoter we knew as Fat Freddy. Pops and I were working as heels, and we came out with all the other heels to surround the ring with all the babyfaces inside the ring. Pops was cutting a promo, and while he was talking, one of the fans reached over and grabbed me.

Old school wrestling rules if a fan comes after a wrestler, the wrestlers cannot back down. If a fan charges you, you stand your ground. If you're a wrestler, you're a fighter, and you must go over to protect the business.

I spun around and nut shotted the guy. Pops dropped the microphone, pushed the guy against the wall, and beat the crap out of him. He went back and picked up the microphone to finish his promo, and we went back to the locker room.

It turns out the guy who grabbed me was a local guy who worked on the shows. He thought he would get a pop from the crowd by grabbing me. Pops was furious, and he let the guy know it. "What the fuck were you thinking out there? You keep your hands off her! Look at me when I'm fucking talking to you?"

The guy couldn't look up. He was hunched over in a chair, still nursing his wound from where I hit him with the nut shot.

We were working for KSW in Pigeon Forge, Tennessee. Mae Belle was with us, and Lisa Funk was working as Momma Smothers. Lisa had planned a spot with a fan. The fan had a mental disability, and he was well known to all the locals.

While we were standing at ringside, the fan reached over and grabbed Lisa, just as he was told. The problem is, Lisa didn't tell any of us about it. I turned around and saw this fan grabbing Lisa, and I attacked him. Mae Belle said what was going on, and she attacked the fan. Then Pops saw what was happening and joined in.

The fan's family saw us attacking him, and they all came after us, along with a bunch of other fans who knew the family. The family knew the fan was supposed to grab Lisa, but none of us did, and I don't think any of the other fans knew, either. We found ourselves in the middle of a riot with Tracy shouting, "Stand your ground!"

The fan had no business being involved, regardless whether he had a disability or not, but Lisa messed up by not telling the rest of us. She could have saved everybody a whole lot of trouble.

Pops and I were working for 304 Wrestling in Huntington, West Virginia as part of a heel faction called The Five Most Wanted with Sean Casey, Onyx, and Shane Matthews. Pops was working an angle with a Juggalo wrestler named Loco the Clown. Pops always won the matches because he had me at ringside to interfere and help him get the win.

In an attempt to settle the score between Pops and Loco, the commissioner brought Mickie Knuckles into 304 as Mickie Knuckles to be on Loco's corner. We had an in-ring contract signing that said if I interfered in the next match, Mickie would be there to take me down.

Mickie and I were both at ringside when Pops and Loco had their next match. The match went out of the ring into the crowd. There were about 500 people in the crowd who all hated our guts, especially mine. I stayed on the other side of the barricade with Mickle nearby keeping an eye on me.

As I was talking shit to the fans, one of the women in the front row spit on me, hitting me right in the face. I got in her face and started to say, "I dare you to—" and before I could finish my sentence, her friend spat on me.

The two women shoved the barricade and hit a small child who was sitting ringside. Mickie saw what was going on and raced over in between me and the fans. "Stop, stop!" said Mickie. "You can't attack her. She'll call the cops!'

"Then you have to beat her up!" the fans said.

"I can't," said Mickie. "I signed a contract! I can't unless she interferes in the match!"

Mickie managed to calm the fans down. Meanwhile Pops and Loco ended up back inside the ring. With Mickie watching over my shoulder, I couldn't interfere, and Loco won the match. The commissioner made his way to ringside with the barber shears to shave Pop's head, but before Loco could start on Pops, Shane, Sean, and Onyx hit the ring. We beat down Mickie and Loco, and then we shaved Loco's head.

Loco had some really long dreadlocks he had wanted to cut off anyway. Pops was the one who convinced him to turn it into an angle, which led to the hair versus hair match to begin with.

Pops and I got changed after the show and were ready to leave, but we couldn't find the promoter, who had our pay envelopes. We asked around and someone told us the promoter was outside talking to the police. The two women at ringside who spat on me called the cops and told them that I spat on them, kicked the barricade, and hit the kid.

The police came looking for me and asked if I minded giving a statement. "Yes, I do mind," I said. "I have a six hour drive. If you want to know what happened, watch the video."

Thank goodness everything was on video that night. The cops watched the tape and saw the women spitting on me, tossing the barricade, and hitting the child. With the tables turned, the cops asked me what I wanted them to do.

"We can let them off with a warning, or we can arrest them for aggravated assault." At Pop's urging, I had them take the women to jail.

Traveling with Pops is always an interesting experience. Pops began riding the roads in 1983, and he's old school. He still prefers a map over GPS. Any time I try to set the GPS, he says, "Have you ever seen one of these? This is a map!"

In all fairness to him, Pops also has an amazing awareness of the roads. He knows how long it should take to get from one place to another. He knows instinctively what time we should arrive where and when during our journey - if we are obeying the legal speed limit. I don't like to drive the speed limit, so this has led to some interesting father-daughter confrontations over the years. If I go off route, he will wake up, look around and ask, "Where are you going? What are you doing? Slow down!"

We were on our way back from the TNA Hardcore Justice show in 2010. Pops was asleep, so I turned on the GPS. The thing I prefer about GPS is not only do you have turn by turn navigation, but you also have real time updates as far as traffic and construction is concerned. Of course as soon as I turned off the route Tracy knew, he woke up. "Where are you going? No, no, no! This is the road you need to take!"

I circled back around and got onto the road he wanted me to take. Pops fell asleep. About two or three miles down the road, we hit a standstill. There was an accident ahead of us. I could see the emergency lights ahead of us, but we sat there for four hours without moving.

Mickie Knuckles was with us along with one other guy. Mickie and I got out of the car and started interviewing people who were stuck on the road with us. We took a video and posted it up on YouTube. Pops missed all the fun because he slept through the whole thing.

Another time we were on a road trip with Ryan Howe, who was part of the 2011 revival of Tough Enough. The two of us were engaged at the time, and even Ryan believed that Tracy was my real dad. I told you, we took it pretty far!

We had been on the road for four days, and our final show of the trip was on a Saturday night. I had promised my mom I would be home Sunday morning in time to go to church with her.

Pops was not about to let me drive. He had had enough of my GPS and my speeding by this point and even told people, "I don't care if we're going on a trip to Russia. I'm driving!"

Pops drove for the first few hours that night. We were all tired, having been on the road four days, and when he got tired, he asked Ryan to take over.

"Do not let my daughter drive!" Pops said, settling into his seat to fall asleep. Ryan, being deathly afraid of the man he thought was my father, promised he wouldn't let me drive.

We made it another three hours when Ryan started to get tired. "I'm going to pull over and take a nap," he said.

We were already running behind, so I said, "No. I'll take over."

Ryan said, "But Tracy said—"

"I promised I would be in church!" I said. "I'm driving."

Ryan gave in, and I took over the driving. I was flying down the road trying to make up for lost time and get home for my mom.

Like I said before, Pops has this thing where he knows at all times where we should be, if we're driving the right road at the right speed. Pops started to wake up at one point and eyed the clock. "Are we in Bluefield, West Virginia?"

"I dunno, Pops," I said. "Maybe. I haven't been looking at the road signs." We were already long past Bluefield, but Pops settled in and went back to sleep.

A short time later, he half-woke up again. "Have we made it to Charleston?"

It was 5 am by that time, and we were seventy miles past Charleston in Ashland, Kentucky. "I don't know, Pops. It's dark. I can't see the road signs."

"Slow down, slow down," he said, going back to sleep. I kept the accelerator on the floor, doing 110 to 140 miles per hour.

The sun was up by the next time Pops woke up, and this time, he was fully awake. By his internal clock, we should have been in Huntington. He looked around and immediately knew something was off.

"Where are we??" he said. "Are we in Kentucky??"

"Ummm," I said.

"We're in Mount Sterling??" I was only doing 90 miles an hour by this point, but we were in a construction zone. Pops started freaking out. "Oh my God! He cursed me with a daughter in the rasslin' business! You were a race car driver in a former life! Slow down! Slow down!"

I said, "Pops, it's okay. The cops that are on duty right now are heading home, and the cops coming on duty are in their morning meeting."

Pops hollered, "Well, if the cops who are coming on duty are in a meeting, why don't we just rob a bank?"

"Well, Pops, we probably could, but it's Sunday," I said. "All the banks are closed." Ryan was in the back seat cracking up listening to us fight.

"Well, why don't we just drive a hundred miles an hour, then?"

"Can I?" I asked.

"No!!" he said. "Slow down!"

Pops was not happy, but I made it to church on time and made my mom a happy lady.

"THAT RASSLIN'S FAKE, ISN'T IT?"

Delivering pizzas may not seem like a glamorous second career for a guy who was hired and fired from every major wrestling promotion on the planet, but I can assure you, there are worse jobs to have. Compared to the time I spent repossessing cars and bounty hunting, I'll deliver pizzas any day. It takes a special kind of man to do that sort of dirty work. Dr. D excelled at it, and as far as I'm concerned, he can have that business!

You're probably wondering if anyone ever recognized me when I showed up to deliver their pizza. Of course they did! I delivered to a lot of businesses and churches and parties over the years, and I got recognized quite a lot.

Every now and then some wise guy who knew who I was would say something like, "That rasslin's all fake, isn't it?"

"Yeah," I said, "This limp I got is fake, too. Every year it gets a little worse and a little more fake."

Sometimes they ask, "So, you on steroids?"

I'll look back at them and answer, "Do I look like I'm on steroids?"

They'll ask if I wrestled this top guy or that top guy, and when I answer yes, they ask, "Did you beat 'em?"

I'll answer, "If I beat 'em, I wouldn't be here in Fort Branch, Indiana delivering your pizza, would I?"

One time I worked a show in Nashville, about four hours south of where I live, and had to turn around the next day to do a show in Michigan near Detroit at a Cinco de Mayo festival. My expenses were covered, but it was a long drive. I had J.D. with me, and J.D. was packing a gun.

People don't realize wrestlers work hurt. They don't realize how much we put our bodies through in this business. We have to keep working so we don't lose our spots. People also don't realize that the days of fans coming after wrestlers never really ended. Some nights, it still happens.

I was worn out when I got there, and I had to work a match

with a big guy named Alcatraz. Because of the festival, there were a lot of non-wrestling fans were there, and they were rowdy. I went out to the ring and did my usual heel act. I was very tired and banged up, and I looked out of the ring and saw four white guys 50 yards away staring at me.

"Hey!" one of them shouted. "Hey you, gimp!"

I didn't look at him but tried to ignore him. "Hey, gimp. Limp, I mean. Hey, you country fuck! Why don't you get your old ass out of the ring and go to the nursing home, you washed up ass muther fucker?"

That hit a real nerve with me, but it got me fired up. "Oh really?" I said. "Why don't you step into this ring and see what I still got, you mother fucker?"

The second I turned around, the guy took off running for the ring. He sprinted 40-50 yards, and I could see he was completely wasted.

"Oh shit," I thought. "I'm not ready for this."

The good news was this guy had never set foot in a ring before. If you've never done it before, it can be hard to get in and out of. I was in the middle of the ring watching to see how he would come in the ring because I've had this happen before - when I was younger.

If he came under the bottom rope, I was going to punt him. Instead, I saw him start to pull himself up to the apron. I ran to the opposite rope and bounce off to get some momentum, then I timed my move, racing across the ring, to catch him right in the chest while he was still in mid-air pulling himself up. WHAM! It was probably the fastest I'd run in a long time.

Somehow my hand got wrapped up in his shirt when I hit him, and I twisted it and broke my hand. My hand is still messed up from that night, and it'll never be completely right again. I still knocked the guy back a good six or eight feet, and not knowing how to take a bump, he hit that concrete floor hard.

He rolled and got back up to his feet, ready to come back for more. I started to climb out of the ring, thinking I would spear him and shoot on him, hoping to knock him out. That's when a security guard, a really big Native American dude, made his way around and told me, "I've got him."

Now, with the security guy between us, I got back into the ring and started baiting him. "Let him in! Let him in!" I could tell the guy wanted to come back, but the security guy finally escorted him out.

Those four guys waited for me a while in the parking lot after, but the promoter finally called the cops and ran them off. Meantime I had a good, stiff, hard match against Alcatraz, fighting with a broken hand. My hand was swollen up like a baseball afterwards, but I was booked on 14-15 shows a month at the time and didn't want to take off. I iced my hand off and on every day and continued my schedule: working out, delivering pizzas, traveling, and wrestling.

Right around the time I started delivering pizzas, I had a memorable match with Jerry Lawler. This was right around the time that LeBron James went from the Cleveland Cavaliers to the Miami Heat. Lawler was a big Cavaliers fan, and promoter J.T. Lightning had me wear a LeBron jersey under my rebel shirt. Jessie Belle Smothers was with me that night, and she went to the ring wearing a LeBron shirt as well. When she removed my rebel shirt to reveal the LeBron shirt, boy, that got a lot of heat!

Lawler gave Jessie Belle a piledriver. I came off the ropes at him with a lot of speed, and Lawler jumped up for a dropkick. Wham! He caught me right in the mouth and knocked my front teeth loose.

My teeth didn't fall out right away, but a short time later, while I was eating a hamburger, they came right out. I ended up swallowing them, and that was that.

The best thing about that incident: it really helped with my tips when I was delivering pizzas! People would ask me, "Well, why don't you get your teeth fixed, you snaggletooth?" They'll make fun of me, I'll tell them the story, and they'll bump up my tip.

People kept bugging me to get partials, and I finally did. As soon as I started wearing false teeth, my tips went down. They cost me about three grand, and right away, I lost them. I decided to leave my teeth the way they were, and I kept on milking the teeth story for extra tips.

Those of you who think it's meth, it ain't meth. Jerry Lawler kicked my teeth out, and that's the truth.

When I first broke into this business, I dressed in a Confederate soldier's coat and started wearing the stars and bars of the Confederate battle flag. Down South in those days that flag was a symbol of

Southern pride. Most people didn't think about slavery and racism like they do now. The Wild Eyed Southern Boys were the pride of the South and as big a babyface act as you'd find down South. There was nothing racist meant by our gimmick. It was Kevin Sullivan's idea to put us over as babyfaces, and in that time and place, it worked.

Times have changed, and so have people's thoughts about that damn flag. As you might expect, a lot of fans take exception to my wearing the flag and carrying it to the ring. A lot of wrestlers have as well, including Abdullah the Butcher. As much as I own it in the ring, the truth is, as I've told Abby many times, that flag isn't who I am.

When people ask me why I still use the flag, I tell them: because it's a gimmick! That's all it is, just a gimmick. Everyone says wrestling is fake, but then you walk out with a Confederate flag and they believe it. I'm part Native American. I do it because I get paid to do it. I was Italian because they paid me to be Italian. Pay me enough money, I'll be anybody you want me to be!

It's crazy to me that even though kayfabe is supposed to be dead, some people really think I'm a racist because of a character I play in the ring. I keep my phone number and email up on my Facebook page so promoters can book me. Shortly after that racist gunman went and shot up a church down in the Carolinas, I started getting threatening phone calls in the middle of the night.

Several nights in a row, the same guy called me around 3 am and started screaming and cursing at me. "You stupid son of a bitch! I'm gonna murder you! I'll bust a cap in you and kill you, you racist!"

After a couple of nights of being woken up, I finally had enough. "Look man," I said, "If you're gonna shoot me or whatever, do it. Got for it. Do whatever you gotta do, mother fucker, but quit waking me up at three o'clock in the morning! First off, I'm a damn Indian. I hate that guy who killed those people as much as you. Second, I have to get up at five to let my dogs out, get in a workout, deliver pizzas for eight hours, go wrestle a show, and then get to bed and do it all over again.

"I have been Italian. I was in the Nation of Domination. I was Jason from *Friday the 13th*. I've been twenty-two other things, and ain't none of them worked, or else, I wouldn't be delivering pizzas! If you're gonna kill me then get your ass down here and kill me already, but if you're not, you gotta at least let me get some sleep."

The guy on the phone started laughing. "Man, you're a trip. I'll leave you alone from now on." He hung up, and I never heard from him again.

A few years ago, I got some massive heat with a very different flag. I was booked as an Italian up in Cleveland with Guido as my partner in a tag team tournament. They advertised us as the Full Blooded Italians, but instead of coming out with my FBI shirt, I wore a Chicago Cubs jersey and carried the "W" flag. This was right after the Cubs had broken the curse by winning the World Series after a hard-fought seven games with the Cleveland Indians. Ask anyone who was there that night, they'll tell you I got more heat flying the "W" flag than I do with the Confederate flag.

The Cubs flag wasn't my idea. It was Chandler Biggins, the same guy who had me wear the Lebron shirt. Chandler was a wonderful man who, sadly, died of a flesh eating virus. He was a big guy when I knew him, and he wasted away almost 200 pounds before he passed. Horrible way to go. God rest his soul.

Jason Flener, Long time fan

I am pretty sure I've seen Tracy Smothers wrestle live more than any other wrestler, going all the way back to the Louisville Gardens days when I was a kid. Tracy can do no wrong. I do not care if he's the heel or not. I am going to cheer for him.

I was at a show in New Albany, Indiana a few years ago with a few friends, and Tracy came out doing his heel act. Everyone was chanting, "Tracy sucks!" except us. Tracy cut his usual promo on the crowd and how much he hated us and Indiana. Everyone booed him except us. We continued to cheer because as I said, Tracy can do no wrong.

Tracy finally came over to our side of the ring, leaned over the ropes and broke character for just a second. "Hey fellas, you need to cut that out. I'm trying to make a living here!"

Jim Finney

The first time I had to ref one of Tracy's matches - oh my lands. As a referee I'm supposed to stay neutral, which means I not only couldn't take sides but I couldn't laugh. I was pulled aside before the match in the back by one of the other guys who told me, "This is a Tracy Smothers match. He's going to make you laugh." I was determined to prove him wrong.

Tracy was working with one of the local guys who was about 350 pounds. He went into the dance off, and Tracy started doing a bunch of moves he knew the other guy couldn't do, including some push-ups. Tracy has a hard enough time just walking around the ring, and his knees were wobbling and shaking, but he still didn't hold back. After about a minute or two, I had to step off to the side and hide my face because I couldn't help but laugh. "Wow," I thought to myself. "This is a Tracy Smothers match."

Tracy Smothers

When you get to be my age, there are things you can't do in the ring like you used to. People who have seen me arriving at a show or walk around at a fan fest know I don't get around as good as I used to. I do a lot of DDP Yoga just to go out and work the match. I'll take some bumps when I'm out there, but while I can't work as hard as I used to, I've learned to work smarter.

Besides my mic work, which doesn't require any movement or taking bumps, I've made the dance contest a regular part of my repertoire. As a gesture of compassion to my opponents, I'll call for the microphone and give them the chance to take me on in a dance contest rather than have me whip their ass at wrestling. Whoever wins the dance contest wins the match. The dance contest idea goes back to Tommy Dreamer at ECW, but all my dance moves come from the Armstrongs, Bob and Steve.

I always go first, and my song of choice is the N-Trance rap version of "Staying Alive." I'll shuffle my feet around and dance around for a bit, and then I offer the babyface a chance to strut his stuff. They always pick their own music, but the ending is the same. Midway through their dance segment, which the fans eat up, I'll jump them to get the heat on them.

The crowd always loves the dance contest, and it's fun watching everyone in the ring try to keep a straight face. Sometimes the unexpected happens, too. One time at Destination One Wrestling in New Albany, I did the dance contest with another veteran named Apollo Garvin. Apollo had recently turned babyface after working along side me for several months, and he was starting to get over with the fans. He had once worked as a male stripper, and he chose Tom Jones' "It's Not Unusual" as his song. He started doing the Carlton dance that Alphonso Ribeiro created on *The Fresh Prince of Bel Air*, and it got over huge. Next thing you knew, "It's Not Unusual" became Apollo's entrance music. He wore a sweater vest as he danced to the ring.

One thing younger wrestlers have to learn is to work smarter, not harder. When you've taken as many bumps as I have, anything you can do to lessen the impact in the ring is a good idea. It's a lot easier on my joints and bones to shake and shimmy to "Stayin' Alive" than it is to bump and run for a full ten minutes a night. It also entertains the fans, which is the whole purpose anyway.

One other gimmick I picked up was my helicopter. I don't recall exactly how or when it started, but one night, I was working the crowd and told them that if they didn't shut up, I was going to get back in my helicopter and leave without wrestling. It got over big with the fans, so I started taking my "helicopter" to every show from then on. It wasn't Austin 3:16, but it got some heat!

DESTINATION ONE

In 2011 I got burned out on the business. As much fun as I was having working with Jessie and Mickie, I was just exhausted. I only took a few bookings in 2011, and I didn't take any in 2012.

In 2013 I got back into it, working a few dates for the Clowns. Joey Grunge called me and started booking me for his company, Midwest Impact Pro Wrestling. Then I got a call from a man named Rick Brady.

Rick was part of a promotion based in Charlestown, Indiana called D1W: Destination One Wrestling along with Tim Denison and Ron Aslam. Rick had started out as a manager for IWA Mid-South in the late 1990s. What started out as a one off booking became a long run with a lot of big names and new names who became big stars. Destination One was once home to WWE's Sarah Logan and Impact's Jake and Dave Crist. It's also a place that helped me rediscover my love for the wrestling business.

Rick Brady

I first met Tracy was at IWA Mid-South, probably 1998. I was just starting out in the business as a manager back then. I would go on to manage with him, manage against him, wrestle with and against him, and work with him as a promoter.

I'll never forget the first night I met Tracy. It was an evening they called The Night the Rats Cried. Tracy was working with Suicide Kid. There were some girls in the crowd who yelled, "Tracy, he's not hardcore!" Tracy smacked Kid with a steel chair and said, "He's hardcore now!"

When I started booking Destination One Wrestling in Southern Indiana, Tracy was the first real name wrestler we used on a regular basis. We had brought a few names before him, but Tracy became a regular from the time he came into D1W until we closed shop. I can't tell you how many times he won and lost the title belt. Tracy always gave everyone a great match, and he never complained when it was time to drop the belt.

I had lost touch with Tracy after those early days at IWA Mid-

South. Then around 2011 I ran into him at the Evansville Coliseum. I was going to go up and reintroduce myself, but he came to me first. "Hey, Rick, how you doing? Good to see you." I was blown away that he remembered me, considering I was just a pissant manager the last time we'd met, but that's just the kind of guy Tracy is.

I had a few big names come in to work for us who would try to get away with doing as little as possible. I never had that issue with Tracy. He never sandbagged it, never phoned it in.

One time we brought in a Hall of Famer to wrestle Tracy for the D1W Championship. The crowd was a lot smaller that evening than we would have liked, and when the Hall of Famer saw the crowd, he told us he wasn't going to do any of the high spots he was famous for.

Tracy looked him straight in the eye and said, "So you're only going to do half your moves? I guess that means you're going to give half your money back. If you want 100% of your money, you better give 100% effort." We ended up changing the match to a six man tag instead of the one on one battle, and the guy went out for twenty minutes. If it wasn't for Tracy, though, we would have only got a half effort.

Tracy helped me to weather a lot of storms on social media during those days. I can't tell you how many promotions took shots at us online, trying to tear us down. I'd get all worked up, and Tracy would get me straight. "Focus on D1," he said. "Don't let them get to you." He was right.

I can't tell you how many nights I'd get a call late at night from Tracy. He was always wound up, and I would just sit and listen. He might have been ranting about something, but I considered it gaining wisdom. If he was ranting about something in wrestling, it's because he knew there was a better way. It was always an education.

My favorite match of all time was Tracy Smothers versus Brian Christopher for D1W in Charlestown, Indiana. What made the match so memorable was something that went wrong that Tracy and Brian turned into something special. Tracy had a chain in his tights that he often used to choke his opponents. That was the plan in Charlestown, but on that evening, the chain slipped around in Tracy's tights, and it looked like Tracy had shit his pants.

Instead of Tracy moving and adjusting the chain, they went with it. He and Brian worked the rest of the match playing up the idea that Tracy had shit his pants! Brian kept pushing Tracy on his ass, rubbing his ass on the ring, and Tracy selling it like he was rolling around with shit in his pants. There were no high spots or flippy-flippy moves or blood and brawling; it was just ten minutes of pure entertainment for the fans.

Tracy Smothers

I got to work with a lot of big top guys at D1W, like Brian Christopher, Tito Santana, Mad Man Pondo, and Tommy Dreamer. I also got to work with a lot of younger guys. Between them and the other promotions, I was wrestling about four times a month while working my job at Sandy's. I'd have Mae Belle, Jessie Belle, or Isabelle Smothers, whomever was available, with me whenever I could get them.

Mad Man Pondo

One night at D1W, they had a raffle, and they picked ten fans to stand around the ring for a lumberjack strap match. The fans who won took off their belts or were given belts, and they were allowed to whip the wrestlers if they rolled out of the ring during the match.

Tracy was working heel in the match, and we had both heel and babyface wrestlers around the ring. The plan was any time Tracy rolled out of the ring, he was supposed to come out where the babyfaces were so we could go easy on him. Tracy didn't do that. He kept rolling out on the side with the fans. The fans beat the shit out of him, and I tried to tell him, "Tracy, don't go over there. Come over to our side." He wouldn't listen. The fans had paid for the tickets, and he was giving them their money's worth.

Rick Brady

Near the end of the D1W run, we had some terrible storms in the Louisville area. My house was flooded, and I lost nearly everything, including a priceless collection of sports cards that were completely ruined. Some of the wrestlers agreed to put on a benefit show for me, and Tracy called asking to be a part of it.

I paid all the wrestlers who worked that night, but when I went to give Tracy his money, he refused to take it.

"At least let me give you gas money," I said.

"No," he said. "But God's given me something to give to you."

Tracy pulled me aside and handed me a hundred dollars. "I know you need it," he said. "You would take it from a fan, so take it from a friend."

A few years after D1W closed shop, Tracy returned to IWA Mid-South to do an unforgettable angle. Even though IWA Mid-South had been where I started, they were D1W's top rival when we were in business. That made me public enemy number one to many of their fans. The fans were thrilled Tracy had come back into the fold, and he was challenging for the IWA Mid-South Heavyweight Championship.

During the match the lights went off. When they came back on, a masked man was standing on the outside ring apron. JJ Garrett grabbed the masked man and ripped off the mask. Twenty years after I left, it was me, standing in an IWA Mid-South ring.

The crowd was shocked. All you heard was one guy yell, "Rick Brady." During the distraction, Tracy used his stick to wipe out Garrett and win the belt. Tracy got on the mic and declared, "This is no longer the IWA Mid-South title. This is the D1W title!"

What happened next surprised even me. Tracy got the fans so angry that they rioted. They chased Tracy and me out of the building. This wasn't 1985, mind you, but 2018.

We had a fun invasion angle at IWA Mid-South over the next few months that included reprinting and selling the old D1W T-shirts and me actually winning "control" of IWA Mid-South and it turned into a launching pad to bigger things for many of them. In the end, Ian Rotten won out, and D1W was finished for good.

On the last IWA show that I worked, the final night of my career in wrestling ended with me carrying Tracy's bags to his car. I can think of no better way to call it a career than carrying a legend's bag.

Tracy was starting to wind down his career at that time, and he had plans to hang up the boots for good. Tracy told me that we helped to revitalize his love for the business and keep him going. I'm very proud of that.

Left: Future star Billie Starkz.
Below: ASW promoter Gary Damron.

Above: With Mick Foley and Ricky Morton. Below: At Heroes and Legends in Fort Wayne. Photo courtesy of Ed Pilipow.

Battling Brian Christopher (above) and Mad Man Pondo (below) at D1W. Photos courtesy of Michael Herm.

Photos courtesy of Kenneth Coker.

Facing off with AEW's Marko Stunt. Photo courtesy of Amazing Maria.

Khloe Belle Smothers.

Above: With Mary Belle Smothers (Amazing Maria), Madi Maxx, and Jessie Belle Smothers. Photo courtesy of Amazing Maria. Below: Isabelle Smothers (Mickie Knuckles), Mae Belle Smothers (Lovely Lylah), and Jessie Belle. Photo courtesy of Jessie Belle.

Dancing with Jessie Belle. Photo courtesy of Pamela Barnett.

AIRPORTS ARE WORK

I'll tell you one thing that is work these days like wrestling used to be - the airport! Not too long ago, I boarded a plane in Louisville bound for Newark for a fan convention. We boarded the plane and sat at the gate for about forty minutes, roasting in this hot plane with no air. People were starting to trip out because some of them had connecting flights and others were just mad about their vacation getting delayed.

Someone finally came on the intercom and said, "We apologize for the delay. We are experiencing trouble with one of the engines. We're going to ask everyone to deplane while we make repairs."

We all got back off the plane, and the maintenance crew moved in. They backed the plane away from the gate and went to work on the engine. An hour later, they moved the plane back up to the gate, and we boarded the plane again.

As soon as everyone was seated and situated, the power went out on the plane. Now people were starting to worry, thinking this is not a good omen! They got back on the intercom and said that we were going to be delayed a little longer. We deplaned again, and finally, about three and a half hours before we were to leave, we took off for Newark.

The convention I was attending ran from 10 am to 2 pm. It was about 12:30 before I finally arrived. Guido was at my table already because we were signing as the FBI. Guido started signing while our vendor host Nicholas kept in touch with me by phone. Everything worked out for the fan fest, and we made sure no one went away disappointed.

My friend Nicholas booked me at the fan fest and took great care of me while I was there, but then it was back to the airport to fly home. I got there early to check in, like they told me, and I stopped to get something to eat and drink. Now here's where the airport really becomes work.

First of all, I had to check my bag, which costs $25. The airline would not accept cash as payment, and I had forgotten my debit card. I asked what I had to do, and they directed me to a vending machine to buy a reloadable card. Of course that $25 card cost me $30, because the credit card company and the government and whomever else has to get their cut. I paid $30 for that card, spent the $25 for the bag check, and got an empty card as a souvenir.

Next I had to go through airport security. I had a small carry-on bag with me with my wrestling gear and a few items inside including a shaving kit, an orange, and some organic peanut butter. They pulled my bag after the scanner, and the guy pulled my peanut butter out.

He said, "Sorry, this can't go."

"Man, that's organic peanut butter," I said. "That costs $10!"

I almost said, "I think the razor you left alone is more dangerous than that peanut butter!" I thought better of it. Last thing I needed was to be arrested at the Newark airport over $10 worth of peanut butter. Those guys are doing their job, and they do good work, but you don't joke around with them, man.

I had already made a joke with that same guy when he saw the Rebel flag in my gear bag. He wasn't too happy about it, and when he looked up at me, I said, "I'm an Indian. I hate 'em worse than you do." I don't know if he believed me, but I'm pretty sure he didn't think it was funny. Maybe that's why he took my peanut butter.

Sadly, this was the second time I had peanut butter confiscated at the airport. A few weeks earlier on a trip to Toronto, I had an orange in my bag that was confiscated. You read that right: I had to leave my orange because they wouldn't allow me to bring citrus into Canada.

Things really get bad once you get past security. There's no going back at that point, and the airport knows you're going to shop, so all the prices are jacked up. Here are a few figures I jotted down:

One beer costs $9.10.

A glass of wine was $12, and a refill was $7.

A bowl of soup was $10.

A salad cost $20!

A regular bottle of water was $8.

I had two beers and a shot. With tax, it came to $32.64. Of course the bar didn't accept cash either, but I talked to a few customers who were willing it put my drinks on their cards while I paid them in cash.

I ended up spending another few bucks for a ride to my gate. One of the airport guys with those electric carts saw how I was walking and offered me a ride. I told him I was okay, but he kept after me and insisted. He was a nice guy, and the ride was free, but I tipped him $5.

"Thanks, Mr. Smothers," he said, "You made my day."

I laughed and said, "I guess I did. You made five dollars only and drove me fifty feet!"

Here's another thing. They can change the gate for your flight and only say it once on the intercom. If you miss the announcement because you're in a noisy bar or talking, you will pay the price if you miss your flight! Doesn't matter if it's another gate or another concourse. This didn't happen to me, but it did happen to Ricky Steamboat flying to Fort Wayne, Indiana for a Heroes and Legends show. His flight to Fort Wayne was delayed, and they made only one announcement abut changing the gate. He ended up having to rent a car and drive from Pittsburgh to Fort Wayne, which meant he had to pay an extra drop fee for the one way trip in the car.

When the plane finally arrived at the gate, a weary looking pilot got off. "We just sat in Indianapolis for four hours and didn't move." So of course the flight was delayed taking off for home. This was early June, so it was vacation time. All the flights were full, and just about every one of them was delayed.

Once I arrived back in Louisville, I had to walk a mile or so to my car and drive home. It was 4:30 am when I finally walked in the door at home. Just because I was curious, I looked online to see how long it would have taken me to drive home. If I had left right after the convention and driven straight home, I would have arrived home at 1 am. It took me an extra three and a half hours to get home because I flew.

This is why I have a helicopter.

D1W was a great place to work, but like so many promotions do, they fell apart. They lost their building in New Albany and some of their key stars, and they just never recovered. I was lucky to have my full-time job still with Spanky's Pizza, and I continued working wrestling shows wherever I could.

I did a few shows for Mark Anthony, including one where I worked Bill Dundee. Cody Hall, Scott Hall's son, was on that show, and Scott and Kevin Nash made an appearance as well. A year later I worked another one for Mark with Shawn Schultz, Al Snow, Ricky Morton, Rob Conway, and X-Pac, who had just come off his WrestleMania appearance with NWO vs. DX, and he sold that place out.

In 2015 I did a show for Jerry Blaylock where I dressed up like a woman. I came out in drag and hit the ring, attacking Jerry Lawler and Bill Dundee and laying them out on the mat. He then booked me in a return match where I wrestled against them in a casino.

Charlene Mcanally

I worked an intergender match one night between Tracy Smothers and Leva Bates for Terry Harper in Jeffersonville, Indiana. Leva is from Kentucky, and any time she was in the area, her family came up to watch her. They were front row that night, and Tracy had Kyle Maverick outside the ring as his second, holding that tree branch he sometimes carries to the ring.

Tracy got the crowd worked up before the match like he always does, and he especially went after Leva's mom and the rest of the family. One of the things he does when he has someone at ringside is distract the ref while the guy or girl outside chokes his opponent. Sometimes they use the ropes, sometimes a chain, sometimes - a tree branch. Tracy distracted the ref, and Kyle grabbed Leva's head to choke her.

Leva's mom wasn't having it that night. She jumped over the barrier, which was just a rope, and went after Kyle. Kyle is a legitimate MMA fighter, but he kept his cool and tried to fend her off. Tracy was a different story. He was furious with Leva's mom, and he lit into her. It was a bit awkward, and Leva's mom was pretty embarrassed by it later on, but looking back, it's pretty funny.

Tracy Smothers

I worked on the very first show for Tried and True Wrestling in Tennessee. Crimson worked Eric Young, Chase Stevens worked Chris Michaels, and I worked in a tag team with Jeremiah Plunkett. They're still going, both putting on shows and training aspiring wrestlers.

Billy Corgan of the Smashing Pumpkins got into the wrestling business up in Chicago with a company called Resistance Pro Wrestling. Billy booked me to work for him a few times along with people like Mad Man Pondo, Sugar Dunkerton, Shane Mercer, and Crazy Mary Dobson.

I did a big show in Jackson, Mississippi in a rodeo rink. Austin Idol was there, along with the Barbarian, Shane Andrews, and "The Nature Boy" Paul Lee. We drew really well at that show.

In 2016 I found out that Chase Stevens had started running shows in my hometown of Springfield, Tennessee. I messaged him and asked if I could come down and work for him. I came to find out Chase had put together a nice little loop of towns, and he offered to put me on it. "Great!" I said.

Wolfie D was booking for Chase, and at first he only wanted me to manage. I wanted to wrestle, so Wolfie worked me in as a wrestler.

The loop was Thursday through Sunday, including Springfield, Murfreesboro, Manchester, Ashland City, and Knoxville. Chase paid me well, and he put together a solid crew including Wes Brisco, Bruce Santay, Damian Wayne, Chris Michaels, Gangrel, Micah Taylor, Tracy Taylor, Rebel, Francisco Ciatso, Stormie Lee, Eric Wayne, Derrick King, and Shane Williams.

Bruce was a big guy, about 6'5" who supposedly got the better of Vader in a fist fight somewhere. Chase and Wes put on some classic matches, and Gangrel was just a hell of a worker for them.

One night in Fairview, Tennessee, we got some serious heat. Derrick King, who is African American, worked against Wolfie D, and Derrick shocked the fans by coming out with the rebel flag gimmick.

Derrick hung Wolfie with the rebel flag, and the people were so mad seeing Derrick waving the rebel blag, they kicked us out and told us never to come back!

We drew really well, and Chase put together some great cards. We had really good promotion at first, but the guy who was supposed to hang posters for us stopped doing it. The lack of promotion hurt us because people didn't know we were there. If we'd had better promotion, whether it was posters or even radio, we might have lasted longer. There was some drama in the office as well, and it ran its course in only six months.

I was still working my job full time while wrestling 15 to 20 days a month. I was worn out, but it was good money, and I had a lot of fun.

In 2016 I was booked to work New Jack in a hardcore match in Pigeon Forge, Tennessee. I had some car trouble getting down there because the fan wasn't working, so I was late getting to the show. As I was putting on my gear, the promoters came over and told me New Jack wasn't there. Instead, I would be working with Tank.

I had no problem at all with the change of plans. Unfortunately for us, nobody told the fans, who were expecting to see New Jack, so I wanted to go extra hard to make it up to the fans and get Tank over as a babyface. They had filled the ring with glass and all sorts of stuff, but Tank and I didn't even get in the ring. We just fought outside the ring.

Someone had put a boat paddle at ringside, and when I saw it, I told Tank, "Hit me on the side of the head that doesn't have thumbtacks."

I called the spot, and I have no one to blame but myself for what happened next. Tank swung the paddle like an ax and hit me so hard, it about knocked me out. It hurt so bad, and I went down to my knees. Tank followed up and hit me in the back, but I didn't even feel it.

You probably already guessed it, but I had another concussion. I stayed over at a friend's house that night. I wasn't feeling right, but I ate some dinner and drank a few beers.

I was still feeling bad the next day, but I decided to drive home. I grabbed some McDonalds on the way, and about two miles from home, I pulled the car over and threw up like crazy.

I honestly thought it was the McDonalds food that made me sick. The next day I ate a small piece of garlic bread, and I fell over, having suffered a mini-stroke. I got sick again, feeling like I was going to pass out. I went home after my shift and threw up again. I was messed up for a while with that injury, but dummy that I am, I kept going. The day after the mini-stroke was a Friday. I drove seven hours to Cleveland to work for Chandler Biggins, and turned around on Saturday to drive down and wrestle in Chattanooga by myself. That really did me in.

I finally shut it down and took some time off at the holidays in 2016, but before I did that, I worked a great match at IWA Mid-South on Thanksgiving night. Ian Rotten put me in the ring with Chris Hero, before he went back to WWE. Chris uses a lot of forearm smashes and that big boot, moves that are rough when you don't have a head injury. I didn't need to be out of the house that night, but I wasn't about to do anything half way, so you can imagine how tough that was.

In late January 2017 I got back in the ring for Frank Rodriguez in Chicago with a former police officer. He was about 40 and just starting to work as a trainer for the police department. I wasn't in the best shape back then, but we managed to have a pretty good match. I really wasn't looking to get back in the ring, but Frank had a good crew, and we had such a blast, it got me fired up again.

I went back to wrestling two to four times a week. Joey Grunge with Midwest Impact Pro Wrestling had been booking me once a month since 2013, and in 2017, he had a brainstorm. He had been using me a lot to teach seminars over the years, and in the spring he founded the School of Smothers. Joey ran about 200 shows over the next two years, and I was there almost every week.

What I liked about that situation was I could pull in Friday night at the building, teach a seminar before the show, teach another seminar Saturday morning before the show, and teach one more on Sunday. I was there from Friday at 6 pm to Sunday 6 pm with no extra travel in between.

Joey had a nice mini performance center set up with a lot of workout equipment and a big screen TV. The local police loved to stop by and workout with Joey's equipment. He brought in guys like Jerry Lynn and Bobby Eaton on special shows, and one time we raised about $3,000 for a girl who had cancer. Guys would bring their air mattresses and stay the whole weekend.

One of the guys I trained was a former soldier named Matt Harmon. While he was in the Army, Matt served for three months and three weeks in the combat zone in Syria. He thought he was headed back home and was put on an airplane headed West. The plane stopped in Germany, and they put Matt and his fellow soldiers on another plane headed to Afghanistan. He spent the next six months in another combat zone before he ever got to go home. Matt said he might have had three weeks sleep total during those ten months. He suffered some PTSD, but he was a natural in the ring who trained hard.

Matt was a bit standoffish with me for a while, but he warmed up to me. We became good friends and still stay in touch.

Joey brought in Shane Andrews, Chase Stevens, Jessie Belle, and a lot of other people who helped work with the trainees. We ran the school like a TV promotion, and we used that big screen TV to play back and critique matches. We taught our guys to call it in the ring and work on the fly.

The name on the outside might have been School of Smothers, but it was really Joey's deal. He's a great trainer, and he's expanded even more since 2017. We drew pretty well for working the same area all the time. He had some fantastic students who were just great in the ring.

We had some locals that were threatening Joey and the rest of us on social media who didn't want us there. I got on social media and challenged them to a fight. Not a wrestling match, but a real fight. I told them to come on down any night, and we'd fight.

That challenge drew money! We had a lot of people showing up hoping to see me take someone on in a real fight at the arena. I was prepared to fight, especially one guy who kept running his mouth, but of course he never showed up despite all his threats.

We had some WWE trolls threatening us online as well. Some of our guys started responding to them online. Johnny Richards went online and would poke the bear, posting things like, "Triple H fears Johnny 'By God' Richards." Next thing we knew, they were running NXT house shows, Raw house shows, Raw TV tapings, and other shows in our area. We told Johnny he needed to back off because they were trying to hurt our business.

One of the young stars Joey and I brought in was a high school student named Corey Storm. Corey was probably only fifteen when he worked for us the first time, but he is a natural in the ring. Corey turned eighteen just as we were starting to do weekly phone interviews for this book, and just a few days prior to writing this chapter, Corey had his debut for WWE on 205 Live with the Singh Brothers.

Alice Crowley came in to work for us when she was just thirteen. She trained with Randi West of the Bomb Shelter, who also worked for us, and Alice was just great. She's already carried the Women's Championship title for IWA Mid-South, and she's still only in high school as of this writing.

Tootie Lynn Ramsey, Rayne Victoria, and Savannah Stone came in to train with us and work on our shows. During out training classes, I'd put them in the ring with each other and also with the guys, just to call a match on the fly. They all learned a lot, and they've all moved on to great things.

One night I got in some trouble on the road. After working a show at the Nashville Fairgrounds, I dropped Doug Gilbert off at his hotel and got on the road to Peoria. It was late at night, and I was very tired. I took a short nap and got back on the road, knowing I really should have slept longer. I started weaving all over the road while trying to read directions on my GPS, and I was pulled over by the police. Without getting into detail, I got into some trouble from the traffic stop. Fortunately, I had a friend who was able to help.

One of the best things to come out of my time with D1W was my friendship with Tim Denison. Tim and Ron Aslam were both attorneys, and Tim put himself on the map back in the early 1990s when he represented "The Teflon King" Jerry Lawler during some legal troubles.

I reached out to Tim, and he was more than glad to help me out. He didn't charge me for his services, and the two of us became good friends. I told Tim I wanted to start taking him on the road with me. He had created an attorney manager gimmick at D1W, and I started using him every time I could.

Tim and I got a lot of heat with him as my manager. He would rail on the fans in Peoria, telling them all their public officials had been locked up (right after the governor of Illinois had actually been locked up) and threatening to issue warrants on the fans.

Tim is a very successful defense attorney in Louisville. He

doesn't need the work, but he loves it, and it gives me a lot of joy to see how much fun he has when we're working together.

Tim is also the guy who convinced me to finally write a book. He introduced me to John Cosper at IHOP in Clarksville, Indiana back in 2018. Without Tim, you wouldn't be reading this book right now.

I had a falling out at Sandy's Pizza in the fall of 2018. I had been there quite a long time, and I knew it was time to leave. I got a job with some great benefits working maintenance at a Flying J travel stop. I was starting to feel sick back then, experiencing a lot of stomach pain, but I thought it was just ulcers. Little did I know it was the beginning of something serious.

In the spring of 2019, I worked a memorable angle with Bobby Fulton in West Virginia working for Gary Damron at ASW in the spring of 2019. Bobby was being inducted into the ASW Hall of Fame, and I came out and interrupted him. Bobby had been working an angle Jim Cornette suggested where he was having trouble with his eye. I asked him which one was the bad one, and when he pointed to it, I poked him right in the eye.

You talk about heat! The people went crazy. I yelled out, "Who sucks now?" Bobby hit me, and then I hit him in the eye. I then took his Hall of Fame plaque and broke it over his head.

I stirred up some more heat on a Game Changer Wrestling show in Nashville with Joey Janela, but this time it wasn't totally intentional.

Jim Cornette had been saying a lot of things about Joey on his podcast, and that night, Joey got into the ring and trashed Cornette, leading the crowd in a, "Fuck Cornette!" chant. Me being the heel that night, I saw an opportunity. I decided to play off his promo to get some heat.

I wanted to let Joey know I was going to do that so he could play off me in return. Joey was working commentary at ringside, so I tried to send word to him what I was going to do. Unfortunately, the word never got to Joey.

I started chanting Jim Cornette's name for starters, and then I started ragging on Joey about the incident with him and Enzo Amore, where the two of them nearly came to blows at a Blink 182 concert. Not knowing I was working, Joey got angry. He got in the ring and responded, "I'm gonna find your daughter, and I'm gonna fuck her!

Then when you're dead in two years, I'm gonna come piss on your grave!"

When he said that, I wanted to beat his mother fucking ass. I didn't, because I knew what had happened. I knew those guys didn't smarten him up like I asked them to do! It was hard not stomping his ass right there in the ring, but I held back and played it off.

I tried to talk to Joey after the show. I could tell he wanted to talk, but he was busy so I just went on. Jessie Belle caught me as I was leaving and told me Joey had loved what I had done in the ring. I told her I didn't like what he had said. She didn't either, but we both knew it was just business.

The next day Nate Webb called me three times. "Joey wanted to tell you he liked what you did and he didn't mean what he said."

"He never should have said it," I said. "And it's because you didn't smarten him up. Don't ever let that happen again."

Tim Denison and I worked a show in Ohio on Thanksgiving night in 2019 while on our way to WrestleCade. This was the weekend when fans started to take notice that I had lost a lot of weight, leading to my cancer announcement on December 17. I wasn't wrestling, but they put me at ringside managing along with Tim. Tim really gets some nuclear heat with his lawyer gimmick. I mean, who doesn't want to hate a lawyer?

"IN THIS CORNER... CANCER"

It was December 17, 2019 when I finally posted an announcement on Facebook about my illness. I had been diagnosed with cancer in September and started treatment in October.

I didn't want to put the word out on social media because I didn't want to deal with all the fuss. I know people mean well, but a lot of them share these kinds of things and make it all about them.

I knew cancer was going to be tough, but I didn't look at this as something that would end my life. This was like a tune up, an oil change, a repair job to set me up for the rest of my life. As it turned out, I nearly died a few times during treatment, not from the cancer but the side effects of the medicines!

The thing that wears you out when you're fighting cancer is not the tumor. It's everything else that hits you when your body is weak. Your immune system goes down, and you end up fighting all sorts of other problems. I picked up a respiratory infection that just wouldn't quit.

I lost fifty pounds in two months, and of course my hair started coming out. I kept all the scheduled appearances I could, but I didn't get in the ring. I just worked ringside and did meet and greets.

John and I worked on the book every week during those early days of treatment. Sometimes I was in the hospital and feeling great, hopped up on the drugs they gave me when I was doing the chemo treatments. Sometimes I could barely speak from whatever respiratory illness had jumped me when my immune system was down. Some nights we did two hours. Some nights I could barely last twenty minutes. All the while, we kept it quiet.

When I attended Wrestlecade Thanksgiving weekend, less than two months into treatment, people started to take notice. Some people were posting photos on social media asking, "What's the matter with Tracy Smothers? Is he sick? Is he dying?" Two weeks later I worked a tribute show for Bobby Eaton and saw a lot of guys I had known for decades. They were all asking about my health, and I knew then I couldn't keep the cat in the bag much longer.

Jim Cornette

I had no idea Tracy was battling cancer until I saw him at a show in November 2019. He had lost a ton of weight, and he was wearing a toboggan on his head. He said, "Jim, look!" He ripped off the toboggan to reveal a completely bald head and said, "Stone Cold Smothers." Cancer had not taken his sense of humor!

Tracy Smothers

I knew when word got out I was sick, it would blow up, and that's exactly what happened. My phone lit up with calls and texts and Facebook messages. I was in the hospital hooked up to the machines doing the third of my chemo treatments at the time, and I got blown up just trying to respond to all the well wishes I was receiving.

A lot of old friends stepped up to help raise money for my medical bills, either by hosting or working on benefit shows for me. Al Snow called to wish me well and offered to reprint my Thug T-shirt through his company, Collar X Elbow. Ian Rotten called and talked to me for about an hour one night. CM Punk texted me to wish me well. I thanked him for wearing my "Everybody Dies" T-shirt, which got me a bunch of sales. Again, it was always just so overwhelming to see the support that I had.

Bert Prentice brought me in to do a benefit show down in Tennessee. Not only did Jerry Lawler and Bill Dundee agree to work the show, I got to see someone I hadn't seen in a long time: Terry Golden. Terry came up, gave me a hug, saying, "You know I love you, right?" He handed me a check, "Use it however you need." I can't begin to say how much I appreciated his generosity.

I never asked anyone to put on any benefit shows. All I did was confirm that yes, I had cancer. A lot of people stepped up to help me because of the help I've given to those people over the years. All I can say to them is I love you and thank you.

John Cosper

Tracy and I met for the first time in the summer of 2018, when Tim Denison arranged a meeting at IHOP to discuss writing this book. Tim had been urging Tracy to do a book for some time, and as you can tell by all you have read, Tracy had a lot to say. I had just released Mad

Man Pondo's book and was in deep research mode on *The Original Black Panther*, but Tracy was in no hurry to get started. In the spring of 2019 I began doing some initial work on this book, and when we crossed paths here and there, I would give Tracy updates.

By late summer of 2019 Tracy was ready. We were both scheduled to be at Kentucky Zone Wrestling in Somerset, Kentucky in September, and we decided to kickstart the book there with an in-person interview. Prior to that initial face-to-face, Tracy found out he had been booked for the biggest match of his life. His doctor informed him he had stomach cancer.

Tracy faced the news with the same grit and resolve he had faced every fight and every challenge in his life. This wasn't a bad night in WCW of WWF, when he could say the heck with it, pack his bag and go home. Like many of the brawls he has experienced in his life, this was not a fight he chose, but it was a fight he refused to lose.

Between our first face-to-face in Somerset and our next in-person meeting at Heroes and Legends Wrestling in Fort Wayne, Indiana on October 5, Tracy was put through a number of scans and tests to see how bad the situation was. We began our bi-weekly phone calls in earnest, every Tuesday and Thursday, and Tracy began to unfold the stories now packed into the pages of the book in your hands.

It was right after Fort Wayne that the fight really began. The initial rounds of chemotherapy proved to be brutal. Tracy gutted through those sessions as best as he could, but they took a heavy toll on his body. The energy and enthusiasm Tracy normally had for telling stories was zapped, and our phone calls became a bit shorter.

One Tuesday night in October, we called it quits just a few minutes into the call. Tracy sounded tired and sickly on the call, and I told him to get some rest. Shortly after we hung up, he collapsed. It was serendipity that his girlfriend Rachelle was nearby and able to help him get to the hospital. Cancer had him on the mat, but miraculously, he kicked out that night.

That was only the first time Tracy nearly lost his battle with cancer. He would spend the next week in the hospital, and he nearly tapped out twice during that time. It was another week before doctors had him stabilized and on the right medicines that he started feeling energy again. Tracy made a big time come back, and he let me know he was ready to keep going.

Our next several phone calls took place during his nightly chemo treatments. The audio recordings of these calls, filled with stories about WCW and Smoky Mountain, are peppered with small talk between Tracy and his medical staff. I can assure you that as rough as he felt at times, he was always a gentleman and a model patient, polite and gracious with the folks helping him battle cancer.

Although Tuesday and Thursday continued to be the goal, there were weeks when health forced us to switch nights. There were also weeks he was feeling so good, we'd talk three or four times, sometimes as long as two hours. We made contact whenever he felt well, and I would stockpile audio recordings to transcribe for the days when he wasn't feeling great. He was wired on nights when they put him on steroids, and he was completely checked out those few nights they gave him Benadryl.

Tracy could have wiped his schedule clear to stay home and focus on his bout with cancer, but that's not who he is. In all that time, in and out of the hospital, only once do I recall him canceling an appearance, a return engagement at KZW in Somerset. The Tuesday before Thanksgiving he told me he was celebrating the holiday Wednesday night with his girlfriend's family, driving to Louisville on Thursday to pick up Tim Denison before driving on to Columbus for an appearance that night. They were then headed to North Carolina for two full days of meet and greets at Wrestlecade. "You oughta come along with us!" he said.

Tracy's body struggled to keep up with his heart, and he got pretty sick after the road trip. The audio file from that first Tuesday in December is pretty hard to hear, with his voice nearly gone, but he had no regrets about going. Cancer picked the fight, but cancer was going to have to fight on Tracy Smothers' terms. Maybe he would go down, like he once feared he would against Ken Shamrock, but if he did, he would go down swinging.

Writing his memoir gave Tracy a reason to fight. It wasn't his only reason, but I could tell it was driving him. If Tracy said, "Let's work tonight," I made sure I was available on his schedule.

I regret to say that I missed seeing Tracy fight in his prime. I was a WWF kid growing up, and I never saw the Wild Eyed Southern Boys, the Young Pistols, or the FBI until long after those days were gone. I can, however, say with absolute confidence I had a ringside seat to the biggest fight of his life. I saw him take everything cancer and chemo had. I watched him get knocked down over and over again. I saw him stand up every damn time and say, "Is that the best you got?"

Tracy Smothers

I've been hospitalized ten times during this ordeal, including six full weeks of chemo treatments. The other four times was because I became terribly ill in between treatments, thanks to a weakened immune system. I've nearly died at least six times, not from the cancer but from the treatment. Sometimes it feels like a lack of care has pushed me to the edge of death.

I've had some good doctors and good nurses, but there have been a few that really just don't care. On the first day of my fifth round of chemo, my stomach was upset. I knew I was headed for some bad diarrhea, and I kept begging the nurses to give me some Imodium before they started treatment. Every time I asked for it, I got the same excuse. "We have to wait for it to come up from pharmacy." I got the feeling the real excuse was, "That's extra work. We don't want to do it." As much as I pleaded with them to dose me before they started the chemo, they never did get that Imodium up from pharmacy. It made for a miserable week.

I would usually lose about ten pounds every week I did chemo and gain it back in the weeks after, but that week I lost thirteen. It was miserable, and it didn't end when I got out at the end of the week. As soon as I was released, I hopped in the car to make a show in Tennessee. I made the show okay, but the diarrhea hit me again on the way home. It happened so fast I had to pull over on the side of I-65 North near Bowling Green and race down a hill. I had an old towel to cover me and then wipe with when I was done. It was cold and miserable. I was back in the hospital just a few days later.

You can tell pretty quickly who the good nurses are. They're the ones that will listen to you and help you and take time with you. Then you get the ones who wake you at 3 am and ask you to swallow a giant fist full of horse pills on an empty stomach. The good nurse will go get you some ice cream or peanut butter to eat with the pills. The frustrating ones won't because that's extra work.

It would be easy to blame it on the newer nurses, who seem to want to play on their phones more than deal with patients, but it's hard to put all the blame on them when they're being paid a third less than the senior staff for doing triple the work. I know I said airports are the biggest work, but hospitals? Everything they do, they charge you for. Every pill, every blood pressure check, it all goes on your bill. They're charging you and your insurance everything they can while paying their staff as little as they can. They cut costs by hiring newer nurses they can pay less and charge you the same amount (or more) for care.

I'm fortunate to have had some good doctors and others who helped along the way. At the end of my fifth hospital stay, I asked for a prescription to keep me from getting sick again. I had one of those "do as little as possible" nurses that day who assures me it would be ready for me and covered by my insurance. The prescription was ready when I got to Walgreens, but I was told it was not covered by insurance!

Frustrated, I explained my whole story to the lady behind the counter. She smiles and said, "We deal with this all the time with that hospital. Let me make some calls." I sat and waited at the pharmacy for two hours, but at the end, I was happy to hear her say, "Mr. Smothers, your insurance covered the prescription." What a relief.

I'm grateful to all the doctors, pharmacists, and yes the nurses who have been helpful, and I am so thankful to all the friends and family who have been there for me. More than anything, though, I'm glad this ordeal is over. Cancer has been the fight of my life. If you were to ask me today if I'd rather fight cancer or three more bears, I'd say, "Bring on the bears!"

FOR "POPS"

John Cosper

I started writing about professional wrestling in 2013 because I was fascinated by its rich history. I kept writing about professional wrestling because I was inspired by the men and women keeping it alive. It was the independent scene that introduced me to people like Mad Man Pondo, Sarah Logan, Aaron Williams, Hy Zaya, Dave and Jake Crist, Ron Mathis, and LuFisto. The heart and the passion and the drive they possess to do what they do week in and week out mirrored my own passion for writing. I found a world of kindred spirits, dreamers who were on a completely different and yet very similar path to my own.

D1W was my favorite promotion in those days, so I saw a lot of Tracy Smothers, and one night in particular stands out in my memory. One of the young heels in an early match made a quick exit, racing up the ramp and flipping the curtain open as he passed through. There was Tracy, sitting in a metal folding chair in just the right spot where he could see all the action.

Tracy wasn't just the old timer, the "name" attraction on the card who would sell tickets. Tracy was Pops. He was the guy who generously poured himself into every kid who wanted to get better. Tracy, I have come to learn, is always positive in his critiques. He focuses on what's good, and offers ideas for improvement in a way that is never harsh or negative. If someone is willing to listen, Tracy is always willing to share his wisdom. It's up to the listener to apply that wisdom, but they know they can tap into the Tracy Smothers learning tree any time.

How influential has Tracy Smothers been to professional wrestling? I'll let his "kids" tell you. There's an army of young men and women, including wrestlers, refs, and promoters, who have been influenced, inspired, and helped by the man. I'll let them speak for themselves.

Mr. Brickster

I grew up in Buffalo, New York during the heyday of ECW, and

Tracy Smothers was one of my favorite guys to watch. My dad took me to wrestling a few times, and I remember Tracy being one of the guys who most inspired me to be a wrestler.

I met Tracy at a show in Jeffersonville, Indiana. I was booked against Teddy King in his retirement match, and I was pleasantly surprised to see Tracy show up that night as well. Tracy worked a match before mine, and he was out at his gimmick table during my match. I went over and introduced myself and asked him what he thought. Tracy was so encouraging, and he really had some good feedback.

I saw Tracy several months later at a show for Capital Wrestling in Nashville, where I now live. I had been out healing an injury for some time at that point, but Tracy had been following me up until my injury. He knew about some of the shows I had worked, and he saw the videos I shot with Cody Rhodes, where I almost became the Librarian for All Elite Wrestling.

Tracy told me he thought I was very close to getting the gig with AEW as the Librarian. He gave me a T-shirt, and he said. "I just want you to know that I believe in you. I think you've got it."

I was going through some really down times, and it was so cool of Tracy to bless me with so much wisdom. "I see you're ready to get back in the ring," he said. "Keep pushing. Keep going. You're going to make it."

Rick Brady

Every time Tracy worked for D1W, Tracy had a chair set up right by the curtain. He watched every single match every single night, and after every show, he would tell me who was putting in the effort and who wasn't worth a shit. Any of the wrestlers who asked for advice got it. He was always positive, always told them what they were doing well and what they could do to get better. I can't tell you how much he cared for those kids and how hard he worked to try to help all of them get better.

Jessie Belle Smothers

I call Tracy "Pops" because he is my wrestling dad. He didn't just help me break into wrestling. He's the one who supported me, encouraged me, and believed in me. I'm not the only one.

Steve C. Branam

I've been in the business for 27 years, and of all the people I've met, Tracy is one of the nicest. True, he's always had that finger ready, looking for an opening to stick it in my ear, but he's always friendly and always comes over to talk to me.

Tracy is always helpful with the young kids who are willing to listen. Any show I've been on with him, he watches all their matches, and he's happy to give advice. Anybody who books him is lucky to have him, because he will do whatever is needed to make it the best show possible.

Jim Finney

The biggest thing I picked up from Tracy was this advice I heard in a seminar: "Basically, every match is a movie. You treat it how you want it. You're as good as the other guy in the ring. Work together and make your own movie."

There's a reason everyone calls him Pops. He treats every guy like a son and every girl like a daughter. Tracy still gets in the ring with kids eighteen and nineteen years old, giving and taking bumps, giving and taking roll ups, doing everything he can to make them better. Tracy has touched so many lives in this business, including mine. He really cares about us, and he is always helpful to everyone.

Charlene Mcanally

I've worked a lot of matches with Tracy. He is always talking, always coaching in the ring. When he's working, I can hear him saying, "Slow down, slow down, okay hold, just a bit longer, now go!" He's so smart at telling a story and building suspense, and everyone who works with him gets a real education in how to put on a great match. I've learned so much working with Tracy.

American Kickboxer

Tracy went out of his way for myself and Tarek when he never really had to. I was a fourteen year old homeless kid at one time, and for one of my heroes like Tracy Smothers to put me over, that was huge. The business is kind of like the mob, and when Tracy gave us his blessing, we were in.

Joel Gertner

Tracy is a prince of a man. He's a man's man and a guy who would always stand up for the boys. He's just a great guy.

Jessie Belle Smothers

It doesn't matter how badly people have fucked him over. Tracy is not one to be vindictive or call people out for what they are. He's such a good person. I honestly would have quit wrestling long before I ever made it to WOW or any of the things I have accomplished if it wasn't for him. He's not my dad, but he is my Dad. He is the only person who ever really supported and encouraged me, and I owe him everything.

Khloe Belle Smothers

One will cut a bitch.

Tracy knows what I mean.

"EVERYBODY DIES!"

People sometimes ask me, "How come you're not as big as this guy or that guy?" It's because I didn't use the steroids or growth hormones the guys on top used. Nothing against those guys. They did what they had to do, but for me it was meat and potatoes and fish. The sad thing is a lot of those guys are dead now, and the substances they used are a big reason why so many died young.

It makes me so sad how many of my old friends are gone. Every time I hear about another one gone, it breaks my heart. A fan once asked me what wrestler's death hurt the most. My answer is, every one of them. Every time someone dies, I find myself not only grieving their death, but reliving my grief of all the other guys who went before them. It seems like every time I get on social media, my timeline reminds me it's the anniversary of another wrestler's death or someone's birthday. Just in the few weeks as we were wrapping up this book, we lost Randy Colley, Charlie Cook, LA Parka II, Kendo Nagasaki, Pampiro Firpo, and Rocky Johnson.

I'm thankful for the years I had in the ring, and I'm thankful every day I wake up still breathing. God took care of me, and I was blessed to make a living doing what I loved for so long.

I was never a top guy. I was never in the main event of a major pay-per-view. I never had a run at the top in a major promotion. I was a utility guy, and I was damn good at it. I knew my role, and because I was happy with who I was, I got to work with a lot of great people in this business.

I used to be able to say without a hint of exaggeration, I've been hired and fired by every major company there is to work for. That's no longer the case, thanks to All Elite Wrestling, but who's to say Cody won't hire and fire me before I'm done?

Even if that doesn't happen, I've been in the biggest companies and worked with the biggest stars the industry has ever seen. I've won dance offs with big stars and rising stars. I've survived riots from Mexico City to the IWA Mid-South warehouse in Charlestown, Indiana that CM Punk once said was his ideal place for WrestleMania. I've kicked cancer's ass, and yes… I've survived three bears.

One other thing that makes me sad is the lack of respect some of the younger wrestlers have towards older wrestlers. Kids who want to get in the business really need to learn the history of the business because there's a lot they can take from past generations.

I remember when I briefly worked for TNA, Ed Ferrara stuck his foot in his mouth disrespecting Dory Funk, Jr. I never had any problems personally with Ed, but when TNA booked what he thought were a bunch of the old timers on the show, Ed had one of the young guys go on TV and call Dory Funk, Jr., an old man.

When Dory heard about it he responded to Ed. "Tell you what, when I get up to Nashville to that show, this old man's gonna walk right up to you and stick his foot up your ass!"

Ed was just playing heel, and he apologized to Dory. I'm pretty sure he was also scared of Dory, and with good reason.

My attitude about guys who disrespect the older guys has really changed while I've been out battling cancer. Back in the day, I'd try to work with them and smarten them up. Going forward, if anyone calls me an old man, I'm just going to beat the hell out of them.

I'm not afraid of any of these guys. I'd rather help them to get better so they can become successful, but if they want to disrespect me, I'll show them what this old man can do. Most of these guys have never been in a real fight in their lives, except maybe playing video games. They could never have survived against the likes of Bruiser Brody or Harley Race.

The business has changed a lot over the last forty years. It's not 1990. It's not 2000. It's not even 2010. The bar is higher than it ever was in professional wrestling, but the bar is also higher in football and basketball. In the older days you had tough guys, but today's wrestlers are more athletic. They can do things physically that guys forty, twenty, even ten years ago could never do. It's different in 2020 than it was in 1990, but 1990 was a hell of a lot different than 1960.

The one thing today's guys don't have that the old guys did was the ability to tell a story and make it believable. It hurts that the cat's out of the bag as far as kayfabe, but guys are also losing the art of putting a match together that tells a story rather than just putting together a series of moves.

I know a lot of the boys and the fans don't like some of the stuff the young guys do. I certainly see what people like my old friend

Jim Cornette are saying when they gripe about guys like Joey Ryan, but the first time I saw Joey do the dick flip, I thought it was funny as hell. It made him a hell of a lot of money, too, and that's what it's all about.

It's a different generation, and they do a lot of things with a wink we would have never done in my day. They can't do wrestling the same because there is no kayfabe, but they're finding ways to make money and have fun doing it. There are so many different promotions with all different styles, and there's really something for everybody out there.

Two of the biggest issues I have with wrestling today are the scripted promos and the inability of guys to ad lib in the ring. The scripted promos just feel phony and don't sound right.

It's sad to me that today's wrestlers in WWE have to take orders from script writers. Watch Monday Night Raw, and then go back and watch some old videos from the pre-WWF days. You can't tell me some scriptwriter from Hollywood knows how to cut a promo better than the guys who used to do it without a script. The WWE should be bringing in guys who know how to do it and having them teach these kids to go off the cuff. Instead they keep hiring these soap opera writers and forcing them to memorize scripts.

As for the ad-libbing, it's becoming a lost art as well. Guys want to map out every move in the locker room before hand, and the problem with that is, sometimes you want to go one direction while the fans want you to go another. If you can call it on the fly, you can feed off that audience reaction and have a better match. Guys need to let go of their insecurities and trust one another and their instincts.

Another thing that's missing today is the ability to sell. Guys go out to the ring, knock the fuck out of each other, and pop right up for the next step. If you want to tell a story, you have to sell. Especially the babyface! Selling is what makes the people care. It's what puts them on the edge of their seat. It makes all those high spots and those aerial maneuvers mean something.

The difference between a guy like me in a modern locker room and a younger wrestler is this: when it's the younger guys, they want to plan their match step by step and get all their shit in. The first thing I want to do is go to the promoter and ask, "Hey, what are you coming back with next month? What happens after this match? What are you building to?" It's not just about that match and that night. It's about telling a story, not just in your match but from one night to the next. Your match should tell part of the story that night, but it should have some sort of "to be continued" that carries over to the next show so the people want to come back!

It's important, too, to know what the other guys are doing in their matches. You don't want every match to have the same spots or similar finishes, and you don't want your opening guys to out-shine your main event. Find out what the other guys are doing, and make sure you do something different in your match.

Above all else, you have to remember you are telling a story. Whether you plan it out in the locker room or call it in the ring, the main point is not to get all your shit in, but to tell a good story. I realize it's not as easy today, when a wrestler may only come to a town once every few months. Back in the territory days, when we were there every week, we didn't concern ourselves with how many moves we got in each week. We knew we'd be back, and we had to mix it up. It still works better when you put the story first and your moves second. That's how you get the fans invested, and that's how you leave them with something to remember.

My favorite part of the business was helping guys learn how to do it. That was my best attribute. Up and down the card, whatever was needed, I could do it. I could play whatever character they wanted me to do. When the business gives you as much as it gave me, you have a responsibility to give back to it. That's why I've enjoyed working for so many independent promotions in my later years.

Whenever I worked with a young kid, let's say Mitchell Huff at D1W in Southern Indiana, the crowd would start in on me yelling, "Tracy sucks! Tracy sucks!" I'd grab a mic and tell them all to shut up. Then I'd give them a piece of my mind.

"Listen up you Hoosier rednecks, I don't care if you think I suck! But if I hear you all say, 'Go Mitch go!' Everybody dies!!!"

Of course, they always dropped the "Tracy Sucks!" chant and immediately switched to, "Go Mitch go!" This was my way of getting the younger guys over. It put the spotlight on them and not me. And nobody died when it happened.

In the end, it's true. Everybody dies. But not everybody lives. After twenty-seven years (plus thirty) on this earth, thirty seven of which I spent in and out of wrestling, I think it's fair to say, I've done a hell of a lot of living.

I ain't done living, either. Now that cancer's behind me and the first chapter of my life is in print, I'm ready to start on chapter two.

Or maybe I'll just go back to school, get my degree, and finally become a football coach.

ACKNOWLEDGEMENTS

First and foremost thank you to Tim Denison for your friendship and all your support. If it wasn't for Tim, I might be in prison. Tim got me out of my shell and made me think outside the box, and it's because of him I wrote this book!

Thank you as well to Jim Cornette. Jim is crazy, and yes, he is old school, but he's also always on the money. He's the best mind in the business, and I can't thank him enough for all he taught me and writing the foreword.

Thank you to my "son" Hy Zaya for contributing a foreword as well.

Additional thanks go to all the people who contributed quotes and stories for the book including: Rick Brady, Steve C. Branam, Jim Finney, Jason Flener, Joel Gertner, Kevin Gill, Randy Hales, Chris Hero, Mad Man Pondo, Nick Maniwa, Charlene McAnally, "American Kickboxer" Frank Mullins, Jessie Belle Smothers, Khloe Belle Smothers, and Tony Myers.

Thank you to all of our photo contributors, including George Tahinos, Jim Cornette, Angela Evans Meadows, Michael Herm, Ed Pilipow, Kenneth Coker, Pamela Barnett, Amazing Maria, Jessie Belle Smothers, Billie Starkz, and Gary Damron.

Thank you to the remarkable Adrian Johnson at Inazuma Studios for designing the cover.

Thanks as well to Jake Manning, Colt Cabana, Hannibal TV, and the Homers Radio Network.

Photo courtesy Angela Evans Meadows.

ABOUT THE AUTHORS

Tracy Smothers is one of the most well-traveled and beloved wrestlers of his generation. He wrestled for WWF, WCW, ECW, Smoky Mountain, Memphis, Mid-South, Continental, New Japan, IWA Mid-South, JCW, and dozens of other territories and promotions around the world. He continues to travel, perform, and share his knowledge with young wrestlers across the country.

John Cosper is an award-winning writer and the founder of Eat Sleep Wrestle, LLC. He has written two books on the history of wrestling in Louisville and the biography of The Black Panther Jim Mitchell. He also co-wrote the autobiographies of Kenny "Starmaker" Bolin, "Dr. D" David Schultz, Mad Man Pondo, and "Hurricane JJ" Maguire. You can purchase these titles and many more on his website at www.eatsleepwrestle.com

Made in the USA
Monee, IL
11 January 2021